Schooling and Work in
the Democratic State

Martin Carnoy and Henry M. Levin

Schooling and Work in
the Democratic State

Stanford University Press
Stanford, California

Stanford University Press
Stanford, California

© 1985 by the Board of Trustees of the
Leland Stanford Junior University

Printed in the United States of America

Original printing 1985
Cloth ISBN 0-8047-1242-5
Paper ISBN 0-8047-0289-1

Last figure below indicates year of this printing:

96   95   94   93   92   91   90   89   88   87

To David and Jonathan Carnoy and Pilar Soler

Acknowledgments

This book has had an extraordinarily long but fruitful gestation. Initial work began in 1973 under a grant to the Center for Economic Studies, Palo Alto, California, from the National Institute of Education for a study of "The Educational Implications of Industrial Democracy." A sabbatical at the Center for Advanced Studies in the Behavioral Sciences in 1976–77 enabled Henry Levin to advance the work considerably, as did a sabbatical for Martin Carnoy spent in Paris in 1978–79. We are especially indebted to our colleagues at the Center for Economic Studies for assistance in the research. These include Bill Behn, Mike Carter, Joyce Crain, David Gold, Marilyn Goldberg, Pia Moriarity, Russ Rumberger, and Kathy Wilcox. Moriarity and Wilcox are responsible for the ethnographic research on which Chapter 5 is based, and Rumberger made important contributions to Chapter 6. We are also deeply indebted to Carlos Torres, Herb Gintis, Sam Bowles, Tom James, and David Tyack, who read and commented on all or part of the manuscript at various stages of our work. We wish to express our appreciation to Gail Meister for the index, and to Catherine O'Connor and Stephanie Evans for the typing of the manuscript.

Contents

Schooling and Work in
the Democratic State

Introduction

Schools and workplaces are organized in ways that correspond closely. Both tend to be large, bureaucratic, impersonal, hierarchical, and routinized. Both tend to motivate performance with external rewards such as grades and wages, rather than depending on the value of the enterprise itself. Schools and workplaces alike are dominated by expertise and formal authority; in both there are schedules that determine the timing of work, and regulations that determine its nature. It has even been suggested that these institutional resemblances are no mere accident—that schools are specifically designed to prepare young people to function in the bureaucratic hierarchies that they will join as adults. Beyond this organizational correspondence, schools and workplaces exhibit similar patterns of success and failure. On the whole, members of racial minorities and low-income groups are less likely to do well in school, and they are also less likely to do well in the job market.

Yet for all these correspondences, schools differ from workplaces in at least one important respect. Even though American education is marked by great inequalities, schools do more than other institutions in the way of providing equal opportunities for participation and rewards. For example, the large differences in status and compensation between men and women in the labor force are not reflected in education. At the elementary and secondary levels, girls do better than boys on test scores in several subjects. Women in universities, much more than men, tend to be concentrated in nonscientific and nontechnical fields, but not to the degree that women are found concentrated in nontechnical occupations within the labor force. And whereas the top 20 percent of the U.S. population in educational achievement receive only about twice as large an educational investment as the bottom 20 percent (Jencks et al. 1972), the richest 20 percent of U.S. income earners not only earn eight times as much as the bottom 20 percent, but own or control about 95 percent of the nation's capital.

In short, schooling tends to be distributed more equally than capital, income, or employment status. Schooling produces relatively more equal outcomes than the workplace and other institutions of the larger society. Furthermore, teachers and school administrators believe that what they are doing in the schools has its own higher purposes, more universal and idealistic than simply preparing youth for a life of unequal work and income. So though schools are organized like workplaces, screening and preparing youth for inequality, they are more equal and participatory than offices or factories.

This paradox has influenced most analyses of American education. On one side are those who stress the role of education as independent of the structure and content of jobs. This position is most commonly associated with John Dewey (1966) and the progressive education movement (e.g. Cremin 1964, Graham 1967). Even many recent critical analyses of American education (e.g. Holt 1964; Kozol 1972; Bourdieu & Passeron 1977; Apple 1979; and Giroux 1981) argue that the school can create values or ideology independently of the workplace. For both the progressives and the critical progressives, then, education shapes minds that in turn condition social relations outside the schools. On the other side are those who take a functionalist view. Talcott Parsons (1959), Alex Inkeles (1966), and Robert Dreeben (1968) all conceive of schools as institutions that prepare youth for later work roles; it is the functional connection to the workplace that gives schools their most important characteristics. Later analyses with functionalist premises (Carnoy 1974; Carnoy & Levin 1976a; Bowles & Gintis 1976) argue that the structure of social relations in the workplace determines how schools will develop social roles for youth; education develops values and skills to fit social relations outside the school. Both versions of the functionalist view, then, downplay the differences between schools and workplaces, arguing that what happens in the one is a function of what happens in the other.

Each interpretation deals with the paradox in its own way, but neither can surmount it. Progressive thinkers imply that though schools may be organized like workplaces, they are independent of them and shape values and skills in their own image. There appears to be no paradox, therefore, because any similarity to the workplace is treated as a secondary feature of schooling. More recent interpretations by critical progressives concede a degree of similarity, as reflected in the school curriculum and the teacher-student relationship, but hold that these features are not directly tied to the workplace and, indeed, have a life of their own. Such arguments diminish the paradox by obscuring the school's role in creating skills and a division of labor.

For the functionalists who simply dismiss the differences between education and work, there is no paradox. Schools merely develop the skills and attitudes needed in work; as work requirements change, so do schooling practices and even the whole structure of education. Such disagreements as exist among proponents of the functionalist view tend to be over the nature of the workplace—therefore over what kind of society the schools reflect and foster—rather than over the matter of the correspondence itself.

None of these interpretations can adequately explain the relationship between education and work. It is not enough to gloss over the central paradox in this relationship. There are similarities between schooling and work in their structure and practices, but there are also differences. Formal education is the principal institution for producing not only values and norms in the younger members of society, but also the skills and division of labor needed for production in a changing economy. At the same time, neither the ideological and pedagogical processes in schools nor the outcomes of schooling correspond exactly to work structure and practice. The aim of this book is to deal explicitly with the paradox, using it as a key to understanding the role of education in American society.

In our view, the challenge today is to explain how the public school can at one and the same time be an institution that reproduces the unequal class relations of capitalist society and an institution that is more democratic and equal than the workplace for which it prepares its students. We reject both a mechanistic correspondence between work and school and a clear separation of the two. Rather, we believe that though schools do reproduce unequal class relations, the fact that they do so imperfectly merely reflects the social conflict that characterizes the capitalist society they serve. What is the relation of schooling and educational reform to social conflict? How is that social conflict related to the dynamics of the workplace? How do schools reproduce social relations? In their institutional role do schools primarily reproduce ideology (the dominant culture), or do they primarily reproduce the social relations and division of labor in production? Ideology and production are difficult to separate, but the distinction is important for analyzing what goes on in schools—particularly for understanding school reform.

We will argue that the relationship between education and work is dialectical—composed of a perpetual tension between two dynamics, the imperatives of capitalism and those of democracy in all its forms. As both a product and a shaper of social discord, the school is necessarily caught up in the larger conflicts inherent in a capitalist economy and a liberal capitalist State. These conflicts reside in the contradiction between the unequal relation underlying capitalist production and the democratic basis of the liberal capitalist State. The school is essential to the accumulation of capital and the reproduction of the dominant capitalist relations of production, and it is valued by parents and youth as a means to greater participation in economic and political life.

This tension illustrates a basic principle, the centrality of contradiction, that we believe characterizes the democratic capitalist State and all its institutions. Contradiction refers to the existence of opposing forces within a particular process. For example, we have indicated that schools must respond to the needs of unequal hierarchies associated with the capitalist workplace as well as to the democratic values and expectations associated with equality of access to citizen rights and opportunities. The contradiction is evident in the fact that these outcomes are largely conflictual, resulting in internal obstacles to the functioning of institutions charged with the simultaneous production of opposites. More generally, the very nature of capitalism and democracy creates internal incompatibilities and conflicts in institutions. We see this relationship as a dialectical one, situated in the context of the overall relations of production and hence the relations of different social classes in American society. A dialectical relation is one that is characterized by change; it represents a social form that is always coming into being; it changes according to the phase of the underlying conflict. Although the form may appear to have permanent features, this stability results from observing the institution over too short a period. It is this dialectic that will be highlighted in relating education to the workplace.

Schools in America are largely public institutions. As such, they are subject to direct political pressures that are conditioned by the overall conflict between capital and labor, by the changing structure of the labor market, and by various social movements seeking greater equality. We contend that as a result of the schools' position as public institutions subject to outside pressures, they are marked by greater equality than the workplace. Even as schools attempt to satisfy their mandate within a capitalist economy, the public as a whole and social movements such as the civil rights and women's movements have made them more democratic and equal than other social institutions. Thus, the way education has been defined by American society—as a means to social mobility and a developer of democratic values—influences social conflict over public education. The fact that education is more democratic than work may create contradictions in production—contradictions that shape the course of social conflict in the workplace and the State.

In the chapters below we will develop our analysis as follows. Chapter 1 examines the historical development of schooling and offers several interpretative perspectives, including our own, for understanding schools in capitalist America. Chapter 2 reviews theories of the State and their implications for evaluating the social role of education. Chapter 3 analyzes the production process in the United States, how that process has been affected by conflicts in the workplace, what trends and variables influence the labor market today, and how schooling influences those trends. The purpose of these three chapters is to locate current educational structure and practice in the history of U.S. capitalist development.

Chapters 4 and 5 focus on the structure and practice of education and how they fit into the reproduction process. Chapter 5 includes an empirical study that compares occupational socialization in two schools. Chapter 6 analyzes contradictions in education within the context of economic and social crises. This chapter looks at social conflict as manifested in the form of labor force "overeducation." It also considers the implications of such contradictions. Chapters 7 and 8 discuss efforts by employers and the State to reform the workplace and educational system in response to contradictions in reproduction and the push of workers and students for more equality and democracy on the job and in the school. Chapter 7 looks at workplace reforms and Chapter 8 at educational reforms. In the concluding chapter we discuss the policy implications of our analysis, including strategies for change and renewal.

The study covers extensive terrain, but even so, it has its limits. We have tried to explore how people learn and work, how social development takes place in one advanced capitalist economy. We think we have made progress in understanding how institutions are related to each other and how social relations are developed through the dialectic of education and work. Our aim is not only to set out convincing research findings, but also to provide practitioners, especially those interested in helping all human beings to reach their individual and social potential, with an analysis that will make them more effective organizers and educators. Theory without practice is a meaningless endeavor, so we can only hope that our efforts to understand education and work will serve the ultimate purpose of developing a more humane and just society.

1

Historical Traditions and a New Approach

Revolutionary America did not have a public school system open to all classes of people, or indeed an extensive system of any kind. An American's opportunity to obtain formal schooling depended on where he lived and how much money he had. Even elementary education, if it was available at all, was rarely free. But the next century saw huge strides made, to the point where, by 1876, some 60 percent of school-age children (five to seventeen years old) were enrolled in public elementary and secondary schools for an average school term of 132 days. By 1876, too, many of the states had passed compulsory attendance laws (U.S. Dep't of HEW 1976: 178; Landes & Solomon 1972). By 1920 schooling was compulsory in nearly all the states; almost 80 percent of school-age children were enrolled; and the school term had increased to 162 days (U.S. Dep't of HEW 1976: 178). By 1972 the enrollment figure was 90 percent, and the school year was 179 days long. Three-fourths of the country's eighteen year olds were completing high school, and half of them were enrolling in postsecondary education (Cartter 1976: 50). In 1974 some 10,000,000 students were attending institutions of higher education, three times the number only 16 years earlier, in 1958 (U.S. Dep't of HEW 1976: 187).

How was it possible that in less than two centuries formal schooling emerged from a relatively minor institution to one of such dominance in U.S. society? Why did such a development take place, and what were the forces that shaped it?

The establishment of schools in the nineteenth century was primarily a local undertaking rather than a broad and coordinated social movement; school systems were shaped entirely by local actors and their perceived needs, and were largely an extension of the family. The length of the school day and school year, the curriculum, staffing, and organization of schools, and their financing differed substantially from community to community. Schooling in Northeastern states such as New York and Massachusetts expanded rapidly between 1800 and 1830 (Kaestle & Vinovskis 1980). Many families wanted to see their children move up the social ladder, and even in revolutionary times education (along with wealth) was looked on as a prerequisite for political leadership and social rank. Also, the "more enlightened" and wealthier members of communities (whose children generally attended private academies) often supported local schools as civilizing institutions. "Left to themselves, the [common folk] were ignorant and vicious men who contaminated children of the better sort and disobeyed the laws, and endangered the state. But good schools would save the society, for even the poor were rational beings who might be guided rather than driven like beasts. Education would uphold law and order, and protect the government." (Main 1965: 251.) Elsewhere, particularly in the South, the founding of local schools was much slower and more haphazard.

Even so, there were unifying themes that helped shape the communities' decisions. Americans believed that education had something to do with social mobility and with civilizing the poor. Both themes had appeared often in the philosophies of eighteenth-century writers such as Adam Smith and Jean-Jacques Rousseau. At the same time, economic reality influenced such perceptions. In the Northeast, industrial expansion and the rapid growth of commerce tended to confirm the belief that schooling led to the best of the new jobs. In the South, a production system based on slavery created a totally different perception of the efficacy of education. Although both regions were part of a thriving transatlantic economy, their different roles in that economy influenced the way their educational systems developed.

Industrialization played no small part in the expansion of

education during the nineteenth century. In 1800 the typical American manufacturer was a master craftsman or miller, the typical employee a handicraft worker, and the typical plant a room or rooms in a craftsman's home or a small building next to a waterwheel. By 1880 the manufacturer was likely to be a factory owner or manager, the employee a machine operator, and the plant an imposing multistoried brick or stone structure equipped to run on steam. Although most people still lived in rural areas, cities sprang up around industries and commerce, inhabited by the illiterate peasants who emigrated in massive numbers from Ireland and southern and eastern Europe to become the principal source of cheap labor for the new industries.

Such a profound change in the nature of work roles and the way people lived was bound to have an effect on schooling. As work shifted from the home and the workshop in small communities to factories in cities or mill towns, the family or family-oriented community school became an inappropriate instrument for socializing the young to the new economic realities of American life. Schooling retained its perceived role for some groups as the path to social mobility and as a civilizing force. By the late nineteenth century the urban poor were not only a significant segment of the population, but also the country's industrial labor base. The earlier lack of uniformity in the provision and form of education gave way to schooling that was increasingly influenced by the organization of industrial production and increasingly the concern of professional educators and state bureaucracies. These professionals turned their attention primarily to controlling the education of the urban poor, attempting to use schooling as a means of civilizing them into a new industrial society (Bowles & Gintis 1976).

The Massachusetts Common School Reform, a program developed by Horace Mann in 1837, became a model later in the nineteenth century for other states. It established a unified and purposive pattern of schooling for all children under the direction of a state board of education. Important internal changes took place: schools became graded by age, and curriculum, textbooks, teacher preparation, and educational proficiency were standardized. But even so, Mann and his disciples had to persuade communities to adopt these reforms, and the communities retained at least some—and often a great deal of— power over school policies.

It was not until the end of the century, after an already enormous expansion of schooling throughout the country, that businessmen and professional educators organized themselves to take control of school boards in cities and began running schools according to modern business practices (Tyack 1974). By 1916, though businessmen and professionals represented less than 11 percent of the nonagricultural labor force, they accounted for almost 80 percent of the school board members in a sample of 104 cities (Bowles & Gintis 1976: 190). Under their guidance, the schools moved away from the concept of a uniform curriculum by initiating vocational curricula, particularly for children from working-class and immigrant backgrounds. Using standardized tests and vocational counseling, schools assigned students to different tracks and ability groups and to different curricula (Spring 1972). These assignments determined their occupational preparation and the level of schooling it required. Instead of the common school experience for all children that Mann had visualized, public education tended to prepare the children of workers and immigrants for one set of occupations in the work hierarchy and the children of professionals and managers for other, higher positions.

This approach to the schooling of the urban poor was reinforced by the method of financing education that was established by the early part of the twentieth century (Coons, Clune & Sugarman 1970). By relying on local property owners and guaranteeing only minimum financial support to any given district, the states established a systematic financial bias against the poor. Wealthier school districts spent five or more times as much per pupil as poorer districts. Racially segregated schools (with far less funds available to the black schools) were legitimated by an 1896 U.S. Supreme Court decision (*Plessy v Ferguson*) on public transportation (Kluger 1975).

These practices reflected the power of business leaders who had a new vision of the relationship between industry and the State (including State institutions such as public schools). Their ability to impose the doctrine of social efficiency on the schools in the name of increasing school efficiency created an educational system that was organized in the same way as the industrial workplace for which it was preparing workers. Even the disenfranchisement of blacks in the South in the 1880's and the 1890's (along with the concomitant segregation of schools) was part of a new alliance between the industrialists of the North and the old Southern landowning class (Carnoy 1974). Indeed, the class- and race-based school system, channeling youth into different curricula for different types of occupations, was organized in the historical context of intense struggles between big business on the one hand and militant labor unions and the Populist movement on the other (Kolko 1963). Part of the triumph of business was the standardized, tracked, "efficient" school that was segregated by class and race.

The democratic, participative dynamic continued even while schools responded increasingly to the new industrial order of American business. Horace Mann's assumption that expansion and compulsory attendance would make for an egalitarian school system seems naive in the face of community social class differences. Yet schools did expand largely in response to social demand and with community financing throughout the nineteenth century. Industrialists had some direct influence over the expansion and the curricula of schools in this early period, but their influence increased significantly only at the end of the century. And the popular pressure for expansion did not end even then. Moreover, the concept of schools as creators of democratic values and ideals gained new life at the turn of the century in the form of the progressive education movement. This was a response to, and to this day remains in open conflict with, the cult of efficiency pushed by businessmen allied with vocational educators (Wirth 1972).

Just as the period 1880–1929 witnessed the emergence and consolidation of the political power of big business in America, the economic crisis of the 1930's saw the decline of corporate power and the success of social movements in winning social reform, especially permanent State intervention in the economy (Skocpol 1981). Although business recovered much lost ground, to take a dominant position in the State again after the Second World War, the social gains of the 1930's created new conditions of capitalist development, conditions that implied a partnership between capital and labor and entitlements for the poor, the aged, and the unemployed. The equality that characterized American society in the war years also had its impact on education in the postwar period. By the 1950's profound changes had begun to occur: there was a growing demand for the protection of freedom of expression in the schools, for more even-handed educational funding, for special consideration of disadvantaged, handicapped, and bilingual students, for school desegregation, and for the elimination of biases in curriculum counseling against female students. The parallel movements for reform in the workplace did not go so far or have as much success as the educational ones.

Freedom of expression for teachers and students was not an important issue in the nineteenth century. In keeping with the idea that schools were an extension of the family, teachers were expected to reflect the values of the community in both their public and their private lives. They were summarily dismissed by school administrators for not meeting community standards or for controversial behavior.

With the bureaucratization of the schools, national political issues came to have no less an impact on teachers than on the community at large. The "red scare" of the 1920's cost many of them their jobs as business-promoted anti-Communism cast its shadow on the schools. The National Education Association responded with a fight for tenure protection, which eventually resulted in legislation in 32 states protecting teachers from dismissal without just cause (Wesley 1957). Over time, the courts came to assert the teachers' right to free expression as long as this did not interfere with their duties (D. Rubin 1972). And in the landmark *Pickering* case of 1967, the U.S. Supreme Court declared that teachers have the right to discuss school policy without fear of dismissal. Students also gained the right to express themselves freely on the grounds that their entitlement to a public education could not be taken away arbitrarily (Kemerer & Deutsch 1979). The Supreme Court's *Tinker* decision (1969) specified that students have the right to due process in cases of dismissal and the right to free expression except where it is educationally disruptive.

These freedoms have no parallel in large parts of the private-sector workplace. Nonunion workers especially are unprotected against arbitrary dismissal for their political views or for virtually any other matter whether job-related or not. The difference, we believe, is that schools are public institutions. Those who work in such institutions have citizens' rights—rights that are much more limited in private institutions. As the State expands its activities, workers' rights are automatically increased because of the public nature of the State. This difference between public and private has shifted much of the conflict for greater rights to the State, and this has tended to expand State involvement in people's lives. Whereas conservative political philosophy regards this increased involvement as coming from a bureaucracy intent on restricting the natural freedoms inherent in the market (the private sector), the growth of the public sector seems to have developed largely in response to demands for services and guarantees not available from the free market. The expansion of schooling and the extension of free speech protection to the schools are simply part of the State's response to such demands.

Educational finance shows a similar pattern of development. During the years of great school expansion there was little concern that financing schools on the basis of local property taxes would create disparities in the quantity and quality of education received by the children of different districts. And as we have seen, the disparities were great, even within large city school districts, where less was spent on schools enrolling students from lower-income and minority backgrounds (Owen 1972; Sexton 1961).

It was not until the 1960's that court challenges and public policies addressed this problem—a clamor for reform that soon moved from the national to the state level (Wise 1968; Coons, Clune & Sugarman 1970). The California Supreme Court's 1971 *Serrano* decision was followed by decisions in other state courts, all declaring the unconstitutionality of financing education based on the wealth of local districts. State legislatures responded by creating new financing schemes that shifted much of the burden to state treasuries and more fully equalized spending among school districts. Simultaneously, federal compensatory education funding under Title I of the Elementary and Secondary Education Act of 1965, and political movements in large cities, went far in reducing the inequalities within large city districts. This period also saw an intensification of governmental assistance for low-income, handicapped, and bilingual pupils, reflecting the vigorous movement toward the equalization and democratization of educational opportunities during the Great Society years. A number of federal and state programs were established to improve the chances for classroom success of students who would normally have learning handicaps. The somewhat later emphasis on educational equity by gender, both in socializing girls in school and in affirmative action for university admission and jobs, was a response to yet another subordinate group's demand for equal treatment through State action. Indeed, as things now stand, the educational system is not only more susceptible to such demands, it is likely to be the most equal institution encountered by the majority of people during their lifetimes.

Education is therefore subject to tension between two conflicting dynamics attempting to influence the control, purpose, and operation of the schools. On the one hand, schools have traditionally reproduced the unequal, hierarchical relations of the nuclear family and capitalist workplace; on the other, they have represented the expansion of economic opportunity for subordinate groups and the extension of basic human rights. Both forces have been evident throughout the history of public education in the United States, but the ebb and flow of social movements has led to one gaining temporary primacy and greater visibility over the other. For example, the democratic and egalitarian movement of the mid-nineteenth century, which attempted to establish schools for the entire population on the basis of a common set of principles, compulsory attendance laws, community funding, and lay control, gave way at the turn of the century to a movement to professionalize, centralize, and bureaucratize the schools, bringing them into line with the emerging labor needs and disciplinary methods of industrial monopoly capitalism. Then with the Great Depression, the weakening of big business, and the resurgence of strong social movements during the 1930's and 1940's schools again became an arena for extending equalization and democratization. The results in the subsequent decades were a greater protection of individual rights and pursuit of egalitarian aims, which undermined many features of the school-workplace correspondence.

The late 1970's and early 1980's witnessed another swing of the pendulum, with the rise of forces trying to bring education into line with the political objectives, labor needs, and social vision of business. Demands for greater selectivity, a back-to-basics approach, career education, and recurrent education, as well as support for tuition tax credits and other private alternatives to public schools, became important components of educational debate and practice. These trends were reinforced by cuts in educational support for the disadvantaged, handicapped, bilingual, and female populations, by the increasing reluctance of federal authorities to enforce school desegregation, and by limitations on loans and grants for low- and middle-income students. These reductions in federal spending were clearly aimed at the elimination of programs that tend to equalize social opportunities for the less fortunate or those traditionally discriminated against. Thus, we entered a new period in which the State began to try to roll back the gains in social mobility and entitlements won during the previous 50 years and to bring the educational system into correspondence with the realities of family resources and the marketplace.

How have educational thinkers accounted for this historical development of schooling, especially as it relates to work? In the rest of this chapter we analyze the interpretative perspectives mentioned in the Introduction—the progressive, functionalist, and critical progressive views of education and work. At the end of the chapter, we develop our own critical interpretation, showing how it builds on and differs from its predecessors.

The Progressive Education View

The progressive view assumes that education is a moral undertaking to shape young minds so that they can create a future society organized along the principles initiated by their schooling experience (Childs 1939). To John Dewey this moral undertaking was a process in which there would be a close integration between the realization of individual potential and the sharing of common experiences, common interests, and common aims based on an intrinsically worthwhile and democratic educational process. For "if democracy has a moral and ideal meaning, it is that a social return be demanded from all and that opportunity for development of distinctive capacities be afforded all" (Dewey 1966: 122). Education was to be a "process of living and not a preparation for future living," where "the best and deepest moral training is precisely that which one gets through having to enter into proper relations with others in a unity of work and thought" (Kilpatrick 1939: 462–63).

Central to Dewey's concern was that schooling should be valued in its own right. He rejected the idea that its role was to contribute to some external objective, such as the preparation of productive workers. To the contrary, he wished to see the industrial system itself transformed by the new generation that would be created by the progressive school (Wirth 1981). As he saw it, the existing system was based on the undesirable fact that work was performed "simply for the money reward that accrues. For such callings constantly provoke one to aversion, ill will, and a desire to slight and evade. Neither men's hearts nor their minds are in their work" (Dewey 1966: 317). But that could be remedied, he argued, by educative changes made among the young, which would produce "a projection in type of the society we would like to realize, and by forming minds in accord with it gradually modify the larger and more recalcitrant features of the adult society" (*ibid.*).

According to the progressive educational perspective, then, the workplace is subservient to the educational process. Progressive schooling, by shaping young minds in a particular way, can change society, on the assumption that education operates independently of existing social and work processes. It is up to educators—or at least it can be up to educators—to educate in ways that go against the grain of hierarchical, oppressive workplaces, and to produce agents of progressive social change. Indeed, historians such as Lawrence Cremin (1964) interpret the history of American education just this way. According to their view, education and educators have been instruments of social progress, new ideas and visions, greater equality, and democracy in American social history.

Critical Progressive Views

The progressive tradition spawned a profound critique of American education, particularly in reaction to the technology and conformity of the 1950's. Educators like Paul Goodman (1956; 1964), John Holt (1964), Edgar Friedenberg (1963), and Jonathan Kozol (1968) all argued that far from being an instrument of social progress, education was actually deadening—much more oriented to producing failure than to developing creative, critical minds that could be the basis for a more humanistic, democratic society. These critics therefore disagreed with other progressives without abandoning the fundamental assumption of the autonomy of education. Although schools reflected the values of a dehumanized, mechanistic, technological, and racist society, they did not have to be that way. Educators could and should change things around.

As early as 1956, Goodman argued that schools had a negative effect on children, subjugating them to the technological, inhuman orientation characteristic of postwar American society. Trying to socialize them into institutions that went against human nature or were not worthy of it could only make it difficult for them to become mature adults. Some years later, he was even more convinced of American education's harmful results, suggesting "that perhaps we have too much formal schooling and that, under present conditions, the more we get, the less education we get" (1964: 3). Goodman was not arguing that schools had to be bad, merely that the organization and purposes of the society as a whole made them adjust to a "mechanistic system" (1964: 26). In the same tradition, Kozol attacked the racism of the big-city schools. In *Death at an Early Age* (1967), he described vividly what it was like to be a black child in an urban primary school taught by racist white teachers.

Still, except for Goodman, these critics wrote more as muckraking traditional progressives crying for increased sensitivity toward children or greater reverence for learning than as analysts with a coherent explanation of why American schooling was the way it was or of what shape a reform strategy might take. Like John Dewey, they did not confront the paradox that they themselves posed: if schools can be, and should be, and often are more humane and just and creative institutions than the workplace (and other social structures), why are they at the same time so much like the workplace, reproducing many of its worst features?

The counterculture youth movement of the late 1960's stimulated renewed interest in Goodman's humanistic approach to schools and learning. Illich (1971) and Kozol (1972) resurrected Goodman (and A. S. Neill 1960) in calling for the "deschooling" of society to free it of institutions that produced unfeeling, uneducated adults. Illich's message was even more pessimistic than Goodman's: since the public schools, like all of the other institutions of modern society, are oppressive because they reflect the oppressiveness, dehumanization, and conformity of the society they serve, it is illogical and impossible to try to change them into something else. To provide education that stimulates creativity, independent thinking, and humanism means doing something different from what traditional schools are organized to do; therefore, it must be done outside the public educational system. Although Illich's analysis, like Goodman's before him, rested on undefined power relations in an all-pervasive, inherently oppressive technological culture, he still implied that a different kind of education and educators could reconstruct society in a creative, activist, participative mold.

The main point made by these writers (and later by the critical functionalists) was that failure, not mobility or success, was institutionalized in the schools for the mass of American children. The educational system taught children to accept failure as the logical result of their own inadequacy, and with that acceptance these children became conforming, passive adults, operating well below their intellectual potential in a social system that had little use for creative, self-aware, self-confident citizens and workers. Education was therefore restricting rather than liberating, undemocratic rather than democratic. What the critical progressives did not do, however, was to distinguish between successful and unsuccessful students—to explain how and why failure was systematized in the schools so that children from different social classes were inculcated with a different pattern of self-realization and different kinds of knowledge.

The Functionalist View

The progressive view of education places the educator and education in the front lines of social change. Schooling as a relatively democratic and humane institution can humanize and democratize the rest of society, including the workplace. Schooling can be and is different from the workplace because it is a different institution. But according to the traditional functionalist view, the opposite is the case. Institutions can be understood only in terms of how they serve society. The school can best be understood by analyzing how it contributes to the making of competent adults. Since the workplace is one of the most important institutions in need of competent adults, the schools' agenda necessarily focuses on the skills, attitudes, and personalities required for acceptable performance there.

According to this view, more traditional societies have no need for schools because the family, church, community, and workplace are perfectly capable of preparing the young for adult roles. Work habits and skills are learned through apprenticeships and various child-rearing practices. But as society industrializes and becomes more complex, a new institution must emerge to prepare people for new social and work organizations. That institution is the school. Inkeles and Smith (1974) have attempted to quantify the school-workplace relationship with a modernity index, defined as a scale of those personal qualities which are likely to be inculcated "by participation in large-scale modern productive enterprises such as the factory, and perhaps more critical, which may be required of workers and the staff if the factory is to operate efficiently and effectively." Education, they found, "was by far the single most important dimension of modernity" (p. 284).

In the functionalist view of the school-workplace relation, it is the workplace that takes center stage. Youth are to be molded by schools to some set of predetermined standards derived from workplace norms. Education is a means to an end, rather than an end in itself. Dreeben (1968: 114–32) ascribes the parallel structures and functions of school and work organization to five major attributes of the modern industrial workplace: (1) its separation from the household; (2) the distinction between the worker as a person and the position he or she occupies; (3) widespread employment in large-scale organizations with both bureaucratic and professional forms of authority; (4) individual accountability for the performance of tasks judged according to standards of competence; and (5) the affiliation of individuals to organizations through contractual agreements. But traditional forces of socialization such as families, churches, and communities do not have these attributes. Therefore, it is the responsibility of the school to create workers by inculcating the appropriate skills, by shaping of "men's states of mind, and gaining their willingness to accept standards of conduct related to holding a job as well as to master its component activities" (pp. 129–30).

The focus of this analysis, then, is the result of the educational process, not the process itself. Schools are seen as functional institutions that satisfy the needs of adult society rather than as Dewey's moral agencies of social growth and transformation. The conditions of the workplace are assumed to be determined by an inexorable process of modernization; hence the schools provide—or at least are expected to provide—competent workers with changing attributes and skills as required by that changing workplace.

The Critical Functionalist View

Although the traditional functionalist view of education argues that school structure and practices correspond to structures and practices in the workplace, it only vaguely addresses—by assuming a technologically determined process of social change—the specifics of why and how this correspondence occurs. A new school of functionalist thinking has tried to fill this gap.

The theory behind this new school of thinking can be attributed to the French philosopher Louis Althusser (1971). For Althusser, the structure of production relations defines the purposes and functioning of institutions. The State (or in his terms the public sector) is ideological in nature, and its ideological apparatuses (the educational system being the most important of these) necessarily function to reproduce the class structure of production—the division of labor and skills and the relations of production. Althusser sees individuals as immersed in the structure of capitalist relations of production; consciousness is a product of these relations and the apparatuses that reproduce them.

Althusser also sees skill production and the division of labor as part of the ideological apparatuses' reproductive function. Thus, he argues that the educational system determines not only the ways people work (the norms, values, and conceptions of society), but also what they do; and both are in turn determined in conformity with the class structure of society and class relations. Skill production and the division of labor have ideological content: "know-how" is divided into different categories for different workers-to-be. Furthermore, the schools also teach different children different rules of behavior depending on the types of jobs they are likely to hold.

Althusser roots the reproductive role of schooling in its inherent correspondence with the workplace. Teacher-student relations, curriculum, the class divisions in school—all are determined by the class structure of capitalist society. Schools reproduce the skills, values, and ideology that contribute to capitalist production, legitimating an economic system in which there are large inequalities and in which the owners and managers of capital control economic and social development.

The French sociologists Christian Baudelot and Roger Establet were the first (1971) to apply the Althusserian concept of schooling to the analysis of a specific educational system (with the added notion that working-class youth appear to resist the inculcation of capitalist values and norms in France, largely because of the activity of countervailing ideological forces, especially left-wing political parties). But the most ambitious and historically concrete work in this direction has been that of Samuel Bowles and Herbert Gintis. In *Schooling in Capitalist America* (1976), they argue that one can best understand the development of schooling in the United States as a process of preparing the young for the social relations of production. By alienating students from each other through an emphasis on individual competition; by subjecting them to a hierarchical structure in which they must relinquish control of their activities to a system of educational production and teachers whose authority devolves from their position; by holding to a system in which they learn to work for grades rather than for their own satisfaction; and by teaching them to accept "matter-of-factness" in their social relations with others—in all these ways the school conditions the young for the relations of the capitalist workplace. Through such preparation workers are divided against themselves, enabling the capitalist to exploit them in a systematic and socially acceptable way.

The importance of Bowles and Gintis's work rests primarily in its attempt to explore in both concrete and historical terms the correspondence between the structures of the workplace and those of the school, as well as the implications of that correspondence. Further, they place these relations in a plausible theory of class conflict in which it is to the advantage of capital to maintain that correspondence. The major problem with their analysis (and Baudelot and Establet's) is that it does not account for the contradictory trends toward equality and democracy in education, trends that were especially prominent in the 1960's and 1970's. Indeed, Bowles and Gintis argue that the "laws of motion" of correspondence are so dominant that democratic or egalitarian reforms must necessarily fail or be limited in their impact. In this respect, their interpretation is functionalist, even though their historical class perspective disagrees profoundly with the traditional functionalists' technocratic view of social structure and change.

The Critical Autonomy View

Among the educators who have reacted sharply to Bowles and Gintis's economic determinism and, by implication, to Althusser's structuralism are Michael Apple (1979; 1982a; 1982b) and Henry Giroux (1981). Rejecting the notion that the school merely mirrors the workplace, they insist that schools have their own dynamic rooted in the struggle over ideology. Their analysis places renewed emphasis on the autonomy of schools, on their crucial role in reproducing ideology rather than skills or the division of labor, and on the dialectical nature of reproduction.

Apple—identifying his own analysis closely with Gramsci's view of relatively autonomous ideological apparatuses and with the "new sociology" in France and England (Bourdieu & Passeron 1977; Bernstein 1975)—argues that there is nothing inherent in the relations of production that ensures a simple correspondence between schooling and work. Rather, schools help create the conditions necessary for the maintenance of ideological hegemony—in other words, for the continued dominance of a particular set of values and norms (Apple 1982a: 17). Ideological hegemony does not just come about; it must be "worked for in particular sites like the family, the workplace, the political sphere, and the school" (p. 18). Although Apple acknowledges the economic function of schools, he is more interested in them as cultural institutions, and particularly in the way they implant society's values in the course of their day-to-day activities.

Apple makes a further argument against Bowles and Gintis's characterization of the school as a mere reproductive instrument by pointing to working-class resistance to school practices. Based in part on Paul Willis's study of English working-class youth (1977), he argues that culture and ideology are in fact produced in the schools, just as they are in the workplace. Moreover, they are produced in ways that are filled with contradictions and by a process that is itself based on opposition and struggle (Apple 1982a: 27). This Gramscian notion makes not only hegemony, but contradictions in it, central to the reproduction of social relations. Interferences with the "hidden curriculum" and school practices are a primary contradiction in the reproductive process.

Giroux (1981: 78–79) argues in much the same vein:

> Schooling must be studied, on the one hand, as part of a critical theory of society which is logically prior to an inclusive or radical theory of education. On the other hand, schooling must be seen not only as part of a "global" dimension of oppression, but must also be studied in its own right. Proponents of a genuinely radical educational theory will have to spend more time in understanding how the many variables at work in the classroom encounter, reproduce, and contradict the prevailing ideologies and social relationships in the larger society.

Giroux also specifically attacks Althusser's (and Bowles and Gintis's) insistence on economic class relations as the dominant factor in society. Such a view, he argues, denies consciousness as an active force. And it also denies the sociocultural forces that mediate between the forces of production and consciousness. Like Apple, Giroux turns to schooling as an "active cultural sphere" that functions both "to sustain and to resist" the values and beliefs of the dominant society. Again, in reacting to

correspondence theory, he emphasizes contradictions in ideological reproduction, specifically in the form and content of
school curricula, in teaching practices, and in school administration, which has its own ideological content (p. 99).

Toward a Model of Educational Change

The dynamic of the American educational system, we suggest,
can best be understood as part of a much wider social conflict
arising in the nature of capitalist production, with its inequalities of income and power. These inequalities lead to struggles
by subordinate, relatively powerless groups for greater equality,
economic security, and social control. In a politically democratic
society, the State provides space for such struggles. In public education, as our historical sketch has shown, the social conflict is
expressed in the conflict between reforms aimed at reproducing
the inequalities required for social efficiency under monopoly
capitalism and reforms aimed at equalizing opportunities in
pursuit of democratic and constitutional ideals. Thus American
education is subject to severe internal tension, since it is pulled
in the two contradictory directions of inequality and democracy—directions that both emerge from the social conflict that
marks the society at large. Continuing skirmishes have led to
changes in both workplace and school, some presumably influenced by the other.

Important as it is to keep this tension in mind in analyzing
the educational system, it is misleading to carry explanations of
culture and ideology too far from the organization of production as the underlying social dynamic. If ideology and production are part and parcel of the same structure of social class relations (as Bowles and Gintis contend), reproduction is no less
so. Schools are ideological apparatuses, but they are ideological
in the sense that they attempt to reproduce the social relations
of production and the class division of labor; schools are an
arena of struggles over ideology and resources. Political power
and belief systems are subject to conflict, as Giroux argues. The
public schools, as a State apparatus, are relatively autonomous
from production. But the contradictions in education arise primarily because education is inherently part of the conflict over
resources—who will get them and who will control the way they

are used. Conflicts in schools are not primarily over the principle of capitalism, but over its practices. It is true that domination can exist without capitalism, but to understand schooling in capitalist countries requires analyzing schools as reproducers of capitalist social relations and the capitalist division of labor.

Contradictions in reproduction are therefore intimately related to production. The social division of labor and capitalist social relations are class-structured and undemocratic; they are created by an economic system that survives by controlling labor and passing on production's social costs to workers and consumers. But it is also a system marked by inherent social conflict over these injustices. Schooling is shaped by class structures and undemocratic capitalist production, but it is also shaped by the social conflict taking place over that injustice and over the political possibilities in a capitalist democracy of expanding democracy itself. Which of these movements dominates is determined by the larger social conflict and the relative political strength of the groups involved.

2

Education and Theories
of the State

Explicit theories of the State—explanations of how political men and women interact, individually and collectively—are lacking from most educational writing, even though public education is primarily a State function and the State has become an increasingly significant part of the production system. Such theories are the basis for understanding the role of all institutions in a society and their interrelation, including the role of education and its relation to society at large. The public sector in the United States now directly controls more than one-third of the national product, one-sixth of all jobs, and one-third of the jobs held by college graduates (Carnoy, Shearer & Rumberger 1983: Chap. 6). This massive participation is not an accident, nor is it the result of an insatiable bureaucracy. Increased State intervention, we suggest, is a product of social conflict.

The present array of social welfare spending, for example, is largely the result of State responses to potential conflict during the economic crisis of the 1930's. There has been a shift of resources from the private sector to the State, which moves conflict away from private production and into the State itself. It is no accident that the civil rights movement, the women's movement, and the antinuclear movement—to take three prime examples of the past quarter century—have focused their activities on changing the State's position toward minorities, women, and military spending, respectively. Even the American labor movement has grown in the last thirty years primarily through organizing public-sector unions.

Education, as part of the functions of the State, is also an
arena of social conflict. If the State in capitalist democracies is
viewed as responsible for providing justice and equity to compensate for inequalities arising out of the social and economic
system, education's role then is seen as improving the social position of have-not groups by making relevant knowledge and
certification for participation available to them. At the same
time, the capitalist State and its educational system must, by
their very nature, reproduce capitalist relations of production,
including the division of labor and the class relations that are
part of that division. The tension between reproducing inequality and producing greater equality is inherent in public schooling, just as social tension is inherent in all institutions structured according to class, race, and gender. The basis of this
tension is not ideology as such, but ideology as it relates to the
concrete reality of social position, material wealth, and political power.

Much of the difference between our analysis of education
and the other views we discussed in Chapter 1 derives from differences in underlying—albeit implicit—theories of the State. In
this chapter, we explore the dominant analysis of the American
State and the alternatives that form the basis of our own view.

Education and Pluralism

The absence of theories of the State in educational analysis is
largely the result of an Anglo-American intellectual heritage
that regards the State as a consensual collective expression of
individual views. This expression is separate and distinct from
underlying social relations in the family and in the private production of goods and services.

Implicit in most analyses of American government and education is the idea that both are intended to serve the public interest even if they do not always do so. Government is the servant of the people, established by the people to perform that
function. American social thought and popular discussion conceive of the State as an empty shell to be filled by some expression of the general will. The State itself, having no ideology and

no underlying purpose except to reflect that will, is the collective creation of its individual members, providing a set of common social goods—defense, education, law enforcement—to a sizable majority of the society. Further individual political choices are not rooted in the structure of production.

The "common good" theory of the State, which posits the State as reflecting the general will, has gone through many changes since its origins in the seventeenth century. Hobbes and Locke were concerned with individual human nature and how, given that nature, men could live in peace and harmony (Hobbes 1968; Locke 1955). They were writing to promote and legitimize change in a social system still in transition from feudalism to institutions more fully consonant with the new capitalist values and economic development. With Bentham and Mill in the early nineteenth century, "classical" theories of the State, which had been premised on a relatively homogeneous rural society of smallholders, shifted to a utilitarian view of democracy that incorporated the newly emerged capitalist class structure and provided an intellectual rationale for it. Utilitarians adopted Adam Smith's argument in *The Wealth of Nations* that, because of the guiding "invisible hand" of the marketplace, unfettered individual economic activity would maximize social welfare, that indeed there was no inconsistency between the unlimited pursuit of individual gain and social good, and that the State should thus limit itself only to the production of such public goods as defense, education, and the enforcement of laws.

Today's "common good" theories have evolved to justify political institutions in a highly developed capitalist society. In its most recent form, called "pluralism," the utilitarian democratic theory—already assigning and justifying differential political power among individuals—is transformed into a market model for public goods (Dahl 1956; Lipset 1963). With the development of utility theory in the late nineteenth century (Pigou 1951) and then more recently of a theory of consumer preferences for public goods (Arrow 1951), political scientists such as Dahl and Lipset have been able to discuss political choices in terms of market criteria. The State bureaucracy and elected officials ultimately decide the course of economic and social development; together with interest groups in society, they frame the issues to be posed. The electorate is left with the power to determine which set of leaders it wishes to carry out the decision-making process and what their stand should be on each issue as it comes along. Although politicians and bureaucrats reflect on issues and make decisions about what to produce, it is the voters who "buy" public goods through the choices they make.

Power, according to Dahl, resides in the voters even though this power is not expressed as majority versus minority will. Each issue calls forth the voters interested enough to vote for a politician on the basis of that issue. Given that political demands are so diverse, some device is needed to translate these demands into election majorities for public officials, or produce a set of decisions most agreeable to the whole set of diverse individual or group demands being made. Political parties fulfill this function by packaging political goods and offering the voters these packages. Individual voters, acting in their own interest (or *not* acting, which also can serve one's own interest—Lipset's functional apathy, for example), unwittingly produce the greatest good for the greatest number.

Pluralism moves away from Smith's argument for a noninterfering State; it rejects his unification in the economic sphere of acquisitive passion with social interest (Hirschman 1977). For pluralist theory, decision making on economic and social development shifts in part from the economic to the political arena. The interested electorate can, for example, choose to increase State intervention in the distribution of goods or even choose to change the organization of production through State constraints on investment policy and intervention in the labor market. Implicitly, pluralism accepts the failure of the market system to distribute products in an optimum way by recognizing as legitimate the electorate's decision to do such things as tax income progressively and provide Social Security.

Pluralist theory reinforces the individual as the basic unit of economic and political analysis. People vote as individuals. They decide to respond or not respond positively on an issue or to a candidate as individuals, not as members of a particular group, even though they may identify with that group on a number of political issues. Thus, pluralists transfer Smith's "invisible hand" to the political arena; the pursuit of individual

self-interest politically (including the decision not to participate) leads to the greatest good for the greatest number.

This view departs from those of Smith and the utilitarians.
Although the utilitarians generally presumed rationality and
adherence to a higher morality as universal human characteristics (see Smith's *The Theory of Moral Sentiments* [1976]),
pluralists find that there are different kinds of rationality. For
example, Inkeles and Smith (1974) place individuals on a con-
tinuum of social and psychological development from "traditional" to "modern." This implies that not everyone in a society
has the same kind of rationality. Traditional individuals are rational in a parochial sense, whereas modern individuals have
universal rationality. On the basis of Weber's value-based theory of action, modernity theory argues that traditional members of society would not be able to make rational decisions
functional in a modern, complex society.

The role of education in a value-based theory of social action
recalls Jean-Jacques Rousseau's suggestions on schooling children in responsible political behavior (Rousseau 1974). Pluralist theory assigns to the educational system and other social
institutions the task of transforming individuals from nonra-
tional to rational social and political actors by changing their
attitudes. Pluralists see political socialization as the means by
which citizens acquire political culture and assimilate "rational" norms and values (Almond & Verba 1963). The schools
inculcate children with the norms and values necessary for
rational" decision making and rational participation in the political culture.

The pluralist view of education, like the pluralist analysis of
the State, is presented as a description of what is happening,
not what should happen. Implicit in this description is a rationale for inequality: Adam Smith saw education as helping to explain why incomes differ and people hold different kinds of jobs
in the production sector (civil society). The pluralists—just as
they view politics as a consumption process—rationalize political inequality through the concept of political socialization.
According to this view, inequality becomes merely a differential
preparation for political consumption. Education (or the lack
of it) can explain why certain people are more likely to participate politically and why the value of an individual's partici-

pation may be worth more or less to a democratic society. Pluralists attempt to explain, in part through differential education, why one individual's political action is more valuable (contributes more to a democratic society) than another's. In this way, it is possible to view "functional apathy" (Lipset 1963) as rational in democratic States, and elites can be viewed as correctly having more to say about defining issues and acting on them (having more political power) than the masses. Because they are more rational and more politically socialized, elites are then seen as being more socially and politically responsible.

Both politically and socially, meritocracy—the evaluation of individuals based on objective and universal criteria—plays an important role in defining not only who gets what, but who has what to say, and the value of that opinion. The schools take on the function of allocating power in society, especially when other institutions are not adequate for the task. The more complex the society, the more schools must assume this responsibility. At the same time, meritocracy becomes a rationale for power divisions in a society on the grounds that power should be based on knowledge (no longer property, as in the classical and liberal models). Knowledge gives one the right to make decisions, because knowledge implies better information and more advanced attitudes. In the pluralist model, experts, as the most knowledgeable people in a society, should and do have a great deal of power. They know the most, they understand best the complexities of modern technology, and they are the best-equipped people to make decisions about that technology and how to use it.

The importance of utilitarian and pluralist theories of the State, and their influence on the educational literature, cannot be minimized. But these theories are fraught with problems that are rarely discussed by American social scientists. First, they assume that the economic sphere, characterized by the free market, represents an essentially just and socially efficient social organization, requiring only minor fine tuning by the public polity. This assumption is based on Adam Smith's premise that unbridled individual pursuit of private gain produces the greatest good for the greatest number. Yet there has never been any evidence to support Smith's premise (see Colletti 1972; Hirschman 1977).

Second, these theories assume that although social classes may exist in capitalist society, there is no conceptual conflict between the existence of a class society and the achievement of the greatest good for the greatest number. Avoided are the issues of the relation between economic and political power, the perpetuation of classes from generation to generation, and the implications of this relation for the public welfare. Also ignored are the effect that enduring class divisions may have on the definition of morality, the control of the State's legal apparatus, and the very development of those virtues that the theories regard as essential to the social functions of humanity.

Third, these theories continue to assume that individuals acting privately in their own material behalf produce the greatest public benefit even though capital has become concentrated in large bureaucratic organizations controlled by relatively small groups of individuals. Individual sovereignty and free choice are still the basis of pluralist theory, despite the appearance of sophisticated advertising and mass media that influence choices and values (Scitovsky 1976).

These difficulties suggest that the State in America is more than just the expression of a general will that is defined as the product of equally weighted individual voting. Voters do have power over the State, particularly when they organize into social movements. But political power is not divorced or distinct from economic power. The economically powerful, although a distinct minority, have somehow been able to reproduce the social conditions that enable them to retain their position and to transmit it to their offspring. The State—and within the State, public education—plays an important role in this process.

To comprehend this dual dynamic in the State (and education) of the democratic general will and the reproduction of economic power relations, we must turn to class-perspective views of the State. It is in these views that the reproductive element is analyzed. But, as we shall see, traditional class-perspective theories are also limited in that they focus only on the reproduction of the relations of capitalist production and the social division of labor. We must go beyond this to incorporate the democratic dynamic into an analysis that takes explicit account of economic power relations and their ability to influence educational change.

Class-perspective Views of the State

Utilitarian and pluralist views of education and society emphasize the role that education plays in altering the characteristics of individuals and the position of those individuals in the economy, social structure, and polity. The focus is on an institution (the school) and its relationship to individual pupils. Nonetheless, that does not mean that each pupil is treated as an individual case; on the contrary, individuals in their collectivity are immersed in a universal pool, and social science attempts to find the universal norms and rules with which to understand the relation between institution and individual in that pool. Individuals are *universal*—they are subject to behavior patterns that cut across culture, occupation, social position—yet are also *separate*, responsible for themselves at this moment in history, separate from past history, past culture, and past interactions.

There is conflict in such an analysis. Being separate, individuals compete with one another. But this competition is resolved by rules and regulations that are universally accepted because they are fair and just. Economic conflicts are resolved by the marketplace, particularly the price and wage system; social and political conflicts are resolved by the legal system, contained in the democratic State; and changes in these systems are devised through democratic consensus in the form of the vote. Education, also part of the State, is similarly an expression of consensus; it is also subject to conflict, but a conflict acted out in the context of democratic decision making and individual choice as to how much and what kind of education and training to seek.

In the class-perspective view of education and society, individual behavior is the product of historical forces rooted in material conditions. As material conditions change, so do relationships between individuals in different social positions, positions determined by the social organization of production and each person's relation to production. The relation of individuals to production determines their class positions. As Marx put it, in the Preface to *A Contribution to the Critique of Political Economy* (in Tucker 1978: 4):

In the social production of their life, men enter into definite relations that are indispensable and independent of their will, relations of production which correspond to a definite stage of development of their material production forces. The sum total of these relations of production constitutes the economic structure of a society, the real foundation, on which rises a legal and political superstructure and to which corresponds definite forms of social consciousness. The mode of production of material life conditions the social, political, and intellectual life process in general. It is not the consciousness of men that determined their being, but, on the contrary, their social being that determined their consciousness.

Thus, the organization of production—the social formation—and its historical development are central to the class-perspective approach. In this organization we find the relations of human life, the meaning and value of individual characteristics, the determinants of political power and social hierarchy. In capitalist production, the control of capital accumulation by capitalists (and more recently, managers) enables them unduly to influence society's development, including its social mores and cultural formation. Both capitalist (business) and labor consciousness are shaped by their relationship in the process of production that sustains the society. This relationship conditions individual social development and life styles. The individual and social institutions are, therefore, historical outcomes of the development of the social formation and the relations of production.

Conflict in this approach cannot be resolved by universal rules because such rules are class-based. Rationality and the notion of the rational action are tainted by class and relations of domination. They tend to serve particular interests—the interests of the dominant class or group. So the market system and the State, far from being consensual, are the product of class domination and class conflict. The business class—through its economic power—is able not only to exploit the working class (those who only own their labor) but also to create a way of life that serves business interests and leaves workers alienated and oppressed. The only resolution of the inherent conflict in this system of production is its replacement by another in which the working class has the political and economic power to reorganize production and develop a more humane way of life.

We consider the dominant class to include both the owners whose capital or property is used in the production process and the managers whose role is to maximize the profitability of that capital and to further its growth or accumulation. Since such managers act in behalf of the owners of capital, we include them as members of the dominant class with similar class interests. The subordinate class is composed of members of the population who must depend primarily on their own labor for their income. They own little or no productive property and must find employment as a labor input into production processes of those who do own such property. Class conflict is implicit in the fact that each class seeks to maximize its share of the product. The dominant or capitalist class can increase its profits only by reducing wages or by increasing labor productivity while holding wages constant. Neither option is in the interest of the subordinate or working class, which can only increase its share of the product at the expense of the owners of capital. (For discussion of class and class boundaries, see Wright [1978], Poulantzas [1975], and Bottomore [1966].)

This brings us to the problem of reproduction and social change. Every society must solve the challenge of reproducing itself from generation to generation. This is no less true of capitalist societies, which must reproduce social, political, and economic relations and institutions. Since class-perspective theories consider capitalist society to be organized in the interests of capitalists and managers, how are the relations of production, the division of labor, and social classes reproduced from generation to generation? In the present version of the "traditional" liberal view (pluralism), reproduction takes place through the selection of leaders who reflect the needs and wants of the electorate—at least that part of the electorate interested in participating in politics and social change. Change takes place through competition between elites with different interpretations of how to achieve the greatest good within generally acceptable goals. Each of the elites tries to mobilize consensus around its view.

In class-perspective theory, this consensus about the structure of society is not a voluntary phenomenon, but the result of power relations whose roots are in the prevailing mode of production. Traditional Marxian theories argue that reproduction is carried out largely by capitalists in the production sector itself—by a series of tactics that keep labor fearful of any attempts to organize against employers and that maintain a division of labor along class lines. These theories also argue that the capitalist State is the repressive apparatus of the bourgeoisie, keeping workers in their place through the judicial system, the police, and the army.

More recent class-perspective analyses, however, give greater weight in the reproduction process to institutions outside production (i.e., to what is called the superstructure)—and this is where schooling comes in. For it is in schooling that reproduction takes its most organized form: children go to school at an early age and are systematically inculcated with skills, values, and ideology that fit into the type of economic development suited to continued capitalist control. It has been argued that the business class reproduces the forces of production (labor, the division of labor, the division of knowledge) and the relations of production through the schools and other superstructural institutions (Althusser 1971).

Reproduction in the interest of one social class implies the existence of class antagonism and the potential for class struggle. When one group in society, by dint of its control of large blocks of investment capital, can exert an inordinate amount of influence over how and how much people work, those who are employed by owners and managers of capital will tend to be in conflict with them. Different interests and degrees of power to control the work process are inherent in the management-labor relationship. This notion of a class struggle inherent in all aspects of capitalist development and institutions forms the basis of a class-perspective theory of social change. Just as capitalists need to organize institutions for reproducing certain kinds of social relations in society, so there is also resistance to their concept of development and their control of that development. The class-perspective analysis of schooling in the context of social change is couched in this overall class conflict.

Fundamentals of Class-perspective Politics

What is the relationship of the advanced capitalist State to social conflict? This issue is central to our analysis of education in America. Marx himself did not develop a single theory of politics and the State, but all writers who take a class-perspective view derive their theories of the State from three fundamentals contained in his writings.

First, Marx viewed the material conditions of a society as the basis of its social structure and of human consciousness. The form of the State, therefore, emerges from the relations of production, not from the general development of the human mind, nor from the collective of men's wills. In Marx's conception, it is impossible to separate human interaction in one part of society from interaction in another: the human consciousness that guides and even determines these individual relations is the product of the material conditions in society—the way things are produced, distributed, and consumed. Second, Marx (in contrast to Hegel) argued that the State, emerging from the relations of production, does not represent the common good, but is rather the political expression of the dominant class. The capitalist State is the expression of the class structure inherent in production. Since the bourgeoisie in capitalist production has control over labor in the production process, it also extends this power to the State and to other institutions. Third, Marx viewed the State as a repressive force to keep class antagonisms in check. This not only describes the class nature of the State, but also its repressive functions, which in capitalism serve the dominant bourgeoisie.

There are two central issues here. The first concerns a primary function of community that is inherent in every society—enforcement of the laws. The second concerns the rise of the State and the repression inherent in that rise. According to Marx and Engels, the State appears as part of the division of labor—i.e., as a result of the differences among groups in society and the lack of social consensus. Repression is part of the State. Historically, the separation of power from the community makes it possible for one group in society to use State power against other groups.

The Autonomy of the State

The principal difference between common-good (classical, liberal, pluralist) and class-perspective theories of the State resides in the interpretation of whom the State represents. According to the former, the State is seen as representing "society as a whole," as "standing above particular and necessarily partial groups, interests, and classes, as having the special function of ensuring both that competition between these groups, interests, and classes remains orderly and that the 'national interest' could not be impaired in the process" (Miliband 1977: 66). In the class-perspective theory of politics, however, the State is an essential means of class domination; it is not above class conflict but party to it.

How is the economic power of the dominant class translated into State power? And to what degree does the State serve the interests of the dominant class? These questions constitute a major problem in class-perspective theory, with many different facets and with important implications for a dialectical theory of education and work.

The dominant class in capitalist society is a social totality made up of different and therefore potentially conflicting elements (this is true of the working class as well); therefore, the State has the essential function of mediating and reconciling these conflicting elements within the dominating class. However, if the State is to mediate successfully among competing interests, it has to have a certain autonomy from any fraction of the "ruling class" (Miliband 1977).

Marx grappled with this problem throughout his writings. In his early work, he proposed that the State had a life of its own, separate from civil society, with a bureaucracy that acted not in society's interests (as suggested by Hegel) but in its private interests. Under Engels' influence and after visits to Paris, Marx translated the class-struggle view of social dynamics into a theory of the State as a class-bound institution. According to Marx and Engels, the State arises out of the contradiction between the interest of an individual (or family) and the communal interest of all individuals. The community becomes the State, apparently divorced from individual and community, but in fact based on connections with certain individuals and groups. All conflicts within the State are "merely the illusory forms in which the real struggles of the different classes are fought out among one another" (Marx & Engels 1964: 45).

The modern capitalist State is dominated by the bourgeoisie. Yet it is unclear to what extent and in what way the State is able to act in the interests of the bourgeoisie "as a whole." The State appears to have power, but this power reflects relations of production in civil society. The State is the political expression of the dominant class without arising out of a class conspiracy. It is a socially necessary institution that is also a *class* institution.

Later, in *The Origin of the Family, Private Property, and the State*, Engels (1968) developed his and Marx's fundamental concept of the relation between the material conditions of society, its social structure, and the State. He contended that the State has its origins in the need to control social struggles between different economic interests, and that this control is exercised by the economically most powerful class in the society. The capitalist State is a response to the necessity to mediate class conflict and maintain order—an order that reproduces the bourgeoisie's economic dominance.

Two levels of State autonomy exist in the writings of Marx and Engels. In the first—the "normal" condition—the State bureaucracy has some autonomy from the bourgeoisie because of the latter's inherent distaste for taking direct charge of the State apparatus and because of the very conflicts among individual capitalists that required the establishment of an independent bureaucracy to act as an executor for the capitalist class as a whole. In the "normal" status of the bourgeois State, therefore, the bourgeoisie can be said to have assigned the task of managing political affairs to a bureaucracy that is neither the bourgeoisie itself nor individual capitalists but that is nonetheless a social formation (unlike its predecessors) subordinate to bourgeois society and bourgeois production. Although autonomous from the bourgeoisie, the bureaucracy is reduced more and more to the status of a social stratum acting as the agent of the dominant bourgeois class. Nevertheless, for Marx and Engels, this downgraded bureaucracy still strives for power (Draper 1977: 496).

The second level of autonomy is achieved when the class conflict is "frozen" by the inability of any class to maintain its power over the State.* In that "exceptional" situation, the bu-

---

*In his analysis of Louis Napoleon's empire (1852–70), Marx returned to his earlier conceptualization of the State, arguing that there are historical instances when no class has enough power to rule through the State. In those instances, the State (executive) itself rules. What are the factors that enable this to happen? Marx wrote that the bourgeoisie, in this case, "confesses that [its] own interests dictate

reaucracy is able to gain autonomy from class control. But even here, State power depends on political conditions in a class society. In this model of the autonomous State, the State is not the instrument of the bourgeoisie; rather, its actions are framed by the conditions of the class struggle and the structure of the class society. The State does not set itself against the ruling powers of civil society; on the contrary, it must be accepted by them, or some bloc among them, to remain in power. Indeed, the autonomous State does not change the configuration of economic power because it depends for tax revenues on bourgeois capital accumulation.

Two issues submerged in the discussion of State autonomy are important to our model of education and work, and to understanding the differences between our model and its predecessors. If we pose them as questions, the first would be, How does the capitalist State serve as the instrument of a dominant class? and the second, How much autonomy does the State have from the dominant class? Both are intimately linked. One answer to the first is that the personnel of the State system have tended to belong to the same class or classes that have dominated other strategic heights of society, notably the economic and cultural ones (Domhoff 1967). This does not mean that State bureaucrats coming from the dominant class necessarily serve particular interests in that class; rather, it means that a member of that class serving in the government would be much more in tune with bourgeois values, concepts, and visions of a future society than would members of other classes. Bourgeois interests would be served by such government bureaucrats even without direct pressures. Empirically valid as this argument may be, however, it does not explain why nonmembers of the dominant class in the State bureaucracy also tend to reproduce capitalist relations of production and to serve the interests of the dominant class, or, vice versa, why some members of the dominant class in the bureaucracy come to represent subordi-

---

that it should be delivered from the dangers of its *own rule*; that in order to restore tranquility in the country, its bourgeois parliament must, first of all, be given its quietus; that in order to preserve its social power intact, its political power must be broken (Marx, *The Eighteenth Brumaire*, quoted in Draper 1977: 398). Engels emphasized, in turn, that Bonaparte was able to take power only after all the social classes had shown their incapacity to rule and had exhausted themselves trying to do so.

nate class interests and attempt to make changes through the State that are vehemently opposed by the dominant class. The class bias of the State is not conclusively determined by the social origins of its leading personnel.

A second answer is that the dominant class wields power over the State by dint of its ownership of and control over economic and other resources, and particularly by its capability to create an "investment strike" and bring the economy to its knees. This is the closest view to Marx and Engels' "normal times" formulation, and most fits the title of "instrumentalism." Through its economic strength, the bourgeoisie—today the owners and managers of giant corporations, both national and multinational—constitutes the major reference point for the capitalist State bureaucracy, which must effectively serve this dominant class in order to survive as the State. This does not necessarily mean that the bureaucracy serves particular interests in that class, but it does mean that the State must reconcile class conflict in ways that respond directly to the needs and dictates of the dominant class.

A third answer argues that the State is an instrument of the dominant class because, given its position in the capitalist mode of production, it cannot be anything else. The behavior of the State depends not on its personnel or capitalist pressure, but rather on the nature and requirements of the mode of production. A capitalist economy has its own rationality—its laws of motion—to which any government and State must submit: that economy's inherent class divisions make the capitalist State structurally a class State, necessarily reproducing class divisions. This third, structuralist, answer has provided an important framework for discussing the State and education. Althusser's (1971) work on education as the principal ideological apparatus of the capitalist State outlines the crucial role that education plays in reproducing the class division of labor and the relations of production. It goes far in helping understand how reproduction can take place without direct control of schools and other social institutions by the business class. Indeed, it suggests that the capitalist class does not have to be composed of conscious class actors acting in consort, but can be a powerful ideological force without such coherence.

In the last instance, ideological structures are determined by the labor process. They attempt to change the nature of the class struggle by concealing from the individual subjects (agents of production) that the relations between capitalists and workers are class relations (Poulantzas 1974: 130). The *State* isolates workers and capitalists into "individuals." It is not the class-structured capitalistic production that does this, for the organization of production inherently moves both capitalists and workers to class identification. Competition is developed among members of the same class by the juridical and political apparatuses of the State, which are at the same time also diffusing the inherent conflict *between* production-based classes by "concealing the class relation." Thus, the capitalist State appears as the political unity of an economic struggle. The State presents itself as representing the "general interest" of competing groups—it is simultaneously popular, rational, and the class State (Poulantzas 1974: 130–31).

If the State tends to diffuse class conflict between inherently hostile economic classes (workers and capitalists) by isolating people as individuals and then reunifying them as a nation-State, how does the capitalist class come to dominate that State? Since the State promotes competition among individuals through its juridical and political apparatus, how do the competing capitalists come to use the State for their own purposes against the equally individualized working class? For it is precisely this, in the structuralist model, that the capitalist class comes to do. Poulantzas calls this the political class struggle (1974: 138). He argues that the political struggle is relatively autonomous from the economic struggle, and that it has to be in order to conceal class relations in the economic struggle from the agents of production. Yet the State allows for the unity of the individualized capitalists, and the dominant capitalist class is able "by means of a whole political-ideological operation of its own" to constitute its strictly political interests as representative of the people and nation.

What about competition between members and subgroups of the dominant class? How is this competition resolved to produce the translation of dominant ideology into dominant class power? The relationship between capitalist State and the dominant classes or fractions pushes them "toward *their political unity under the protection of a hegemonic class or fraction.*

The hegemonic class or fraction *polarizes* the specific contradictory interests of the various classes or fractions of the power blocs by making its own economic interests into political interests and by representing the general common interests of the classes or fractions of the power bloc. This general interest consists of economic exploitation and political domination" (Poulantzas 1974: 239; italics in original). In this structuralist formulation, the State is not a place of class struggle, but rather a product and shaper of class struggle in the civil society.* It represents an "equilibrium" of political power in which the dominated classes have little influence over the structure and operation of the State.

Structuralist theory is important for our own analysis because it provides insight into the reproductive role of the capitalist State and its educational system. But it is an incomplete analysis, and, some would argue, misleading and incorrect (Miliband 1970; Gold, Lo & Wright 1975). Although arguing that the State is autonomous, structuralists define autonomy as only "relative." The State bureaucracy is not a direct instrument of the dominant class but rather the site where the dominant class organizes and reproduces its hegemony. The working class and other subordinate groups have little or nothing to say about the State, even in capitalist democracies, as long as they remain isolated as individuals, losing their class identity, and as long as the ideological apparatuses successfully cause them— as individuals—to internalize dominant class values. Change can come only from outside the State apparatuses, and only from mass organizations that manage to separate themselves from dominant class institutions, including corporate political parties and schools.

An alternative formulation argues that the autonomy of the capitalist State is much more concrete. The State is not merely the site where the capitalist class organizes its hegemony; the State bureaucracy does the organizing, often against the perceived short-run interests of the various fractions of the capitalist class. This formulation, developed in Germany by Claus Offe (1972, 1973, 1974, 1975, 1976), theorizes a State that simultaneously reproduces capital accumulation as being "rep-

---

*This determinism represents the basis for Bowles and Gintis's as well as Baudelot and Establet's analysis of dominant class domination of educational change.

resentative" of capitalist interests as a whole (without being directly controlled by the capitalist class) and legitimizes this role by increasing the value of labor, primarily through allocating funds for education and training programs. The important feature of Offe's theory for our analysis is the independence that he assigns the State and his assertion that the capitalist class does not exist as a class except as its interests are manifested in the policies of the capitalist State bureaucracy. That bureaucracy depends for its revenues on economic growth. By smoothing out the process of capital accumulation, the State is, in effect, "creating" a coherent capitalist class position. Nevertheless, to remain in power, the State must also be legitimate, so must give in to labor demands as part of its project to promote capital accumulation and class reproduction.

Offe posits a State that consists of the institutional apparatuses, bureaucratic organizations, and formal and informal norms and codes that constitute and regulate the public and private spheres of society. As the embodiment of relations of domination, the State apparatuses consist of a set of complex, differentiated organizational structures whose unity resides in their claim to legitimate authority and their monopoly of coercive forces. In keeping with Marx's early Hegelian views of the State, and the subsequent Weberian interpretations of bureaucracy's relation to civil society, Offe's analysis emphasizes the relative autonomy of the State to the point that bureaucracy becomes the "independent" mediator of class struggle inherent in the process of capital accumulation. Contradictions arising from the various mediating roles of the State itself (and the inherent characteristics of bureaucracy) make the State the principal arena of the "crisis of legitimation" and the place where the crisis is resolved or exacerbated.

Education, for Offe, is the principal means by which the State can reproduce capitalist relations of production and simultaneously gain legitimacy by providing greater employability to labor. Yet Offe's analysis of education is unidimensional. He defines the school's role solely in economic terms, as a source of increased possibilities both for the capitalist to accumulate capital and for the laborer to enhance his employability by capital. Neither does Offe's theory account for capitalists' private power over media and other ideological apparatuses, or for the power of social movements to alter the ideological conditions under which the State is forced to deal with labor and with capital.

The view of the State as a "third force" between a fractionalized business class and an equally fractionalized working class—both of which have inherently opposed interests but are sufficiently disorganized to give the State bureaucracy a great deal of independent policymaking power—has its adherents in the United States (Wolfe 1977, 1981; F. Block 1977, 1980; Skocpol 1981). The State for them, as for Offe, is more the independent shaper of the social conflict than the site where the capitalist class organizes its influence over society. If the State reproduces capitalist relations of production, it is because the State bureaucracy depends inherently on continued capital accumulation for its own expansion. And it is the State that is central to the definition and expression of capitalist class interests. State policies shape capitalist development in a way that makes it less harsh and therefore more acceptable to the working class. For American writers, more than for Offe, the ideological aspects of State policies are crucial to the legitimation of capital accumulation. Expanded education (like other social services) is thus more a means of providing a form of direct consumption to the working class in a form that is ideologically reinforcing of capitalist relations of production than a means of making workers more employable.

But from our standpoint, this "political" view of the State places the State and education above the political action of business interests and social movements that so profoundly influence State policy. Offe, Block, Skocpol, and Wolfe make a significant contribution by placing more emphasis on the State itself as an arena of conflict and by making State policymaking an important object of study. However, their analyses cause us to lose perspective on the changing social forces that shape State action.

We argue that the State bureaucracy is not only a "third force" operating on its own and subject to particular historical conditions, but also the scene of conflict both between the dominating and dominated classes and within the dominating class, whose fractions compete to organize that class and establish its social dominance. The State not only develops its own dynamic, it is subject to the competing dynamics both of a capitalist class attempting to reproduce capitalist relations of production and of social movements trying to expand their economic power and social and political rights.

In this formulation, the State apparatuses are the materialization and condensation of class relations (Poulantzas 1978b). Power struggles originate outside the State, but insofar as they are political struggles, they have to include the State. And whereas the State attempts to represent dominant class interests in these conflicts, the structure of the State—its hierarchical and bureaucratic organization—includes the presence of dominated groups and their struggle. It is impossible to understand the organization and functions of the State without including its role as an area of conflict between dominant and dominated groups. The State attempts to divide and disorganize dominated groups, but at the same time it reaches a compromise with many of their demands. "The State is not a monolithic bloc but a strategic battlefield" (Poulantzas 1978b: 152). The State itself becomes an arena of struggle.

Although the contradictions between the dominant and dominated groups are reflected in the structure of the State (and in the power relations expressed in that structure), there is not necessarily agreement at any given time among the fractions of the power bloc on how to deal with such contradictions and the conflicts with subordinated groups. All this is condensed in the internal division and contradictions in the State, among and within its diverse branches, networks, and apparatuses.

The State, in all its functions (ideological, repressive, and economic), is marked by contradiction because a struggle is taking place in its very heart even as it attempts to maintain an external dominant class hegemony. The State is neither an instrumental object of dominant class power nor a subject possessing an abstract power of its own outside the class structure. It is a place for the dominant class to organize itself strategically in its relation to the dominated classes. It is a center for the exercise of power, but it does not possess its own power.

Social Conflict, the State, and Education

The social-conflict theory of the State provides a framework for developing a dialectical analysis of education in capitalist society, because it views social movements as playing a vital role in affecting educational policy. Educational institutions are not just reproducers of dominant class conceptions of what and how much schooling should be provided; public schools also reflect social demands. Attempts by the capitalist State to re-produce the relations of production and the class division of la-bor confront social movements that demand more public re-sources for their needs and more say in how those resources are to be used. The capitalist State and its educational system are therefore more than just a means for co-opting social demands, or for simply manipulating them to satisfy dominant class needs. Social demands shape the State and education.

These demands usually emerge from the defensive position in which subordinate groups find themselves in a society domi-nated by business-class values and norms. The reforms de-manded may therefore appear as co-opted or manipulated. But to assume that they are completely manipulated is, we suggest, to underestimate subordinate groups' consciousness of their dominated position in capitalist society. Such an assumption relegates all popular action to the realm of an unconscious and inevitable reproduction of capitalist relations of production. Popular action—the social-conflict theory argues—speaks au-thentically to mass needs. That the reforms achieved by such action may be partially altered by capitalist-class power acting through the State apparatuses does not negate the authenticity of the social movements themselves.

In the social-conflict theory, the struggle of dominated groups to change the conditions that oppress them and the at-tempts of dominant groups to reproduce the conditions of their dominance are the key to understanding changes in the econ-omy, in social relations, and in the culture. These changes, in turn, are reflected in State policies and in public schooling, both prime targets of the conflict.

The nature of conflict in each historical period is qualita-tively different because the structure of production, the State, schools, and other institutions keeps changing as a result of previous conflict. For example, the conflict between labor and capital in the nineteenth century contributed to a transforma-tion of the dominant form of capitalist enterprise from a small, competitive firm to a giant corporate oligopoly. With the crisis of corporate capitalism in the 1930's and the conflict that was part of that crisis, the State became involved in the production process (albeit indirectly) especially in the distribution of output. After the Second World War, transnational capital became the dominant form of capitalist production. Labor struggles have changed and so have social movements. They condition social change and are also profoundly conditioned by it.

Various fractions of the capitalist class attempt to fashion education and other State apparatuses for the reproduction of capitalist production, and social movements attempt to fashion these same institutions in ways that would better serve workers, women, and minorities. As capitalism changes, some of the demands made by capitalists on the schools also change, although the underlying theme of reproducing the relations of production remains the same. Similarly, the demands of social movements have changed with social change, even though the underlying theme of extending their rights as workers and citizens has not. Education can thus be understood in the context of social conflict, as part of a social conflict that changes as a result of previous struggle.

The changing organization of work is central to this understanding because social conflict is so deeply rooted in work organization. Capitalist production is marked by a social division of labor that separates intellectual work from manual work, by a separation of technology from the process of work, by the use of science and technology to rationalize power, and by an organic relation between knowledge and power.

As part of this reproductive dynamic, the State incorporates these divisions into all its apparatuses. Moreover, the State helps reproduce capitalist relations of production under changing conditions of work by taking knowledge and attempting to transform it into language and rituals that separate that knowledge from consumers and workers. The State regularly legitimizes business ideology by transforming self-serving economic and social views into technocratic "facts" and decisions allegedly based on "scientific" studies and "expertise." In the State, the knowledge-power relation is not only an ideological legitimization; the capitalist separation of intellectual from manual work concerns science itself. The State incorporates science into the mechanisms of power; intellectual experts as a body of specialists are controlled through their financial dependence on modern State apparatuses. Most professionals have become State functionaries, in one form or another. In the United States, 33 percent of all university graduates are directly employed by federal, state, or local government, many in public education itself. Twenty-five percent of scientists and engineers depend directly on military spending alone (DeGrasse 1983: 101).

At the same time, social movements make demands on the State for increased protection *against* experts and technology, as well as for increased access to information. For example, the ideological battles on U.S. Vietnam policy were fought over information and expertise reaching the American public. A similar struggle is taking place over the issue of U.S. involvement in Central America. The antinuclear movement has challenged expert opinion on nuclear power plants and arms. The struggle over knowledge and information is carried out in the State apparatuses, through legislative challenges and agencies whose charge is to protect the public against excesses of the private market.

As part of its democratic dynamic, therefore, the capitalist State can produce knowledge that protects the public and extends democratic control over private production. The democratic dynamic also conflicts with the State's use of knowledge for reproduction. Some State agencies may produce knowledge and expertise that contradict that of other agencies. Thus, reproductive and democratic dynamics conflict within the State itself.

Education is, of course, part of the State apparatus. Besides contributing, first, to the reproduction of the class structure through the distribution of youth into the various functions of the labor force on the basis of their educational qualifications and, second, to the reproduction of the relations through an ideological inculcation of bourgeois values (see Althusser 1971), the educational system provides the technical skills and know-how necessary for the continued accumulation of capital. The schools not only distribute knowledge, they produce it. Workers pay for the education of their children, and part of the return to these expenditures goes to maintain the rate of profit.

The production of knowledge is carried out not only through teaching students, but also through State spending on research in public and private universities and research institutions. The State plays an increasingly important role in guiding the direction of innovation by investing heavily in research and development. The space program, defense expenditures, grants to universities—all contribute to a particular direction of innovation, one that assists in the extraction of surplus value by private capital, but also one that expands development, raises wages, and increases access to higher education for working-class youth.

Furthermore, the educational apparatus itself is an important source of employment for subordinate groups in society. In advanced monopoly capitalism, the teachers and administrators of the school system form part of the "new petty bourgeoisie" (Poulantzas 1975), which is drawn from sections of the working class and provides upward mobility for women and minority males. More than half of all women and minority men professionals in the United States are employed by the government, mostly in local government, and primarily in the educational system (see Carnoy, Shearer & Rumberger 1983). The schools are therefore also employers and contribute—through that employment—to expanding opportunities for subordinate groups.

The educational system is not an instrument of the capitalist class. It is the product of conflict between the dominant and the dominated. The struggle in the production sector, for example, affects schools, just as it conditions all State apparatuses. Furthermore, because the State, including the educational system, is itself the political arena, schools are part of social conflict. Education is at once the result of contradictions and the source of new contradictions. It is an arena of conflict over the production of knowledge, ideology, and employment, a place where social movements try to meet their needs and business attempts to reproduce its hegemony.

Because public education is not completely obedient to the capitalist imperative, it may not contribute optimally to creating a work force that contributes to smooth capital accumulation. In that case, employers will attempt to reproduce those relations either through tightening discipline of labor in production, through pressuring the State bureaucracy to act in a way that disciplines labor and other subordinate groups, or through bringing the educational system back into line by means of business-inspired educational reform. Thus, the development of contradictions in education is not the end of the dialectical process created by the tension between the democratic and re-productive dynamics; the process continues from one round to the next.

3

Education and the Changing American Workplace

Schooling is shaped by work, and for more than a century in the United States the nature of work has been defined by the development of industrial capitalism. This relationship between schooling and work is not direct, however. It is transmitted through the prism of the State. Formal education, as a major State institution, is simultaneously a reproducer of capitalist relations and a source of social mobility, greater knowledge and skills, and even self-respect for some. American schools play contradictory roles, but what goes on in them is still rooted in an inherently unequal production process and a hierarchical workplace. One of the schools' chief functions is to reproduce work divisions and work relations. We will see later that schooling is much more democratic than the workplace, and that, as part of the State, it is susceptible to political demands. But these demands for a more democratic education—usually expressed as a demand for more and better schooling—are also closely related to work and the division of knowledge associated with different jobs.

Before we analyze the contradictory role of education it is important to examine the characteristics of the changing nature of work. This context shapes the schooling process at several levels. First, work in a capitalist society conditions the fundamental relations in schools—of teachers to school administrators, students to teachers, and students to students. Second, who gets how much schooling is related to the division of labor in the production process. This division, in turn, is the product of conflicts in production and the way those conflicts have been resolved historically. The workplace changes as workers contest the conditions of work and they attempt to increase the rewards they get for their labor, and as employers adopt new technology to increase output per worker. Third, what is taught at different levels of schooling is influenced by the skills and attitudes required by jobs in the labor force.

Understanding the changing nature of work provides a background for analyzing the kinds of reforms that those forces supporting the reproductive dynamic may try to introduce in schools in the future. The changing workplace also gives us insights into the changing nature of social movements and the kinds of reforms they may push for in schools.

What are the underlying relations in the American workplace? What is the present division of labor and how is it changing? We can only give brief answers to these questions, for our goal is limited to developing guidelines for understanding changes in schooling.

What Is the Nature of Capitalist Production in the United States?

The American workplace is all but static. The most important changes in the American workplace over the last two centuries have been the shift from self-employment to wage employment and from employment in small to employment in large enterprises. Today, the vast majority (over 90 percent) of the labor force work for corporations, government agencies, and other organizations in exchange for wages and salaries rather than working as their own bosses. That is, most people are dependent for income primarily on their own labor, which is purchased by those who own the facilities and tools that are needed for production. At the time of the founding of the nation, some four-fifths of the nonslave labor force worked in agriculture, most of them self-employed (U.S. Dep't of Commerce, *Historical Statistics* 1978, Table Series D 167–81). By 1900, this proportion had been reversed, with only 40 percent of the labor force in agriculture. Most nonagricultural workers worked for firms that owned the means of production and that "hired" their labor (*ibid.*).

The size and nature of the workplace have also changed. Rather than working in the small workshops, farms, and commercial establishments characteristic of the late eighteenth and early nineteenth centuries, most employees began concentrating in large bureaucratic firms by the late nineteenth century (Nelson 1975). These entities have come to dominate both the markets for their products (on a regional, national, or multinational basis) and the demand for labor in the areas where they operate. Most individuals in the labor market do not face a large number of employment opportunities among large numbers of employers; rather, there are relatively limited employment prospects concentrated among relatively few potential employers. The size of these economic entities prevents new competitors from arising, since the former dominate their markets and can engage in various types of anticompetitive practices. Relationships with both government regulatory agencies as well as such large government entities as the Pentagon enable them to influence the government to help ensure their profitability (Baran & Sweezy 1966).

The organization of work has become more complex over time, but it has remained hierarchical and fragmented. Typically, the workplace is organized with a large number of relatively low-paid workers at the bottom, a smaller number of more highly skilled and supervisory-level workers in the middle, and relatively few people representing the various levels of management at the top (Braverman 1974). This pyramidal form of organization is based upon a fragmented division of labor in which work tasks are divided into minute and routinized functions that permit the use of relatively unskilled workers at the bottom, where most of the employees are situated. Such fragmentation of the productive process often occurs even at higher levels so that only at the very top of the organization are a few managers or executives able to comprehend the entire production operation.

Most workers, whether blue collar or white collar, are required to perform repetitive and routinized activities. They are ignorant of the larger production process, and they do not experience the satisfaction of producing a whole product. Furthermore, their activities are highly restricted and regularized by the nature of the job, and there is little opportunity to learn new skills or to make independent judgments. Most workers have very little control over the process of their work activity and have little or no opportunity to express their own ideas, insights, and individuality (Blauner 1964). Although workers and managers have more independence at the higher levels of organizational structure, some restriction on activity is characteristic even there.

As work has become increasingly characterized by wage employment, most workers have come to toil for external rewards rather than intrinsic satisfaction. Income to be used for consumption is the most important form of external reward. Workers are forced to relinquish control over the nature of their work activities as part of the wage-labor contract, so wages and salaries become the focus of their work effort. Because most employees no longer expect to receive much satisfaction from their work, they place their hopes in rising levels of consumption of goods and services. Work is looked upon as the drudgery necessary to obtain a meaningful life in the sphere of buying and consumption. It is the prospect of higher levels of consumption that provides the major motivation for work rather than factors inherent in the work itself.

It is little wonder that the biographies of workers suggest that work is stultifying to personal growth, injurious to health, and for most people a very disappointing experience (Terkel 1974; U.S. Dep't of HEW 1973; House 1974; Kasl 1974). Most work lacks any intrinsic meaning that makes it worthy of doing for its own sake. It is commonly assumed that such a condition is necessary for a modern, high-technology society capable of yielding our high "standard of living." However, several historical studies suggest that technology and organizational practices have responded to the quest for domination of the workplace by its capitalist owners and for capital accumulation at the expense of workers (Marglin 1974; Gintis 1971; Edwards 1979). A highly centralized and bureaucratic workplace in which jobs are fragmented into repetitive and routinized tasks simplifies the extraction of labor from workers. Each employee need only follow a specific set of functions at a prescribed speed established by the organization and its machinery. Supervision is simplified, since productivity can be readily observed (Alchian & Demsetz 1972), and the elementary nature of the tasks means that workers can be easily replaced if they do not do what is expected (see Haber 1964 on the "scientific management" approach of F. Taylor).

Thus, the internal discipline and control of the workplace by the few at the top of the organization are cemented by both hierarchy and the division of labor. Workers are set apart not only from those above and below them, but also from fellow workers at the same level. Under conditions of high unemployment, workers see themselves as fortunate to have a job or to have steady work. The possibility of promotion up the pyramid depends on few rising, so workers are placed in a competitive and antagonistic position toward one another. Not only has this mode of organization undermined the establishment of trade unions, but it has also pitted groups of workers against each other: skilled workers become jealous about maintaining their wage and other advantages over unskilled ones; and race and sex antagonisms are also exploited and exacerbated as workers are forced to compete for jobs and benefits.

Interestingly, recent studies show that productivity (although not control of the work force and the extraction of profits through its labor) would be higher according to other modes of work organization. The recent study of *Work in America* (U.S. Dep't of HEW 1973) identified a large number of experiments that modified traditional work relations and increased productivity. Studies of industrial worker cooperatives have shown similar results (Jackall & Levin 1984; A. Johnson & Whyte 1977). Although capital accumulation on behalf of the owners of productive property has expanded at a rapid rate historically, the cost of this expansion to the work force has been conditions of work that do not permit a healthy personal and social development or a satisfying work experience.

The Legitimization of Labor Organizations

The workplace, then, is organized to reproduce capitalist relations of production and the concentration within a small segment of the population of capital accumulation and ownership.

But characteristics of the workplace have been and continue to be shaped by conflicts between employers and labor. In the United States, the workplace is healthier today than it was fifty years ago, and workers have more rights, primarily because labor organizations have struggled for greater protection on the job and for increased job security. Much of this struggle has come to be directed through the State.

Employers, by contrast, have sought throughout the industrialization process to find new ways to increase the difference between labor's productivity and wages. Labor's response to these efforts has been to organize to resist and, in some cases, to oppose the capitalist system. With the advent of the Depression, the threat of labor militancy reached such proportions that employers reluctantly accepted the recognition of labor organizations as legal entities (Skocpol 1981). These organizations indirectly became associated with apparatuses of the State, joining schools and other State institutions as arenas of conflict between the democratic and reproductive dynamics of capitalist society.

The history of the trade union movement in America since the turn of the century is not only a history of worker struggle for higher wages and better working conditions in the place of production, but also a history of struggle for increasing worker influence over the State in order to raise the possibilities for economic gains and protection against employer antilabor practices. In the context of that latter struggle, choices were made both by the State and by labor organizations around the issue of the *kind* of labor organizations that would represent workers in America and the role of labor in the production system.

In an effort to mediate the capital-labor conflict of the post-1890 period (a conflict characterized by frequent violence and the potential for a widespread labor revolt) in favor of a peaceful continuation of capitalist development, the State gradually recognized the need for organized labor to have an effective role in the capitalist production system. Labor gained recognition and influence in wage and production policy because of its willingness to engage in political and economic conflict with the owners and managers of capital. Recognition was certainly a labor victory, yet not all worker organizations were recognized by the State. As recognition and inclusion were being extended to the American Federation of Labor (AFL), the State was simultaneously destroying the Industrial Workers of the World (IWW), which opposed many of the employer's prerogatives associated with property ownership. The State chose to include those labor leaders who were willing to help preserve capitalist social relations of production and to participate "constructively" in the preservation of a State that fostered such production. Thus the AFL (and later the CIO) agreed that the role of labor unions in the production sector should be limited to bargaining with employers over clearly defined issues of wages and working conditions, not over control of production or the relationship between employers and employees. These State-sanctioned bargaining units took on the function of enforcing the division of labor worked out by the corporations and of channeling worker militancy into legal activities. Collective bargaining under the National Labor Relations Act (NLRA) and the Wagner Act regularized the interaction between labor and business, particularly the large corporations.

The State-recognized union is bound by collective-bargaining agreements to make workers adhere to contracts negotiated with management. This is part of the regularization of the labor process. American labor unions not only are limited to confronting the system of production through collective bargaining, they are part of the labor-market control mechanism for the corporate hierarchy (Aronowitz 1973). Whereas small competitive firms face difficulties in dealing with labor unions because they usually cannot pass on wage increases to consumers in the form of higher prices, large corporations, dominating a high fraction of the market for their products, can pass on a large part of those negotiated wage increases to consumers. Although large domestic firms may face competition from abroad, extensive foreign investment covers their interests in foreign markets and in the importation of American-manufactured goods using foreign labor. Thus, the State's recognition of unions as bargaining units, though often fatal to small firms, provides the large firm with stability in the supply of labor and control over the labor force through worker organizations themselves.

Most important, since the unions have a stake in corporate

capitalism, they serve as a buffer against the rise of worker groups hostile to corporations. The union hierarchies that emerged in the 1930's have monitored radical challenges to corporate control of the production system. They have "educated" their workers to limit their demands to collective bargaining and to channel their grievances through the conventional arbitration machinery rather than taking direct action. They have ostracized radicals who question the system. And they have strengthened the segmented labor markets that separate unskilled from skilled work, and unionized from nonunionized labor. Yet such unions, as organizations of workers, are always in a certain amount of conflict with management over the distribution of revenue—favoring higher wages and benefits rather than management's desired higher profits and capital expansion. Unions have, for example, consistently backed higher minimum wages and, more recently, the Equal Rights Amendment (equal pay for women).* Unions have also lobbied for greater State-financed benefits, such as Social Security, unemployment compensation, and welfare assistance. These increases in the social wage may have also cut into the share of capital controlled by the private sector (Bowles & Gintis 1982).

These activities pose contradictions for capitalist reproduction. They illustrate how even corporate worker organizations are inherently in conflict with corporate management. The two may share an interest in smooth capital accumulation, but they also represent different interests: higher wages and better working conditions versus control of profits and returns to stockholders. This explains why, in the early 1980's, management—with the cooperation of a pro-business regime in Washington—has attempted to dismantle the power of American labor unions, and new firms have fought to keep unions out.

---

*The antagonism between relatively high wage union labor and lower wage fractions of the working class is not as all-embracing as the contradiction between capital and labor. For example, unionized labor in general has an interest in establishing higher minimum wage standards for all members of the labor force and higher levels of public assistance, whereas capital has an interest in reducing these. In the long run unionization has probably contributed to raising the standards of living of all workers through union political activity, although its direct economic effect has likely increased relative differences in wages between union and nonunion labor.

The State as Employer

As the union movement grew under State recognition, the State greatly expanded its own role as employer. Indeed, both legally sanctioned collective bargaining and public employment were a response to the threat of massive labor unrest during the Great Depression. In 1920, the State employed 9 percent of the labor force; in 1930, 10 percent; in 1940, 13 percent; in 1970, 18 percent; and in 1980, 16 percent (Carnoy, Shearer & Rumberger 1983: Chap. 6).

The growth of government employment took place largely at the state and local levels. Growth of the school system was a particularly important factor in increased public employment. Since the Second World War, government has also tended to employ an increasing fraction of college graduates, minority males, and women—especially college-educated minorities and women—and pays blacks and women more than the private sector does for similar jobs (Carnoy, Shearer & Rumberger 1983: Chap. 6). When differences in education, age, and work experience are accounted for, blacks and women receive more in the public than in the private sector, whereas white males receive less than in the private sector (*ibid.*).

The State sector, therefore, provides opportunities for minorities and women that the private sector is apparently not willing or able to provide. The State does this in response to pressures on the public sector to fulfill the mobility aspirations created by the American ideology of a classless society characterized by equal opportunity for all. Women's employment in education, social welfare, and other public-sector service jobs results also in part from a historical and cultural process of using educated women to deal with children and indigents. The State's willingness to respond to the failure of the market system to provide equal employment opportunities for less advantaged groups seems to reinforce the unequal relations of production in the private sector. But it also undermines those relations by providing and legitimating alternative employment based upon more egalitarian criteria.

This direct intervention into labor markets creates contradictions in the public sector. Since unemployment has been a continuing American economic problem, as minorities and women become better educated the public sector must absorb increasing numbers of marginalized workers. Rising costs have created increasing resistance to maintaining this role. Furthermore, public employees' unions, once organized, have attempted to raise wages, thus increasing public employment costs even more. The State is in a dilemma of having to employ more and more highly educated workers who cannot find jobs elsewhere but of being unable to raise taxes to cover the cost of that employment, particularly given demands by monopoly capital interests for a strong U.S. military posture (O'Connor 1973).

The most important characteristic of recent government expansion is the increasing role the State has played in the economy. Whereas in 1980 16 percent of Americans were directly employed by the government sector, it was estimated in 1979 that another 7–8 percent were employed in quasi-private firms that depended on government contracts (*National Journal*, May 5, 1979: 730). Thus, one in four members of the labor force is directly or indirectly a government employee. Furthermore, another one-half percent of the labor force is in prison, at an annual cost of approximately $13,000 per prisoner in 1978 (U.S. Dep't of Commerce, *Statistical Abstract 1981*: Tables 313 and 333), and (in 1979) the government paid out $1,120 per capita in social insurance and welfare (social security, federal retirement, disability benefits, unemployment compensation, Medicare and Medicaid, and veterans' benefits [see Carnoy & Shearer 1980: 340]).

The Present Structure of the Labor Market and Its Contradictions

The current foundations of work in the United States, based upon private ownership of capital and contracted wage labor, contain inherent tensions. These arise—as we suggested in Chapter 2—from the antagonistic social relations that are the central feature of such a system. The response of management to these tensions has been to segment the labor force—a segmentation that is compounded by racial, gender, and age divisions in labor. As part of this segmentation, unions have come to play a dual role, of regularizing production for employers and of struggling for greater worker power both in individual firms and through the State in the political and economic structure as a whole. The State has also intervened directly in employment, providing mobility for educated minorities and women who would not have been absorbed as professionals in the private sector.

The same processes of capitalist development that have characterized the United States since the early eighteenth century—the increasing division of labor and the attempt to lower labor costs—provide the basis for continuing contradictions. With the end of free immigration in the 1920's, cheap labor had to be recruited from minority groups and women, both of whom had been at the margin of the labor force before the First World War. The percentage of women in the labor force increased particularly rapidly after 1940: from 24.4 percent in 1940, to 28.5 percent in 1948, 32.8 percent in 1959, 38.5 percent in 1973, and 43.5 percent in 1982 (*Economic Report of the President* 1983: Table B-30). For the most part, both minorities and women have been relegated to low-paying, low-status jobs, with little prospect of upward mobility in the private sector.

Nonetheless, the relatively high wages of even women and minorities in the United States compared to those abroad is driving many competitive industries to relocate production in low-wage countries for export back to the United States. In effect, this reduces the employment possibilities for the marginal groups here, increasing the reserve army of the unemployed despite the restriction on immigration. Furthermore, monopoly industries have shifted from exporting their goods to foreign countries to producing them there for sale in the local market. Transnational monopolies have extended the division of labor in the firm to the international level. Workers are separated not only by departmental ladders, but by national boundaries, language differences, and long distances.

Changes in the technical and social organization of production in the last century have therefore divided the job structure into segments or clusters. Each segment has different wage levels, entrance requirements, and promotion patterns, and each is predominantly staffed by workers from particular backgrounds (see Carnoy 1980; D. Gordon, Edwards & Reich 1982).

The great majority of workers are divided not only into job segments, but also into different types of firms. In the private sector, one group of firms is marked by capital-intensive technology and long-term planning horizons (monopoly firms), whereas the other group is marked by relatively low capital per worker, short planning horizons, and even a short firm life (competitive firms).*

These segments are overlaid by the discriminatory character of present-day capitalist production. Considerable evidence supports the view that women and blacks (as well as Spanish-speaking minorities) are discriminated against in the labor market on the basis not of their skills but of their gender, race, or ethnic background (Gwartney & Long 1978; Reich 1981). There is a close relationship between race or ethnic group and class.† But discrimination against women cuts across social classes and is rooted in another historical phenomenon—patriarchy—that preceded capitalism but now under capitalism appears in new forms (for example, see Hartmann 1979). Even so, women and minorities (especially blacks) are concentrated in competitive industries and the public sector, which gives a particular character to those industry segments.

For analytical purposes, today's work structure can be divided into three segments, each typified by different work conditions and required worker characteristics. The first is a well-paid segment of jobs requiring high levels of general education that cuts across both competitive and monopoly sectors of the economy (this is the "high-education" segment). Technical

*The central factor relating monopoly-sector workers and other workers or potential workers is that the former can only sustain historically higher wages in the face of technical change by insulating themselves from competition with lower-wage labor. As technical change and the increasing division of labor lower special skill and experience requirements, the pool of potential substitutes for jobs held by skilled, experienced labor expands. The larger this pool of potential substitutes and the lower the wage for which such people are willing to work, the more imperative organization on a broad base becomes for the workers who have historically established higher wages. Only through organization can the monopoly-sector workers retain this deterrent and prevent the erosion of their wage differentials through gradual substitution.

†Much more than sex and class, race and class have become entwined in American social life. Nevertheless, the fact that racial discrimination has been shaped historically by particular institutions such as slavery does make it different from a "pure" class issue. The best recent analysis of race in the American economy is Reich 1981.

change constantly creates new jobs within this segment, but it eliminates or simplifies many jobs formerly requiring high education. There is job competition on an individual basis within this segment, but the high education requirement has, until recently, restricted access to males from middle- and upper-class backgrounds.

Employees in this segment have the most autonomy, the highest pay, and the most job security of any group of workers in the economy. Although there are substantial individual differences in income and power within this segment—and considerable competition among workers for the most important and best-paid jobs—the relatively privileged position of the group as a whole contributes to a strong sense of identification with the profitability goals of the employer, and with the general principles of division of labor, hierarchical control of production, and private property. Currently, however, circumstances that have bolstered the privileges and job autonomy of the high-education segment are dissolving. The separation of planning from execution is increasingly applied to mental as well as manual work. Intellectual work itself is increasingly subdivided into relatively routinized tasks that require a high level of education but little job-specific experience, and that involve only minor or moderate individual responsibility for capital value.*

Furthermore, the traditional role that the public sector has played in absorbing highly educated minority and women workers is also being attacked. The fiscal crisis of the State has stimulated attempts to reduce public-sector employment at both the federal and the local levels. This means, in effect, that women and minority professionals (as well as lower-segment public workers) will be thrown into the private labor market, where relative wages for those groups are lower and the number of professional jobs fewer. The data we have cited showing the importance of the public sector in enabling more highly educated minority and women workers to move up occupationally and receive higher salaries also suggest that the cuts in public-sector employment for those groups will produce a large sur-

---

*Teaching in primary and secondary schools is an excellent example of a high-education job that is systematically being reduced to simpler components through programmed workbooks and, in some cases, educational media.

plus of labor for the more highly educated segment of the private sector. Whether public-sector workers forced to take lower-income jobs in the private sector will do so smoothly is another question.

Second, there is a "unionized" segment characterized by unionization, internal hierarchies, and relative job security for employees with seniority. Although the jobs in this segment do not necessarily require more experience or education than jobs in the competitive sector, they are more highly paid than those jobs. Workers in this segment have historically been able to capture some of the gains from the increased labor productivity brought by mechanization and have been able to maintain higher wages through nonmarket mechanisms that have restricted the entry of lower-wage labor.* A central unifying feature of jobs in the unionized sector is that their content can be more or less routinized and codified in a set of rules and standard operating procedures. Jobs in this sector are finely subdivided components of larger processes. Though there are some jobs that involve individual operation of large machinery and thus retain some scope for individual feelings of mastery and accomplishment, many more are repetitive assembly-line tasks. By their very nature, these jobs afford the worker little intrinsic satisfaction, so that the motivation to perform them must come from outside the job—from its circumstances rather than from its content. The major circumstance rendering work in this sector tolerable is, of course, the relatively high salary level. On the average, salaries are still below those of the high-education sector; but for levels of education through junior college, jobs in the monopolized union sector pay relatively better and afford more stable employment than jobs in the competitive sector. There are also established standards of productivity and working conditions on unionized jobs to protect against arbitrary dismissal or speedup.

Education can become a liability in the unionized sector. A highly educated employee is likely to view routinized jobs as even more stultifying and boring than otherwise, and is likely to be more ambitious for upward mobility and new experiences

---

*Unions also have an interest in requiring some educational credential for entry into the sector, as this requirement helps to keep the most disadvantaged low-wage labor out and thus helps to prevent erosion of wage levels.

than the fixed seniority systems in this sector can accommodate (Quinn & Baldi DeMandilovitch 1975). What is required on these jobs is a willingness to relinquish meaningful work experiences to obtain income and job security. Fulfilling activity will only be sought outside the workplace.

Third, there is a "competitive" segment characterized by the lowest wages, least steady employment, and poorest working conditions and advancement opportunities. This segment includes not only jobs in competitive firms, but also clerical jobs in monopoly firms. The latter have developed only with the growth of monopoly and mass production itself. From the outset they were separated from production jobs in the monopoly segment and were never the locus of struggle by a previously entrenched group of workers. Hence, employers were able immediately to recruit low-wage labor for them. Jobs in the competitive segment are overwhelmingly staffed by women, minority group members, and other relative newcomers to wage labor.

The overwhelming majority of workers in the competitive segment of the labor market are those who have not obtained or cannot obtain jobs in higher segments. These categories include workers without at least a high school diploma, workers with a high school diploma who have been denied entry into the unionized sector by discriminatory regulations and practices, young workers waiting for an "opening" into the monopolized, unionized sector, or workers who either desire or are constrained to work less than full time. Workers who fall into one of these categories are not just a random sample of the labor force. Women, blacks, Chicanos, Puerto Ricans, illegal aliens, recent immigrants, and workers from impoverished rural backgrounds contribute a disproportionate percentage of adult labor in the competitive segment. Teenagers who work are almost exclusively confined to competitive-segment employment, regardless of race, sex, or socioeconomic background; teenagers from minority groups are frequently unable to find employment at all.

The competitive segment, then, is a low-skill, generally low-education market. Although dependability and discipline are desirable and may command a slight wage premium even in this market, employers must take what they can get and depend on tight supervision and the threat of dismissal to extract labor from their workers. Submissiveness and passivity are the traits most characteristically required by such jobs.

Finally, there is a dwindling crafts segment, jobs requiring traditional manual skills that can only be learned through lengthy practical experience. Craft workers are largely organized in craft unions, which through licensing and certification procedures attempt to restrict competition for members' jobs. They are located in both the monopoly and competitive spheres, and many craft workers are self-employed. Craft workers are relatively well paid and exercise more autonomy over their work activities than any workers except those in the high-education segment, but technological advances constantly undermine the need for craft skills.

These differences in social relations imply that different sets of skills, values, and attitudes are relevant to productivity in the different segments. Neoclassical models of labor markets generally assume that wages are closely related to productivity; therefore, the relationship of worker characteristics such as education and age to earnings represents a relation between worker attributes and worker productivity. The level of wages and the return for additional education and experience in work are assumed to reflect the contribution to output of more schooling and more experience. The firm pays workers in accordance with their marginal product because of competition in the job market for workers by employers and for jobs by workers.

This notion is a theoretical, rather than an empirical, construct (Carter & Carnoy 1976). There is no convincing way to verify that wages equal productivity across jobs or firms producing different products. Since people with higher education and experience do tend to receive higher wages, we can infer that, unless employers are completely irrational or maximizing something other than output, there is some correlation between productivity, education, and experience. Yet, this relation can only be assumed to meet the productivity claim of neoclassical economics under conditions of perfect market competition and full employment. No one argues that such conditions are an accurate picture of reality. We already know from numerous studies that the relation of education and experience to earnings *is* different for different sexes, races, and occupational groups (Gwartney & Long 1978; Rumberger & Carnoy 1980).

The Contradictions in Labor Market Segmentation

The expansion of the labor force in the 1970's has taken place under particular economic conditions. Absolute employment grew rapidly (2.5 percent annually) between 1970 and 1980, but real weekly wages declined 16 percent over the decade (Carnoy, Shearer & Rumberger 1983: Chap. 3). The spread between productivity increases and real wage increases grew even though productivity growth slowed down. Yet profits did not rise significantly, probably because the costs of nonlabor inputs—particularly energy—increased rapidly, and demand decreased.

However, there has been a trend toward maintaining or raising profits in the 1980's by holding down wages, even to the point of absolute wage reduction. Part of this strategy is reflected in the union-busting policies of the Reagan Administration. More generally, the increase of women in production work, the incorporation of illegal aliens into the competitive segment, runaway shops, and the rapid incorporation of highly educated workers into the labor force are all facets of the reaction on the part of capitalists to the need to maintain or increase the profitability of capital. But all also create contradictions in the production process.

Women are apparently less likely to organize into unions (in 1978, according to U.S. Dep't of Commerce, *Statistical Abstract 1981*, Tables 636 and 391, only 13 percent of women in the labor force were unionized as compared to 28 percent of men). This may be attributable to women's high representation in the semiskilled jobs, where it is easy for employers to discipline them with the fear that they will be fired if they attempt to organize. It may also reflect women's more tenuous attachment to the workplace. Women workers in this stage of their incorporation into the labor force also seem to consider paid employment as a positive good, giving them a chance to earn some extra money for the family and to get away from an oppressive situation in the home. Under these circumstances, they are less likely to make demands on employers. Furthermore, women may be socialized in the family and in the schools to be more docile and compliant, and to set a lower value on their services than do men.

Though bringing these lower-paid, more compliant workers into the labor force is favorable to profitability in the short run, it produces important contradictions for capitalist development. Increasing the percentage of women in the labor force may contribute to the demise of the nuclear family. Fewer and fewer women identify themselves solely with home life and dependence on their husbands for income. As daughters see their mothers working, their own aspirations gradually increase and their docility in the labor market should also gradually decrease. This suggests that women—who in the last few decades have provided such a large percentage of the increase in the labor force—are less likely to be a source of low-paid, compliant labor in the future. The destruction of the traditional male-dominated family, and with it the destruction of an important socializer of female labor, will eventually have profound effects on the institutions (including schools) that attempt to reproduce relations in production, since such institutions are interdependent.

The incorporation of illegal aliens into the labor force, and the shift of capital to low-wage foreign countries to increase profits, successfully avoid attempts by organized labor to increase its bargaining power by restricting immigration. Expanding foreign production by U.S. firms places downward pressures on wages in all segments that are affected by competition with foreign workers. In effect, these moves often make possible union wage concessions in the United States to save jobs, increasing the profitability of U.S. production. However, such developments also create contradictions. High rates of unemployment in the United States result in part from the unwillingness of private corporations to hire domestic labor at conventional wage rates, since this would reduce profits below what firms can earn by going abroad or employing illegal aliens.* If the civilian public sector had not grown so rapidly since the Second World War, unemployment would have been

---

*In the early 1960's, about 45 percent of the U.S. labor force was part-time or part-year, and most of these workers were women, blacks, and young white males (Morse 1969).

even higher, particularly among professional women and minorities (Carnoy, Girling & Rumberger 1976). The continued existence of high unemployment in the 1970's and 1980's thus implies the necessity of increased government intervention, either as an employer of last resort or as a provider of sufficient public assistance for the unemployed to have a steady income. But this in turn increases taxes on those who are already employed, either directly or through inflation, which has led to taxpayer revolts (O'Connor 1973) and recent cuts in welfare and social programs. As formerly unionized work is shifted to foreign labor markets, a politically volatile group of workers threatens to expand in numbers. Without increased government intervention in the labor market, the large numbers of the unemployed pose a possible threat to the capitalist system. As social benefits are lowered, social movements like those of the 1960's could be the response.

The reduction in job opportunities for highly educated workers also creates the contradiction of alienation and frustration among workers who had high expectations when entering the labor market. Higher education has traditionally entitled its recipients to a secure, remunerative career holding jobs with a high degree of autonomy, responsibility, and status. As college graduates with these job expectations have been confronted with the reality of routinized, standardized work, they have felt frustration and alienation. Increased production of college graduates can only exacerbate the contradiction between expectations and reality, between socialization patterns and actual workplace reproduction requirements. In part, this contradiction will probably result in the division of the high-education segment itself into traditional and unionized compartments. Many workers will continue to hold the high-education jobs of the past, but a large portion of what used to be high-education jobs will be deskilled in the monopoly and public sectors. At the same time, our model predicts that business interests will attempt both to change education to reduce students' expectations when they graduate from high school and college, and to expand the "vocational" character of higher education to prepare students for the new, routinized jobs they will be getting.

These changes in education were already observable in the mid-1970's. Recent years have seen increased differentiation in postsecondary education and increased efforts by people in the highest echelon of the postsecondary system, the universities and elite colleges, to go on to graduate schools, particularly professional schools. The change in labor market conditions has had a disciplinary effect on undergraduate students, leading them to concentrate more on grades and less on political activity.

The Changing Nature of Social Conflict

Our analysis suggests that as private employers attempt to hold down pay in the face of labor pressure for higher wages, conditions in the labor market change in ways that have significant implications for social conflict in general and for the educational system in particular. Some of the changes of the last fifteen years include a continued increase in the percentage of women in the labor force, high rates of youth unemployment (especially minority youth unemployment), and increasing average education both of the unemployed and of those workers employed in menial, repetitive jobs. Associated with all these factors is continued government social-welfare spending to soften unemployment, and private-sector inability or unwillingness to absorb more highly educated minorities and women at wages approximating those of white men. Government social-welfare spending and direct employment have changed the labor conflict in recent years and distinguish the economic crisis of the 1970's and early 1980's from previous crises. We have suggested that the social crisis of the 1930's changed the conditions of capitalist production, involving the State in mediation and allocation of its increasing share of total national resources. As the American labor movement continued to confine itself to traditional wage-bargaining struggles, refusing to raise the labor-corporate conflict into the political arena except by backing particular candidates, organized labor as such gradually lost its vanguard position in social movements. The legitimization of unions within the State shifted the dynamic of conflict away from private production and the traditional wage struggle. The new social movements—the civil rights movement in the 1950's and 1960's, the antiwar movement in the 1960's, the women's movement in the 1970's and 1980's, the environmental and consumer movements in the 1970's, the antinuclear movement in the 1980's—all focused directly on the State. These movements affirmed more than ever before the direct interventionist role of the State.

But the State collects its revenue mainly from individual income, property, and sales taxes. Under the New Deal accords, labor and employers could both gain from economic growth. Employers' profits remained high and permitted capital investment that raised worker productivity to offset increasing real wages. And as long as the economy grew steadily with real wages at about the same rate as increasing productivity, prices remained stable and tax revenues also increased. Labor and capital did not resist higher taxes as long as wages and profits were increasing.

In the late 1960's, this delicate arrangement began to break up. Government spending increased rapidly to pay for an unpopular war in Southeast Asia. At the same time, massive domestic spending on programs for inner cities was used to head off urban unrest. In an already tight labor market, profit rates fell and wages as a percentage of gross national product (GNP) rose significantly. The wage bargains achieved by many unions were lucrative. Employment increased at record rates. All this, combined with the riots in the ghettos of major cities in 1964–68, and the antiwar movement in 1967–71, changed the way business viewed the future of the New Deal accords (Carnoy, Shearer & Rumberger 1983). Not only did growth slow in the United States after 1972, but there was a shift of private investment from productivity-increasing to wage-reducing investment. The oil crisis reinforced the trend. The primary concern of business is profits. Unlike the postwar period when profits were rising even with increased real wages, the 1970's saw employers essentially abandon the old accord in favor of reducing real wages (hence increasing profits) through political struggle.

Labor, in turn, attempted to hold its position by pushing up the State's social welfare spending. But now increases in such spending had to be eked out of a declining growth rate. Social spending did rise in the mid-1970's, yet the rise was not great enough to offset falling wages (Bowles & Gintis 1982). The mass of Americans translated their frustrations with falling purchasing power into anger against the State, particularly against inflationary spending and rising tax rates. In James O'-Connor's terms (1973, 1974, 1981), the State's expansion of government spending for defense and as a response to falling real wages flew in the face of voter resistance to increased taxes, leading to the "fiscal crisis of the State." Voters saw inflation as a government spending problem rather than the result of a labor-capital conflict that labor was losing.

The backlash was first manifested in tax resistance—for example, the passage of Proposition 13 in California—which resulted in a severe slowing in the growth of real public spending on education and other locally provided services. Then the Reagan Administration came into office promising to cut government spending and taxes as a means of stimulating general economic recovery. Social-welfare spending and taxes were cut, but military spending was increased substantially. The State had also become unabashedly anti-union and the unemployment rate had increased to almost 11 percent by the end of 1982. In addition, the tax and spending cuts together changed U.S. income distribution in favor of the rich.

The tax revolt and voter support of conservative economic policies have had an impact on education. As the generation of postwar babies began to leave schools, the middle class showed itself less and less willing to pay for more education through taxation. Proposition 13 in California lowered property taxes, which in turn resulted in less real spending per capita in California schools and a sharp slowdown in per pupil real spending even though the number of pupils in California public primary and secondary schools dropped from 4.4 to 4.1 million between 1976 and 1981 (Calif. Dep't of Finance 1982: Table F-8). Spending per pupil (in 1976 dollars) rose from $1,546 to $1,767 between 1976 and 1981; spending per capita fell from $357 to $299. Class size has increased and the number of class periods in each day has decreased. Federal aid to education—which had been central to expanding education since the early 1960's—has been cut sharply. Reductions in student loan programs and in funding for social science research have hurt colleges and universities. There have been moves to "privatize" education through legislation that provides tax credits for tuition paid to private schools (James & Levin 1983). Simultaneously, the Reagan economic package cut other social welfare spending and federal employment. These cuts have indirectly and directly reduced government employment outside education, so that social mobility for women and minority groups through such employment has been reduced drastically (in 1980, about 50 percent of college-educated women and minorities were working in the public sector—see Carnoy, Shearer & Rumberger 1983: Chap. 6).

This assault on public education and State employment is a direct attack on the New Deal interpretation of capitalist ideology—an interpretation in which the State both provides the educational means to social mobility and underwrites the American dream through its employment and income policies. The assault also represents an attempt to restrict the democratic aspects of schooling and expand schooling's skill production in a more strictly class-reproductive structure. In that structure, parents with enough income would have many options about where to send their children to private school, whereas public schools would become—even more than they are now—holding operations for less employable minorities, with correspondingly lower expenditures per pupil.

The conflict over public spending and taxation is an expression of a social conflict that is being carried on largely in the political arena of the State. Corporate leaders themselves are divided over the extent to which a conservative policy on such spending should carry the day. Many are concerned that high rates of unemployment and a sharp redistribution of income could lead to a popular attack on corporations and then to structural change. Also, employers in such education-intensive sectors as research and development and the high-technology industries worry that eroded educational expenditures will reduce America's comparative advantage in technology and world commerce. Most employers, however, continue to focus on reducing labor's bargaining power and on increasing the proportion of State resources going to capital rather than labor to raise profits and expand corporate control of economic development. This strategy has worked in the early 1980's because labor has been divided on the issues of taxation, social-welfare spending, and the fiscal crisis of the State. But the result has been to make employment and education major issues and points of conflict.

In their role as taxpayers, voters charged with paying for the fiscal crisis of the State have turned against the State. The social movements of the 1960's failed to impose themselves politically and produce alternative solutions to the crisis that would preserve and extend the democratic gains of the postwar period. With that failure, corporate economic power reasserted itself in an assault on those gains. Part of that assault, with direct assistance from a frustrated working class, was on the educational system. As funds were cut from education, the groups that hoped for improved access to better jobs were increasingly cut off from those jobs. At the same time, the availability of any kind of work for minorities was reduced by a traditional conservative economic strategy of disciplining the labor force through higher unemployment rates and anti-union policies. The effect on the schools of educational spending reductions, increased unemployment, and falling real wages has been to reduce their "democratic" side and make them increasingly oriented toward reproducing the relations of capitalist production and its class division of labor.

We have shown in this chapter that conflicts over education emerge from conflicts over the direction of capitalist development, particularly the distribution of its benefits. Stresses in workplace relations and changes in the division of labor place new demands on the schools, as do new social movements, which increasingly focus on schools to provide expanding access to resources and democratic rights. In the next chapter we show how the dynamics of reproduction and expanding democracy were manifested in the growth of American education, and how in different periods of history one or the other of these dynamics prevailed to produce particular educational reforms.

4

Social Conflict and
the Structure of Education

Workers are made, not born. First and foremost, they are molded by the workplace. The nature of the class structure and its inherent conflict are formed in this arena. Worker values and skills are also developed there. Yet molding takes place in other institutions besides the workplace, some of which, unlike capitalist enterprises, are charged with reproducing a more equal and more democratic society in addition to reproducing unequal relations of work. Young people are prepared for adult roles in such contradictory institutions well before reaching the workplace. The education system is the principal public institution organized for shaping youth into working adults, but schools are subject to conflicting forces over their purpose and operation. Public education both reproduces the unequal hierarchical relations of the nuclear family and capitalist workplace and also presents opportunities for social mobility and the extension of democratic rights.

A main proposition of this book is that schooling, like all the institutions of capitalist society, operates in the context of social conflict. Schooling is shaped by the nature of that conflict, and what schooling does helps shape the conflict. Even as schools reproduce capitalist class relations, contradictions to capitalist development emerge from that very reproductive process. The State tries to help employers raise profits, but at the same time it has to legitimate itself by providing benefits to labor and making society more just. Set in the arena of social conflict, the

State therefore disseminates a contradictory ideology that tries to build faith both in capitalism and in democracy. Public education is both a subsidy to employers and a way for workers to gain social mobility; it trains young people to be good workers and good democrats, reproducing a class-structured labor force to fit into a historically defined division of labor, but also inculcating aspirations about the nature of work in a democratic society.

We have shown that the functionalist analysis stresses only the correspondence between work, society, and education—the lack of autonomy in social institutions. By contrast, the progressive analysis stresses the "contradictory" nature of schooling—its autonomy from the workplace and from the injustices of society as a whole. As an autonomous abstraction of society, the progressive school tried to shape youth's values and norms to make society more equitable, democratic, and humane.

In our view, the educational system of a democratic State tends to serve the changing imperatives of both the workplace and the norms of a democratic society. The infusion of class tensions into State apparatuses—including education—means that the educational system can be in part dysfunctional to capitalist development, even creating contradictions in production and altering the work process.

In this chapter and the two that follow we analyze the inherent tensions in schooling. These tensions have shaped the development of education, just as young people, in turn, are shaped by the resulting education process and the tensions in it—tensions inseparable from the reproductive process itself. This is why it is possible for Lawrence Cremin (1964, 1976) to view American education as a shaper of social development, whereas Bowles and Gintis (1976) view it as reproducing the relations of production. In our view, Bowles and Gintis have correctly identified the development of capitalist work relations as a significant dynamic influencing educational change, but American public education has been subject throughout its history to competing forces seeking on the one hand to reproduce these relations and on the other to expand economic opportunity and human rights. During some periods one dynamic has gained ground at the expense of the other.

In this chapter, we will focus on the structure of schooling and its historical development. Because the structure of schooling has been shaped not only by the schools' role as a key institution in preparing the labor force for the capitalist workplace, but also by the larger conflicts occurring in capitalist society, this will necessitate our considering the history of capitalist transformation, egalitarian movements, and the struggle between the two.

There are two levels at which the schools are involved in reproduction. At the first, the school system's structure has developed in the context of capitalist production and class conflict. To the extent that employers have been able to exert their influence, assisted by a State committed to capitalist development, schools have been directed toward producing a labor force that would be functional for a changing workplace. At the second level, school practices have attempted to produce general values and norms consistent with the reproduction of relations of production and differentiated behavior and knowledge for young people who are destined for different segments of the labor force.

Class-based reproduction is derived from the structure of production: the family, church, and school in varying degrees prepare people for the organization of work and the labor market requirements unfolding in any historical moment. The class-based reproduction process attempts to prepare young people to accept capitalist development by reconciling themselves to their role in it. Such reproduction also attempts to prepare people of different social classes for certain broad categories of work. This does not mean that every individual in a particular social class ends up working in the same job category or earning the same level of income; rather, it implies that institutions of socialization are such that someone from a lower social class is likely to take less schooling, obtain different knowledge, and work in lower-paying categories of occupation than someone with parents in highly skilled production work or professional jobs. The class-based process we describe does not have its origin in the lower intelligence, motivation, or organization of those who end up in lower-paying work (as neoclassical economic, sociological, and psychological theory would have us believe); rather, it originates in the nature of capitalist production and the legitimizing role of the capitalist State.

The democratic dynamic underlying education is well reflected by the fact that public schooling has generally been accepted by the mass of Americans as a legitimate social institution. State-run schooling—like the community schools that preceded it—has been formally autonomous from production, administered by educational professionals, and subject to parental review. School expansion, we will argue, occurred primarily because of pressures from working- and middle-class parents and school personnel themselves. Once schooling became an important way to allocate young workers into different kinds of jobs, and once more schooling became synonymous with access to higher-paying, less physically demanding work, the State had to expand schooling in response to demands from a middle- and working-class public seeking social mobility for its children.

The expansion of education in the United States and its increased influence in the reproduction process have also been rooted partly in the changing skill requirements brought about by capitalist development, and in the need of industrial capital to incorporate and socialize labor into a changing organization of production. As the United States moved from agrarian to industrial capitalism, employers supported educational expansion and reorganization (especially in urban, industrializing areas). This effort tended to develop, first, a reserve army of literate labor inculcated with behavior patterns necessary for factory work (and later for office work) and, second, a pool of highly educated, trainable labor to serve in the expanding technical and managerial stratum of production. Especially after the turn of the twentieth century, employers also pushed for an educational system that would teach people to accept their designated role in the production process, that would socialize young people into a class-stratified organization of production.

Rapid increases in the average level of schooling have not been matched by increased skill and responsibility requirements in the workplace. This has resulted in an "overeducation" or "underutilization" phenomenon that may be creating significant contradictions for capitalist production. The schools have also become centers of a youth "counterculture" not consistent with the work ethic and of union activity on the part of increasingly proletarianized teachers. (These and other contradictions will be analyzed in detail in Chapter 6, where we discuss specifically the contradictions for capitalist development of school expansion.)

Our thesis in this chapter is that educational growth in the United States was conditioned by the class conflict underlying capitalist production and the changing nature of the workplace. Schools expanded as part of a production-centered historical dynamic in which they reproduced the developing conditions of capitalist production while simultaneously responding to the demands of labor and growing school bureaucracies. The growth of schooling is intertwined with the changing workplace *and* with social demands for upward mobility and increased democracy; the tensions created by such competing demands—tensions that until recently were sometimes eased by educational expansion itself—have continually shaped the role and structure of schooling.

There is considerable controversy about the reasons for school expansion and even about how school expansion should be measured (see Kaestle & Vinovskis 1980; Katz 1980). But, as Michael Katz has argued (1980), the complexity of educational history should not keep us from trying to find a unifying explanation for educational expansion and reforms. In the following pages, we explore the major premises of such a unifying explanation to show how the American educational system developed in the context of changes in the workplace and in the nature of the workplace-centered social conflict as described in Chapter 3. Specifically, we argue that public schooling in the nineteenth century began its expansion largely in response to social demands at the community level. By the end of the century, however, as employers began systematically to homogenize and discipline the labor force in order to gain increased control over work within the firm, and as the class lines of the social conflict became more clearly drawn, employers moved to increase their influence over the schools. Yet even when this influence was established, school expansion was driven as much by middle- and working-class demands on the State for greater participation in the fruits of economic development as by employer interest in a socialized, trainable labor force. It is this tension between education as a source of social democracy and as a reproducer of capitalist production that we view as the underlying dynamic of school expansion and reform.

The Development of Educational Structure: A Brief Historical Interpretation

Early nineteenth-century U.S. capitalism was primarily agrarian, the household was the most common production unit, and the village or small town was the center of trade and nonhousehold social activities. As a result, the socialization of children into work was carried out almost entirely by the family and the community. Both cognitive skills and behavioral patterns were passed to children from parents and other adults in the household. This knowledge transfer was a relatively simple task, not because the skills to be learned lacked complexity, but because they were virtually unchanging from generation to generation, and because the transition to the work world did not require that the child adapt to a wholly new set of relationships.

The child learned concrete skills and adapted to the social relations of production within the family and community. "The pre-industrial family was . . . the chief unit of reproduction, production, consumption, socialization, education, and in some contexts, religious observance and political action. It was the institution to which the individual ordinarily turned to cope with the problems of age, sickness, and incapacity. Effective membership in society at large was attainable in many circumstances only by membership in a family through which a claim could be mediated" (Wrigley 1977: 72).* In pre-industrial America, education by family and community consisted primarily of apprentice-style learning in the home—a "relentless round of imitation, explanation, and trial and error"—plus some systematic religious interpretation and discipline by a community-approved clergy, and, least of all, learning of reading and writing in a school (Cremin 1976: 12–13). Most chil-

---

*Aries claims that the community—including family—was more important in determining the individual's fate than the family itself, but he does not address Wrigley's point that the family determined the limits of the domain which the individual could establish and even the community to which the individual belonged. (See Aries 1977: 227.)

dren in the eighteenth century did not go to school at all or only attended for a few years, perhaps to pick up the rudiments of reading and writing in English or Latin.

These early elementary schools were extensions of the home. "Dame schools" were usually conducted in the kitchen of a literate woman and provided most of the basic formal education available in the original thirteen colonies. Co-existing with the dame schools were the so-called "writing schools." They were ordinarily held outside the home, but, like the dame schools, stressed basic literacy and computational skills. Like the dame schools, too, the internal structure of the writing schools was informal.

By the end of the eighteenth century, as early capitalism matured, some important changes began to take place in the socialization process. An ideology developed around capitalist production, preaching an economic order based on the rational behavior of individuals acting in "natural liberty" to maximize the welfare of the society as a whole. Parallel to this ideology, ideas about raising children changed significantly, moving toward an increased emphasis on the love relationship between socializing adult and child. More and more the child was being differentiated as an entity separate from the family (Kagan 1977: 42). Schools became more widespread in the eighteenth century and, if not more systematized, then at least more secular, as evidenced by the successive eighteenth-century editions of *The New England Primer* (Cremin 1976: 36). Literacy in the colonies also increased rapidly, so that in 1776, Thomas Paine's *Common Sense* sold 500,000 copies in a population of 2.5 million. Colleges multiplied and became centers of bourgeois revolutionary ideas instead of religious learning (Cremin 1976: 38).

These changes were gradual, just as changes in American capitalism were occurring slowly. At the beginning of the nineteenth century, free farming by the family unit was still the predominant form of production in the North, just as it had been at the beginning of the previous century. But the increasing size of the towns, the beginnings of industrialization, the new emphasis on children's individuality, and the deepening of bourgeois ideas about individual choice and achievement influenced the socialization of children into work roles. As schooling gradually became a means to attain professional positions or entry into the mercantile class, it began displacing the church as the principal socializer outside the family.

The churches resisted this trend toward the secularization of education and the increasing importance of schools. Although the secularization of education was complete by the 1830's, according to Cremin, the evangelism of the 1830's and 1840's was a massive effort to respiritualize education, and "insofar as that effort was successful, agencies such as schools and colleges continued to teach the ideals of the revival long after the revival itself had lost its momentum" (Cremin 1976: 49). So despite religion's continued importance, the access to more prestigious and better-paying jobs provided by public schools gave them great social impact. Increasingly, the churches had to influence the schools in order to reach youth. At a different level, however, the churches were much more successful: in an effort to reestablish themselves as the fount of ideology, they became more patriotic. In the early nineteenth century, they were able to connect a patriotic American ethic to Protestantism. Thus, Protestant values continued to be one of the principal bases of American ideology despite the separation of church and State (Tyack & Hansot 1982: 20–25, 34–39).

The percentage of children enrolled in these early community schools increased steadily in the period 1800–1830, at least in such states as New York and Massachusetts (Kaestle & Vinovskis 1980). Many of these schools were private, but about half were already public schools. Thus, well before industrialization, a relatively high fraction of children in the North attended school, even if only for a few years and for less than 150 days annually.

Schooling and Industrial Capitalism

With industrialization, the family no longer constituted the dominant unit of production. Production was increasingly carried on in large organizations in which an employer directed the activities of the entire work force and owned the products of its labor. The social relations of production became distinct from the social relations of reproduction. Even more important, the organization of work in the factory was different from the structure of work in the home or in the artisan shop, and conflicted with many of the bourgeois values taught by family and church, mainly ideals of individuality and self-sufficiency. These continued to be the political and ideological bases of American laissez-faire capitalism, despite the fact that the factory system required punctuality, reliability, and willingness to follow directions unquestioningly. The factory was neither democratic nor tolerant of individuals who acted out of turn or attempted to change the conditions of work. The family and the church were unsuited to the task of socializing children to be good factory workers, both because production in the factory was much different from production on the family farm or in the home, and because the home and the church stressed a socialization much more relevant to a self-employed farmer or artisan who owned his tools, determined his pace of work, and chose the products he wished to produce and how to produce them.

There were other factors that analysts like Bowles and Gintis (1976) and Field (1976) argue contributed to the "need" for a new institution to socialize children. The factory system itself tended to break up the fabric of the traditional community. Factory towns had a more transient population than the traditional town or city, with its subcommunities based on the type of work people did. Factory workers had little time to be involved in any community life. The growth of factories therefore created communities that had little of the sanctioning power of the traditional town. The factory also often contributed to the breakup of the family unit (Wrigley 1977: 80–81). Many of the workers in the factories were young women and children who were sent by their rural parents to earn a living in the mills. Although the Fall River textile system employed entire families, the Lowell system employed almost exclusively women and children, providing housing for them and tight control over their lives in the company dormitories (Cremin 1976: 71).

The Irish immigration that began in the 1830's and grew to a flood after 1846 created doubt in the minds of Protestant capitalists and reformers that the family unit, even where it existed intact, could provide the proper values for a decent Protestant society. Irish children had to be inculcated with proper norms

by State (read Protestant) institutions in order to maintain social order and control (Bowles & Gintis 1976: Chap. 6).

The Massachusetts Common School Reform (1837) is therefore seen by some historians as a response to that state's emer-
gent industrialization and the need felt by employers for new
institutions of socialization. Field (1976: 549) cites the views of
Massachusetts manufacturers in 1842 that schooling led to
punctuality, reliability, an ability to follow directions, and a reduced propensity to be unreasonable during periods of labor
turmoil. Along with Bowles and Gintis (1976), he contends that
the development of cognitive work skills was of secondary importance in explaining the rapid increase in primary schooling
at this early stage, since factories needed only a small percentage of skilled laborers and in fact probably required fewer
skills than artisan production (Field 1976: 544).

According to Field, increasing industrialization and the
Common School Reform resulted in rapidly increasing enrollment in Massachusetts primary schools in the 40 years after
1837. Attendance rose from 49 percent of the school-age population in 1837–38 to 67 percent in 1880 (Field 1976: 527).
Kaestle and Vinovskis argue, to the contrary, that enrollment ratios did not increase in this period, but rather fell slightly from
about 55 percent to 45 percent of the population under 20 years
of age (1980: 34–35). These authors maintain that industrialization thus did not result in increased enrollment. Katz (1980)
notes that Kaestle and Vinovskis's data are biased because of
the larger number of children below 5 years old in schools in
the early years by contrast to the later years, when children
were kept home because of changing attitudes toward schooling the very young. Nonetheless, the data of Kaestle and Vinovskis show that enrollment rates still fell (albeit slightly)
when controlled for children under 5 years old.

More importantly, even Kaestle and Vinovskis report a rapidly increasing number of days spent in school by Massachusetts youth after 1840, especially in urban areas. Thus, the
amount of public schooling taken by school-age youth in Massachusetts did increase after the 1837 Common School Reform,
and the increase was associated with industrialization and ur-
banization. The question is whether the reform itself and the

subsequent expansion of schooling in Massachusetts and other states can be attributed to the influence of manufacturers. According to Bowles and Gintis, and Field, forward-looking manufacturers recruited Horace Mann to develop the reform and were solidly behind him and the Massachusetts State Board of Education, which implemented and controlled public school expansion and curriculum changes. The composition of the State Board, and data from local school committees as well, indicate that manufacturers did participate directly in the politics of school administration. They struck a low profile, however, perhaps because of the suffrage, and left much of the field open to professionals like Mann. Although professionals might be aligned with manufacturing wealth, they were less publicly tied to property and could thus elicit wider support for the expansion of schooling. Both professionals and manufacturers viewed schools as primarily agencies of social control and moral regeneration and made few references to technical requirements for skilled or educated labor (Field 1976: 548).

Thus, even for Field the role of manufacturers was indirect and their influence important primarily as it coincided with the views of educational professionals with broad social interests. That these professionals' vision of the future was tied to capitalism and a "moral" industrialization not associated with slums and poverty is borne out by Mann's writings. But that their educational policies were intended to serve manufacturers' interests per se is much less clear. It is one thing to argue that increased schooling in this period is associated with industrialization and rapid economic growth grounded in increased manufacturing, but quite another to argue that school-system expansion was orchestrated by manufacturers.

Mann sought an overall school system that would be public, tax-supported, and nonsectarian. In addition, the heavy demands of social reform and amelioration being placed on the educational system required that virtually all children be induced if possible, and forced if necessary, to attend school. The school term would be expanded to increase the impact of education. Particularly important was Mann's conviction that children of diverse background should attend the same elementary school. By developing Common Schools, as they were called, Massachusetts would achieve a free school system that

"knows no distinction of rich and poor, of bond and free, or between those who in the imperfect light of this world, are seeking through different avenues, to reach the gate of heaven"
(Messerli 1972: 493). Such a system, a writer in the *American
Annals of Education and Instruction* had earlier argued,
would enable the poor "to look upon the distinctions of society
without envy" and be "taught to understand that they are open
to them as well as to others and to respect them for this reason"
(Curti 1963: 93).

Furthermore, there is some question about how much direct
impact professionals such as Mann and even the State Board
had on schools in this period. Schools expanded at the community level and were subject to a great deal of local control.
There were certainly struggles over school expansion, but the
fact that schools were financed out of local taxes made those
struggles local. And since secondary schools benefited the children of some groups more than others, the struggles often cen-
tered on whether a community should have a local secondary
school paid for by all the citizens (Katz 1968). Manufacturers
had little, if anything, to say about these decisions. In fact, if
State Board decisions were to be implemented, they had to be
approved by local communities. Though Mann certainly was a
leader in school reform, his powers depended much more on
persuasion than coercion. The direction of school reform was
probably as much influenced at this time by social movements
as by manufacturers—social movements based on religious and
class conflicts: between Protestants and immigrant Irish Cath-
olics, and between farmers and artisans on one side and the
new wage labor on the other (see Tyack & Hansot 1982).

Mann was successful in introducing changes in schools, but
he did so by going along with the majority sentiments of the citizenry. The changes corresponded in some cases to the emerging organization of factories, but it seems much more logical to
argue that all institutions in industrializing America were becoming more like factories in many ways, that changes in capitalist production were influencing all spheres of social life in
America. Capitalist industrial relations of production became
dominant in the Northeast during this period, but capitalists
themselves were far from organized into a coherent class. Even
when some of them were, it does not appear that they had a co-

herent concept of what kind of labor force they wanted or how schools should be organized to produce that labor. As schools became larger in urban areas, the State Board, intervening as an innovator in public education, introduced changes that were influenced by the organizational expressions of the new social relations sought by capitalists in an expanding economy. For example, school reforms included the graded school in which children were grouped according to age and proficiency rather than assembled in a single room. The graded school allowed a more standardized curriculum, graded texts, and the establishment of standards of individual progress or productivity.

Through his newly formed normal schools, Mann's teacher training also strongly urged a modification of classroom methods to tap the affection, loyalty, and other "higher" motives of students. The replacement of male by female elementary teachers during this period constituted a step in this direction. The fact that female teachers were much cheaper to hire than males may have provided the main impetus for the feminization of the teaching staff and may have allowed many communities to lengthen the school year. But the shift in hiring policy was probably at least as much a reflection of the view that schools should be an extension of the family or even a substitute for it.

Most parents, then, paid their taxes and sent their children to school without coercion. When working people did resist educational expansion and reform, they appear to have done so because the schools blatantly did not serve their needs. The Irish, facing discrimination in the schools and the workplace, manifested their indifference to the State's school system and its reform by their children's nonattendance (Field 1976: 546). The rural population, not yet accepting the new industrial order, found the Massachusetts State Board of Education meddlesome and a likely source of increased taxes that they did not want to pay (Katz 1968; Bowles & Gintis 1976: 171). Efforts were made to attract nonenrolled students through the differentiation of curricula and of types of schools. Examples included evening schools and half-day schools for teenage workers, as well as intermediate schools to bridge the gap between elementary and grammar school for those whose education was irregular. Since children of poor and immigrant families attended such schools, education reflected and reinforced social stratification (Kaestle & Vinovskis 1980: 37).

With the beginning of industrialization, then, schooling began to rise to the forefront of the reproduction process. But the connections between the emerging business elite and that reproduction process were much more indirect than direct. As industrial capitalism gradually became the dominant economic form in the Northeast and Midwest, schooling as a reproductive institution became organized in ways consistent with the values and norms inherent in industrial capital-labor relations, but it also incorporated features desired by a part of the working class, those who sought upward mobility for their children through the growth of the manufacturing system. The Common School Reform incorporated the rhetoric of Jacksonian democracy while preparing artisans' and farmers' children to fit into a new form of capitalist production. Although Mann himself did not believe in the class system, or even the existence of classes, he did provide a reform that helped legitimize the emerging capitalist division of labor and its class structure, all within an ideology of equal opportunity.

Changes in Capitalism and the Response of the Schools

The dialectic of education and work is perhaps nowhere more clearly observable than in the second major U.S. educational reform, beginning in the 1890's. In the second half of the nineteenth century, schools expanded rapidly everywhere in the United States. The South continued to have relatively fewer schools than the North and West, and it was also much less industrialized. By the end of the century, an increasing fraction of young people attended secondary school; in Massachusetts, the ratio of primary to high school students declined from 17:1 in 1855 to 11:1 in 1880 (Field 1976: 538). Yet the 200,000 pupils in U.S. public high schools in 1889–90 represented less than 1 percent of the total school population (86 percent were in public primary schools and the rest in private schools). More girls than boys went to high school (58 percent of pupils and 65 percent of graduates were girls), and high schools were available almost exclusively to urban dwellers. And although studies made in the 1880's indicated that all social classes were represented in local high schools, dropout rates were so high (only about 10 percent of the total pupils were graduates) that the likelihood of poorer children finishing was probably small (Krug 1969: 11–14).

With young people receiving an average of five years of education in the 1890's (Tyack 1974: 66), schools had increased their role in Americans' lives substantially since the 1840's. Schooling had begun to become a means to higher income and a better life. Although the factory labor force was entering a period of homogenization and new forms of labor discipline, the growth of large firms, retail sales, the service and commercial sector, and even the school system itself increased the number of nonfactory, white-collar jobs available. As secondary-school education became the basis of competition for these higher status jobs, it began to expand rapidly. Also, the growth of both primary and secondary education in urban areas had been so great that the urban schools were, by the 1880's and 1890's, an important political base for community groups and local politicians. In 1890, public school expenditures were $141 million, or 1.1 percent of GNP. Almost 13 million children attended primary schools. The reform of the 1840's not only had taken root in state after state, it led to such growth of primary schooling that in urban areas business elites lost control of the schools.

This was the setting, at the end of the nineteenth century, for America's second major school reform. The reform was associated with the beginnings of major monopoly corporate expansion and a corresponding transformation of the labor force. It was also big business's response to the political force of Populism, especially its expression in working-class militancy and urban politics. The nature of the class conflict in America had changed. Labor was much more militant and saw itself much more clearly as having a class interest (for example, the AFL was formed at this time). Large monopoly corporations emerged, and business saw the State as a potential ally in the conflict against labor (Kolko 1963). Businessmen also saw themselves more clearly as a class. But the reforms also came about because of the great expansion of schooling and the fact that schools were public and were therefore situated in the arena of the State. As part of the State, education could and did slide into the control of local groups of voters. Schooling had become an important social good and source of political patronage. In our theoretical terms, the democratic dynamic of schooling had become significant as schooling had expanded. So the first item on the business class's reformist agenda was to regain control of schooling.

The reformers regained control of urban schools through the broader municipal reform movement, which was aimed at reducing the political power of the "ethnic enclaves" of the urban working class. School reform was part of a wider class conflict and represented upper-class moves to regain direct power over the institutions of social reproduction. Under the banner of honesty and good government, small groups of businessmen, newspaper editors, and professionals in city after city succeeded in altering the structure of urban government. According to Samuel Bowles and Herbert Gintis (1976: 187): "The objective of the school reformers was to centralize control of urban education in the hands of experts. They sought to replace ward elections for school boards by citywide at-large elections, to grant autonomy to the superintendent, and to develop a more specialized and well-defined hierarchical bureaucratic order for the improvement and control of the schools. Schools were to be as far removed as possible from the sordid world of politics."

To a remarkable extent the reformers got their way in running the schools. Following the reform of the Boston school system, the superintendent enthusiastically noted the lack of conflict in the board: "the work of the board is conducted in a conversational tone" (Tyack 1972: 65). The reforms of this period, so well described in Callahan's *Education and the Cult of Efficiency* (1962) and Tyack's *The One Best System* (1974), ushered in an era of tight supervision from above and substantial independence from popular control. Bureaucratization became the watchword of the schools. Though the older decentralized village pattern of schooling was still viewed by some reformers as the ideal, all agreed that the increased numbers of students necessitated bureaucratic control in the modern era (Tyack 1974: 58–59).

In its second phase, educational reform shifted to the rapidly expanding high schools. New divisions in the labor force were translated into differential preparation and socialization for work in secondary education. This was the era of "progressive" education in which educators such as John Dewey and Alfred North Whitehead aimed to change the pattern of children's socialization in school. But the nature of the more general Progressive movement was inherently conservative, as the historian Gabriel Kolko has shown (Kolko 1963). Within the big-business bias of that larger Progressivism, the second phase of reforms was primarily a reaction to social changes induced by economic growth and capitalist development, including growing labor militancy. There was new urgency in the social control arguments popular among the proponents of education.

Once reformers had regained control of urban schools and bureaucratized them under the administration of professional educators, they set about developing criteria for tracking and curricula for different tracks, both based on the social class structure and the new forms of motivation and discipline required in the emerging corporate order. The eugenics movement and the development of occupational testing contributed significantly to the reform in the years after the First World War (Bowles & Gintis 1976: 196–98).

The working class pressured for expansion of secondary education. Professional educational reformers organized the expansion into two tracks: a high track to prepare a middle-level, white-collar bureaucracy for growing big business, and a low track to train skilled workers to maintain the expensive machinery of the new technology and supervise production at the shop-floor level. Secondary schools were called upon to develop new attitudes, particularly an internalization of loyalty to corporations, and new skills, particularly those associated with different technology and bureaucratic control functions. This expansion of education was also pressed by the Progressive movement, which hoped that it would prove an effective antidote to urban poverty, and by organized labor, which, with the closing of the Western frontier and the declining possibilities of self-employment and cooperative trades, increasingly viewed education as the only remaining path toward mobility and security.

The transformation of industrial labor in this period was reflected in the vocational education movement. At first, the vocational movement was directed toward providing industrial and farming training for the large number of those who never attended high school—young people who left school because it did not offer them what they wanted and who did not have a trade upon leaving (Krug 1969: 227). In the late 1890's and early 1900's, the movement gathered the political support of major educators and the financial backing of a number of leading capitalists, J. P. Morgan and John D. Rockefeller among them (Bowles & Gintis 1976: 192). With the founding of the National Association of Manufacturers in 1896, the movement gained what would become its most important advocacy base and acquired a strong anti-union orientation. From the late 1890's until the First World War, virtually every NAM conference passed resolutions advocating vocational education.

Employers seized upon vocational education as a means of breaking workers' control over skills training. In 1906, the NAM Committee on Industrial Education reported: "It is plain to see that trade schools properly protected from the domination and withering blight of organized labor are the one and only remedy for the present intolerable conditions" (Cremin 1964: 38). Moreover, vocational education offered a useful method of credentialing the growing stratum of foremen associated with the deskilling of production workers (Bowles & Gintis 1976).

Until the turn of the century, organized labor took little part in the discussions of vocational education (Bowles & Gintis 1976: 193). The anti-union advocacy of vocational education by the NAM hardened labor's opposition, and by 1900 Samuel Gompers and the AFL had taken a firm position against the movement. However, with the growing momentum of vocational education in the next ten years (Krug 1969: Chap. 10), labor's position shifted. Faced with the likelihood of a federally funded vocational education program, organized labor sought to gain some influence over its direction by joining the movement. By the eve of the First World War there was virtually no organized opposition to federal aid to vocational education. The movement culminated in 1917 with the successful passage of the Smith-Hughes Act. Though in most respects reflecting the views of the NAM, the Smith-Hughes Act was not all that some employers had hoped for. Federal aid was to be restricted to those over 14 years of age, thus dampening the hopes of some advocates that the newly formed junior high school could become the "vocational preparatory school of the future" (Bowles & Gintis 1976: 194).

The vocational education movement began as a response to the specific job training needs of the rapidly expanding corporate sector. When faced with opposition from the labor movement and many professional educators, it gradually became, in the years before the First World War, a vehicle for transforming a previously elite educational institution—the high school—into one that could accommodate the need to reproduce the class structure. Particularly important was the use of vocationalism to justify a tracking system that would separate and stratify young people in ways reflecting race, ethnic origins, and class backgrounds (Bowles & Gintis 1976: 195). As large numbers of working class and immigrant children began attending high schools, educational reformers proposed a system of stratification within secondary education. The older ideology of the common school—the notion that the same curriculum should be offered to all children—increasingly came under attack. In 1908, Charles Eliot, in a change from his earlier position that the schools should be limited to developing mental discipline, declared that schools should be used "to sort the pupils and sort them by their evident or probable destinies" (Krug 1969: 226).

The proposal to sort students and give them different training to meet different "needs" was accompanied by the concept of "social control" pushed by Progressives such as David Snedden and Edward Ross. This concept envisioned knowledge as something to be selectively distributed to various groups. Girls were one such group; the so-called "rank and file" was another. The traditional curriculum might be appropriate for college-bound students, but it was not for those who were going to complete only high school (Krug 1969: 252). Proponents of social control also saw formal education succeeding religion as "the method of indirect social restraint" and the schools as the "only educational institutions which society, in its collective and conscious capacity, acting through the state, is able to control" (Krug 1969: 252–53).

The "scientific management" movement also entered the

schools, calling for the retention of certain subjects and the elimination of others on the basis of "performance" (Krug 1969: Chap. 13). The merger of scientific management and social efficiency and control produced curricula with socialized objectives and the differentiation of curricula aimed at different groups—groups stratified primarily by social class, race, and sex. Pupils were sorted out through the development of the junior high school, vocational guidance, and vocational testing. This class-biased guidance and testing—though purporting to be fair—channeled students into different courses within the same high school on the basis of their ostensible vocational aptitude. But this aptitude was correlated with pupils' class-based social experience. Within the school, some progressive reformers' attempts to bring students together and to forestall differentiation were limited to extracurricular activities. But no amount of schoolwide assemblies, clubs, or athletics—all of which were institutionalized in this period—could bridge the racial, ethnic, and class divisions symbolized and reinforced by curriculum tracking.

The legacy of the urban school movement in this period reflects both its strongly upper-class bias and its commitment to social control as the overriding objective of schooling. The essence of the reforms was the rationalization of the process of reproducing modern, industrial social classes. The professional, expert educators of this time viewed the growing emphasis on efficiency in economic activity as desirable and forward-looking—indeed, the best antidote to the provincialism and elitism of U.S. culture. For some, Taylorism (see Chapter 3) in the schools was seen as an ideal. For others, the unified and centralized high school with the differentiated curriculum represented the most efficient accommodation to the new exigencies of modern economic life (Callahan 1962).

The general acceptability of this reform to the public lay in its promotion of the expansion of education and the making of secondary education available to the urban working class. So, whereas reform reproduced class structure for the increasingly segmented division of labor, it did allow the children of many workers to use education to move into corporate bureaucracies. This was not simply a concession to the working class; the more skilled white-collar workers available to those bureaucracies, the greater the downward pressure on white-collar wages and the easier the extraction of labor from the bureaucracy. But education appeared to serve labor as well as capital; the reform was not obviously designed to keep workers in their place and to aid capital in the extraction of surplus. The educators who participated in the "business" and "scientifically managed" organization of schooling probably thought that rather than reproducing capitalist production they were using proven techniques from industry to increase educational output and to make the educational system more efficient in increasing children's cognitive knowledge. The fact is, however, that business interests with the cooperation of professional educators were able to channel educational reform toward their own ends, all the while proclaiming the liberal rhetoric of equal opportunity and social mobility.

The educational expansion that occurred during and after the Progressive era was massive. In 1870, high school graduates represented 2 percent of the population of 17-year-olds; in 1920 this figure had reached 16 percent; and by 1940 it was 49 percent (U.S. Dep't of Commerce, *Historical Statistics* 1978). But the increased enrollment these figures represent is only part of the story. In 1920, elementary and secondary public-school expenditure per pupil in average daily attendance was $106 (in 1970 dollars); in 1940, the amount had risen to $238, with most of the increase in the years before 1930. In 1870, a mere $63,000,000 was spent on elementary and secondary public education—about 0.9 percent of GNP. In 1920, 1.1 percent of GNP was spent, and by 1940, 2.3 percent of GNP. Thus, there can be little question that public education—already an important feature of American fiscal life by 1920—became especially important just before the Second World War. And because of the dependence of American school finances on the local property tax, the brunt of school spending was borne by the parents and neighbors of children attending school.

To summarize, employers and professional educators shaped the organization and curriculum of schools to meet the needs of developing capitalism. They pushed for the tracking of students in high schools and the hierarchical development of secondary education in conjunction with segmented labor markets. But at the same time, the educational system expanded rapidly to incorporate the demands on the part of parents for greater access to public secondary schooling for their children. By the 1920's and 1930's secondary education was considered a right by most American families. As the curriculum and tracking system were being shaped to accommodate a segmented labor-market system, educators were pressured even more to open up secondary education to working-class families desiring social mobility for their children.

The New Deal and Educational Expansion

The economic crisis of the 1930's changed the relationship between the State and the private sector. The State stepped in to legitimize labor unions and protect Americans against the excesses of a severe economic downturn. Voters made it clear that they would no longer accept capitalist business cycles as an inevitable part of capitalist development. At the same time, labor gained considerable power within the State apparatuses during the Depression and the World War that followed, and it pushed for a "new social contract" between the State, the unions, and business. The underlying basis for the New Deal accord was the government's acceptance of the responsibility for insuring a "proper" level of demand for reasonably full employment; labor, for its part, acquired legal collective bargaining rights on the production side. The government's spending for social programs increased greatly as part of its intervention on the demand side of the market, but more important was the new context in which the working class found itself: because of the depth of the crisis, the State itself was responding to many of labor's demands.

It is significant for our analysis that the demands that took shape during this period—specifically those for government employment guarantees—led to the GI Bill, which provided for federally subsidized postwar training for almost 8 million Americans. Fear of postwar unemployment and working-class demands for expansion of education created a large increase in secondary and university education after the war. More than one-fourth of the 8 million GIs who took advantage of the GI Bill after the Second World War went to college (O'Neill & Ross 1976: Table 7). After the Korean War, 51 percent of the 2.4 million GIs trained under the Bill went to college. In 1940, 186,000 bachelor's degrees had been granted; in 1946, this figure had dropped to 136,000; but in 1950, 432,000 degrees were granted. The number decreased again, but university expansion had become part of the general educational expansion of the postwar period, fueled by Korean War and later GIs. In 1955, 285,000 bachelor's degrees were granted; in 1960, 389,000; in 1965, 530,000; in 1970, 827,000; and in 1980, 929,000 (U.S. Dep't of Ed. 1982: 130). In 1945, one-fifth of the 18–21-year-olds were enrolled in colleges; in the 1970's, almost one-half were enrolled in postsecondary institutions (U.S. Dep't of Ed. 1979: 92).

Between 1950 and 1970, the real spending per pupil in average daily attendance in primary and secondary schools rose by over 130 percent after adjusting for changes in the price level, in large part owing to increases in teacher salaries. The total expenditures on primary and secondary education reached $15 billion in 1960, $40 billion in 1970, and $96 billion in 1980—3.0 percent, 4.0 percent, and 3.6 percent of GNP respectively. Including expenditures at the university level, the American government spent $57 billion on education in 1970 and $137 billion in 1980 (U.S. Dep't of Ed. 1982: Table 14).

This expansion was a continuation of the New Deal program of increased public services and government intervention in labor markets. Yet, as in the past, once the expansion began, big business stepped in to shape and try to control the structure of education and the curriculum—this time in large part at the postsecondary level. The liberal arts tradition of promoting scholarship and unfettered inquiry was appropriate when college students were destined for leadership positions, but with an increasing percentage of the age cohort continuing schooling after high school, college had to become a training ground not only for leaders but also for technicians, teachers, and clerks. Postsecondary education was thus gradually organized to produce labor for a segmented labor market. The growth of large corporations and the State bureaucracy demanded trained white-collar workers, and as that demand increased and as the number of college graduates also rose, so did the complexity of educational requirements for jobs. People were now chosen for jobs on the basis of whether they had completed high school and college, on where they had gone to college, and ultimately, on whether they had graduate or professional training and where that training had been acquired.

The transformation of postsecondary education into a more generally attainable level of schooling and the demand for increasingly schooled employees led to a dilemma: would the leadership and inquiry-oriented socialization of the liberal arts college produce the kind of highly trained but nonmanagerial employee now needed? As Gorz (1973: 121) put it: "Big business, in short, is seeking to reconcile two opposites: on the one hand, the need created by the modern process of production for a higher development of the human capabilities; and on the other hand, the political need to prevent this development from leading to an increased autonomy of the individual that would threaten the existing division of social functions and the distribution of power."

As a response to this problem, postsecondary education was stratified into a number of different levels. Unlike earlier high school stratification, however, which occurred within the high schools through curriculum differentiation, postsecondary education was differentiated primarily by institution. Even so, certain courses of study within the same college or university, such as education, generally attracted lower-class, minority, and women students, whereas costly programs such as medicine drew higher-class students. Yet, the main divisions have developed between institutions in the form of a multi-tiered system dominated at the top by prestigious private institutions and great state universities, followed by state and lesser private colleges, and ending with the rapidly growing community colleges (see Karabel 1972; F. Pincus 1980). This system reflects both the social status of the families of the students and the hierarchy of work relations into which each type of student will move after graduation.

Comprehensive national data collected by the American Council on Education reveal sharp disparities between the social origins of students and attendance at various types of institutions. Even the more egalitarian state systems exhibit this stratified pattern. Data from California, for example, show that over 18 percent of the students at the campuses of the University of California in the mid-1960's came from families earning $20,000 or more. Less than 7 percent of the students in community colleges, by contrast, came from such families. (And less than 4 percent of the children not receiving postsecondary education came from such families.) Similarly, whereas only 12.5 percent of the students attending the University of California came from families earning less than $6,000, 24 percent of the students attending community colleges and 32 percent of the children not receiving postsecondary education came from families at that income level (Hansen & Weisbrod 1969: 68).*

The segregation of students not destined for the top has allowed the development of procedures and curricula more appropriate to their future "needs," as defined by their actual occupational opportunities. The vast majority of students in community colleges are programmed for failure; great efforts are made through testing and counseling to convince students that their lack of success is objectively attributable to their own inadequacies.

Bringing student hopes into line with the realities of the job market is facilitated by a tracking system within the community college much like the channeling system for high schools: four-year-college transfer programs for the "promising," vocational programs for the "dead-enders." The magnitude of the task of lowering student expectations can hardly be exaggerated: at least three times as many entering community college students want to complete four or more years of college as actually succeed in doing so (Karabel 1972: 531–32). Less than half of the community college entrants receive even the two-year Associate of Arts degree.†

In the junior college, the student does not so clearly fail, unless he himself wishes to define it that way, but rather transfers to terminal work. . . . The terminal student can be made to appear not so radically different from the transfer student, e.g., an "engineering aide" instead of an "engineer," and hence he goes to something with a status of his

---

*A similar study of Florida higher education (Windham 1970) confirms this pattern. Moreover, the nationwide 1969 Bureau of the Census survey shows that college students from families earning less than $5,000 a year are over twice as likely to be enrolled in two-year (as opposed to four-year) colleges as students whose families earn $15,000 or more.

†Though the proponents of community colleges make much of the opportunity for students to transfer at the end of two years and receive a bachelor's degree from a four-year college, of the entering freshmen in community colleges only a small minority actually do so (Karabel 1972).

own. This reflects less unfavorably on the person's capabilities. . . . The provision of readily available alternative achievements in itself is an important device for alleviating the stress consequent on failure. . . . The general result of "cooling out" processes is that society can continue to encourage expectations (Clark 1960: 569–77).

For those who stay, studies at the community college are—much more often than in four-year colleges—explicitly vocational, emphasizing such middle-level training as nursing, computer work, and office skills. The connection between the needs of business and the curricula of community colleges is fostered by business representation on advisory boards. Community college administrators are more than willing to help out. When "corporate managers announce a need for skilled workers," writes Arthur Cohen, director of the ERIC Clearinghouse for Junior Colleges, "college administrators trip over each other in their haste to develop a new technical curriculum" (A. Cohen 1971: 6). The student is allowed little discretion in selecting courses or pursuing a liberal education. Systems of discipline and student management resemble those of secondary education more than those of elite universities.

The Structure of Education and Social Mobility

The postwar educational expansion was part of the successful struggle by the working class for increased social-welfare spending and higher wages. At the same time, through the very success of the New Deal accords, America entered into an era of fairly steady economic growth and high mass consumption. The real wages of the average worker increased 60 percent between 1948 and 1973. The growth of education in the labor force was deemed an important factor in achieving increased productivity and hence these higher wages (Denison 1962, 1979).

The expansion of American education in the postwar period was therefore an important part of the ideology of growth and consumption. Schooling's role was more than just a means to individual mobility; it was an essential element in the Keynesian solution to capitalist development and a part of middle- and working-class participation in the growth process. Secondary and postsecondary education increasingly became a consumption as well as an investment good. The ideology of growth and higher consumption thus came to include education.

The role of this ideology and the position of education and social mobility in it seem to be vital elements both in the expansion of schooling and in the reproduction of capitalist relations of production and the division of labor. The ideology of mobility through schooling influenced school expansion. To what extent does schooling lead to social mobility? What is the relationship of ideology to empirical reality?

Status Attainment Models

Status attainment models represent statistical attempts to assess the contribution of schooling, social class background, academic achievement, and other variables to income and occupational status. The economists' version of such models—human capital theory—indicates that schooling is one of the most important factors in determining future income and occupation, and even access to further training (see, for example, Griliches & Mason 1972; Sewell & Hauser 1975; Duncan, Featherman & Duncan 1972; Chiswick & Mincer 1972). Taking account of ability and social class differences, an additional year of schooling in the Sewell and Hauser Wisconsin sample of young nonfarm white males resulted in earnings that were 4 percent higher; Kohn's work (1969) using the Parnes' survey of 18–24-year-olds (both whites and nonwhites) showed a similar increase of about 4 percent in hourly earnings for an additional year of schooling. Although this increase may seem small, the samples in which the relations were found dealt with very young workers—earnings later in working life for people with more schooling are a good deal higher. And although the education-to-earnings relationship is weaker for females than for males, it remains positive and significant for them too (Carnoy, Girling & Rumberger 1976).

Schooling apparently plays a more powerful role in explaining occupational status than earnings; Sewell and Hauser (1975), in three separate studies using different sets of U.S. data, found educational attainment to be the most powerful variable explaining a son's occupational status even when father's education, occupation, and son's I.Q. were accounted for. They also compare the estimates of the relationship between social class, mental ability (I.Q.), and economic success (occupational status and earnings), using the major sources of 1960's data in the United States. In that comparison, they show first that parents have a definite effect on a son's future work role, primarily through the amount of schooling that the son receives. The effect of parents is much greater on occupational status than on earnings. Second, they show that schooling has a significant effect on work roles in addition to the influence of parents' social status and the effect of measured ability. Something happens in school that influences work roles beyond universal measures of ability and beyond the parental effect. By taking more years of schooling, both males and females do better economically, even when we control for effects of ability and parents' social status.

These ideas and the empirical work supporting them have been assaulted by Christopher Jencks (Jencks et al. 1972), but there were so many questions raised by Jencks's data and his use of them that even Jencks himself recanted in a later study (Jencks et al. 1979). Although schooling, social class, and mental ability apparently account for only a small percentage of the earnings variation of young people in the labor force, these variables are much more powerful in explaining incomes at higher ages, and much more important in explaining a person's occupational status even when young.

Thus, the ideology of mobility associated with increased schooling seems to be rooted in an empirical reality. The social pressure for more schooling as a means to higher incomes and occupational status has a foundation in the way New Deal capitalism works, even if it has been State employment—especially for women and minorities—that has largely provided that foundation.

But there is another side to this issue. The view that schools are important in mobility because they increase cognitive achievement is refuted by a number of empirical studies. Virtually all the statistical studies attempting to determine the causes of achievement have concluded that most of the explainable variance in test scores is attributable to out-of-school influences rather than in-school ones (Coleman et al. 1966; Averch et al. 1972). Though it is clear that children and young adults acquire many skills and cognitive proficiencies in school, they also acquire many of them outside school. The amount of such cognitive proficiencies acquired, and the nature of the noncognitive socialization that takes place both in and out of the school, seem centrally related to the social class origins of the child.

Other studies have attempted to determine what aspect of schooling is related to success in labor markets. We know that educational attainment (in terms of years of schooling), on the one hand, and earnings and occupational success, on the other, are closely related statistically. If the true effect of schooling on earnings and occupation were attributable to an I.Q.-type of cognitive effect of schooling (a continuous cognitive effect universally—although not necessarily equally—valued everywhere in the labor market), we would expect that the statistical relationship between years of schooling and work success would be attenuated or eliminated once we controlled for the cognitive test scores of workers. That is, the cognitive theory of schooling's effect on such outcomes as earnings suggests that years of schooling have an important impact because educational attainment is a surrogate for the kind of cognitive development measured by test scores.

Attempts to explain the variance in earnings by both test scores and educational attainment have shown mixed results. Several studies indicate that the inclusion of test scores in the analysis diminishes only slightly the statistical effect of years of schooling (Gintis 1971; Griliches & Mason 1972; Bowles & Gintis 1972–73). But other studies show a high correlation between I.Q.-related scores and educational attainment (Sewell & Hauser 1975; Duncan, Featherman & Duncan 1972). These latter results are for younger workers, though. In any case, even when I.Q. is included in the earnings and occupational-status equations in these latter studies, schooling is a more important variable than I.Q. and is a significant explainer of earnings and occupation in its own right. Accordingly, it appears that education affects labor market success more than simply through the effect of I.Q.-type cognitive abilities. Indeed, a recent study of high school graduates found that when one compared students at the fiftieth percentile with those at the eighty-fourth percentile on test scores, there was only a difference in earnings of five to ten cents an hour (Meyer & Wise 1982).

Socialization in the Family

Studies of family socialization and educational aspirations also tend to support the concept that there is an interaction between what goes on in school and in families and peer groups, and that the decision to take more schooling or not is heavily class-based through family and peer influence.

Kohn (1969) and MacKenzie (1973) show, in several different samples, that parents' conceptions of which skills, values, or qualities it is important to instill in their offspring will be crucially influenced by their own experiences and situation in the adult world. "Insofar as middle- and working-class parents have occupied significantly different positions in the social structure, they have practiced distinct modes of child rearing, which have, in turn, contributed to the maintenance of class differences and boundaries within a complex society" (MacKenzie 1973: 51).

Both Kohn and MacKenzie find that white-collar workers, particularly those in managerial positions, appear more concerned with raising their children to be individuals with internalized values and standards of behavior, so that they will be self-reliant and have a sense of independence and integrity. Working-class parents, by contrast, emphasize conformity to externally imposed rules and standards. MacKenzie found the latter true even among craftsmen, the "aristocracy of labor." Kohn found that middle-class parents are more likely to emphasize children's self-direction, whereas working-class parents are more likely to emphasize their conformity to external authority (Kohn 1969: 34).

Kohn explains these different values for children as stemming from differences in occupational circumstances. In Kohn's terms, this "does not necessarily assume that parents consciously train children to meet future occupational requirements; it may simply be that occupational experiences affect people's conceptions of the desirable" (Kohn 1969: 141). He found that men who work under conditions that facilitate the exercise of self-direction are likely to value self-direction for their children; men who work where self-direction is inhibited or precluded are likely to value conformity. He found this to be true for both the middle class and the working class. The class difference in fathers' values for children is largely attributable "statistically" to the experience of occupational self-direction. Even some substantial part of the class difference in mothers' values is attributable to their husbands' differential experiences of occupational self-direction (Kohn 1969: 151).

This means that "higher-educated" workers are likely to transfer a different set of values to their children than unionized-segment or secondary workers; it also means that secondary workers probably impart an even more well-defined line of conformity and respect for rules and externally determined direction than do unionized workers. Thus, the family acts, through the parents' work experience, to help reproduce the class structure by imparting values to the children that are useful largely in the same type of jobs the parents hold.

Sennett and Cobb (1972) argue further that workers in the higher-education segment impart a greater feeling of pride in their occupational position than do lower-status workers. The self-doubt and lack of self-pride in the lower-status workers are transmitted to the workers' children and make them want to get a higher-status occupation than their parents, but those same feelings also inculcate in them the sense that they are not as good as middle- and upper-class children.

Differences in Gender Socialization

The occupational socialization of girls in the family is different from that of boys. Despite differences in emphasis in gender socialization in different social classes, there are unifying themes across classes. Perhaps the most important of these is that marriage and a family are the primary goal for many girls entering adulthood and occupational concerns are secondary, whereas for boys the order is reversed (L. Rubin 1979). Thus, women may subordinate their work roles to those of their husbands and view their own economic functions in terms of their principal role as wife and mother.

Gender socialization takes place in the school by reinforcing different approval-seeking behavior patterns among girls and boys and by orienting girls and boys into different curriculum paths. But schooling, much more than families and the church, is inherently an institution tied to labor force preparation. Hence, the antipatriarchal ideology of the women's movement has found its way quickly into schools, where it has taken the form of upsetting the traditional marriage-first, work-second attitudes among young women. This has been reinforced by the fact that the labor participation rates of married women are directly related to their educational attainments (Bowen & Finegan 1969; Cain 1966).

Anyon (1983) found that schoolgirls seem to take on the docile "female" behavior expected by teachers, but now aspire to occupational success more than marriage. She calls this "accommodation and resistance." Yet historically, schools have always promoted academic achievement as a means to occupational success. Girls have traditionally been channeled into seeking "occupational success" through marriage, but schooling itself transmitted knowledge that could be used by women directly for getting jobs. It is the labor market that sets the conditions for women's work; school preparation reinforces gender attitudes and behaviors that steer women away from male-dominated jobs. But with a greatly increased participation of women in the labor force and an active women's movement changing women's attitudes, it is logical to expect an increasing number of girls in school to see their preparation leading to jobs first and marriage second.

So different gender socialization in schools and families explains neither job segmentation by gender nor lower female salaries; however, in the context of capitalist society, male hegemony includes the ideology of work primacy for men and the primacy of marriage and child-raising for women. Since women are defined as subordinate to men, women automatically play a secondary role to men in the labor force. For example, married men earn more than single men in the American labor market, even accounting for age and education differences, but single women earn more than married ones (Carnoy, Girling & Rumberger 1976). This structure of rewards meshes with women's hegemonically defined role as wives first, wage-earners second, to produce a fulfilled prophecy, a "coherent whole." The women's movement challenges the underlying relations of this coherence. And, as Anyon suggests, the challenge manifests itself in schools through how girls and young women perceive using the knowledge and certifications they are acquiring.

Summary

Schools are more democratic than the workplace and many other institutions. They do provide the means of social mobility for subordinate groups, but at the same time mobility is sharply constrained by the economic system and schooling practices. The reasons that schooling can expand and still reproduce an unequal social structure—i.e. that the school system can provide increased access to subordinate groups without seriously challenging the nature of social relations—stem from the strength of the social relations outside the school and their influence on the family socialization process. Schools are rarely independent innovators in challenging the unequal class, gender, and race relations outside the school. But as social movements challenge those relationships, schools—as a legitimate instrument of social mobility—are often the first State institution where structure and practices change to reflect the political power of those movements.

The structure of schools reproduces social inequalities even as school expansion is associated with working-class struggles for greater equality and social mobility through education. How this happens is inherent in the role of schooling in an unequal capitalist society, and it is inherent in school practices themselves. We have suggested in this chapter that public education reflects larger class, gender, and race conflicts that characterize American capitalist development. School development is continually shaped by those conflicts.

The reality faced by families in the workplace heavily influences their views on what their children should learn in school and how much and what kind of education are appropriate for them. By the turn of the century, when business ideology was particularly strong and business-oriented professionals controlled the schools, the importance of schooling for occupational success had become readily apparent in America. Business successfully imposed a view that just as discipline and order, hierarchy, lack of control of the work process, and motivation through the use of extrinsic rewards were increasingly dominating work, such characteristics should also dominate schooling. If the young were eventually to succeed in their occupational advancement in the expanding industrial economy, the schools had to provide them with the skills and values that would enable them to meet the dictates of the workplace.

But families and students are also part of social reproduction, so their expectations and demands also influence the reality of the schools. In historical periods when social movements are powerful and seek social change through education, subordinate groups—for example, blacks during the civil rights movement—gain increased say over what goes on in schools. Family pressure within the context of these movements tends to force educators to pay increased attention to the needs of pupils from those groups.The schools respond, much more than the private workplace, to the increased aspirations, combined with the increased political power, of those in the movement. The school and the classroom become arenas where that power is tested.

In historical periods when social movements are weak and business ideology strong, families and students are forced to accept, explicitly or implicitly, the class-reproductive role of schooling. Their pressure on schools in the absence of such movements has little effect. The tension in many subordinate-group families between higher educational aspirations and the low expectations implicit in the attitudes and values transferred to their children continues to exist, but it is the low expectations that prevail in such periods.

Thus, social mobility and other facets of the democratic dynamic in education depend largely on the political and ideological power of movements outside education. To the degree that these movements have been effective, education, despite its role as reproducer of capitalist relations of production and the class division of labor, does produce some social mobility. However, as we show in the next chapter, schooling practices readily reinforce class, race, and gender differences in the absence of such movements. The individual subordinate-group family, acting alone, is trapped in the attitudes and values associated with its position in the work structure.

5

Reproduction and the Practices of Schooling

Schooling practices are inseparable from class and social conflict, passing as they do through the prism of school bureaucracies—the administrators and teachers who represent formal authority to both students and their families. School bureaucracies are part of the State, which forms the larger context in which class and social conflict are related to school practices. In previous chapters we emphasized the historical struggle between schools seen as sources of the reproduction of workers on the one hand, and of the expansion of democratic rights and egalitarian outcomes on the other. Traditionally, the needs of the workplace have been impressed upon the schools through the demands of employers in labor markets as well as through the pervasiveness of capitalist work organization in molding the vision of what has been considered good educational practice (Callahan 1962). These needs have been reinforced by administrators, teachers, parents, and students as they translate workplace requirements and procedures into their own educational decisions.

By contrast, the push for greater student and teacher rights, for social mobility through education, for educational expansion, and for programs to improve educational equity have come through political and social movements. These movements have pressed the courts, the legislatures, and local school boards for an expansion of educational rights and opportunities. We have argued that an understanding of educational policy requires an analysis of the nature of the struggle between these dynamics as well as of the strategies and resources of the contestants and the stage of conflict as it has been historically conditioned by the "temporary" resolution of earlier skirmishes.

Although schooling practices change over time, depending on the relative strength of the democratic and reproductive dynamics, at any point in time within schools we observe only the reproductive nature of schooling practices and, possibly, resistance to them. Any historical analysis looking at various individual cases must be, by the very nature of the analysis, restricted to explaining reproductive practices and any observable resistance to reproduction (Apple 1982b). The larger interplay of social change and how it affects schools over time cannot be captured by an analysis that focuses only on a moment in time.

Yet studying schooling practices at such a single moment does yield important insights into the reproductive aspect of schools. Observing the relationship of teachers to pupils and of parents to teachers and administrators suggests, for example, the difficulty of individual family action (outside social movements) to try to change reproductive practices. Such individual action is circumscribed by rules, regulations, and attitudes that can only be changed by collective social action. In a collective group with common interests and purposes, individual parents, teachers, and students can attack the structure in which practices are situated.

It has been asserted that American schools reproduce the social class division of labor from generation to generation so that children tend to be inculcated with the occupational skills, values, attitudes, and expectations associated with the occupations of their parents (Bowles & Gintis 1976; Apple 1979). Children of lower socioeconomic origins are likely to receive less schooling (Rumberger 1983a; Jencks et al. 1972: 23–29) and have less money spent on their education (Coons, Clune & Sugarman 1970; Owen 1972) than other children. But schools differ in other ways than just the resources allocated to the education of their students. As Friedenberg (1963) has stressed, the educational process itself tends to differ according to the social class origins of children. In this chapter we present the results of a study of two first-grade classrooms, one with upper-middle-class children and the other with lower-middle-class children, designed to assess differences in occupational socialization. Although capitalist ideology views the individual as the unit of change, we argue that it is only a longer-run coalescence into social movements that can meaningfully oppose and alter these practices.

A Study of Differential Reproduction

In order to understand differential reproduction according to social class origins, two members of our research team, Kathleen Wilcox and Pia Moriarity, undertook an ethnographic study of two first-grade classrooms, one in an upper-middle-class neighborhood and one in a lower-middle-class neighborhood (Wilcox 1977). The purpose of the study was to explore how and why the educational experiences of children from different social class backgrounds might create systematic differences in occupational orientations. The study was designed to compare how the different educational experiences of first graders drawn from two different levels in the middle class might relate to the reproduction of the work values required for entering occupations similar to those of their parents. Accordingly, two first-grade classrooms were selected for the investigation; the specific dimensions of educational experience chosen for study were linked to occupational values; and a method for collecting and analyzing the data was established.

After an exhaustive screening of 31 classrooms in ten different schools, two first-grade classes were found that met the criteria for the study. These criteria included the socioeconomic backgrounds of the students, the apparent representativeness of the teachers and schools, and accessibility for an in-depth study. The two classes were in schools about fifteen miles apart in the suburbs of San Francisco. The school serving the upper-middle-class students will be referred to as Huntington, the one serving the lower-middle-class students as Smith. A majority of the fathers of the children in the Huntington first-grade class were lawyers, physicians, business executives, or investment counselors, and over 60 percent of them had received advanced college degrees beyond the bachelor's level. The Huntington School was in an upper-middle-class suburb known for the quality of its schools.

By contrast, the Smith School was located in a working-class neighborhood where two-thirds of the fathers of students in our first-grade class either worked as mechanics, technicians, machine operators, and truck drivers, or held other nonprofessional jobs. The average level of education was about 12.2 years—slightly below the average for the state. The school district in which the Smith School was located was highly regarded for a nonaffluent district. Although slightly above the state average in school resources, the district in which Smith was located had an expenditure level for each pupil about 40 percent lower than that of the district in which Huntington was located. Further, students in Smith's district scored at about the 67th percentile on the state reading test, in comparison with the 99th percentile for Huntington's district. These data tend to underline the fact that the two schools represent different levels of the middle class rather than the extremes of poverty versus wealth.

The first-grade teacher in Huntington was Mrs. Newman. She had taught students at the elementary level for over 20 years and had taught at Huntington for eight years. She was a resident of the Huntington neighborhood, and her own children had attended the school. She had obtained a master's degree from a prestigious university and was considered an exemplary teacher by many parents who sought her out for their children. At Smith, Mrs. Jones had taught at the elementary level for ten years, although she was only in her thirties. She had been raised in the Smith neighborhood and was taking courses toward a master's degree on a part-time basis at a state institution. She was highly regarded by other teachers and the principal.

Mrs. Newman's class had 20 students, equally divided by sex. Only three of the children came from minority backgrounds, two black males who were bussed to the school from another neighborhood and a girl whose mother came from Central

America. With the exception of one girl who transferred into the school at midyear, the membership of the class was stable; most of the students had gone to kindergarten together at Huntington, and many had gone to nursery school together. Mrs. Jones's class had a maximum of 28 students during the year, with five children leaving and another five entering between September 1974 and March 1975 (when this study was undertaken). During most of the observations, the class was composed of 19 boys and nine girls. Two-thirds of the students were Caucasian (19), with the remainder being Chicano (six), Filipino (two), and Samoan (one). All of the children were English-speaking and came from homes where English was spoken, although a few spoke Spanish as well.

Occupational Values

Four attributes that relate to different levels of the work hierarchy were selected: (1) external versus internal standards of authority; (2) future versus present orientation; (3) verbal self-presentation skills; and (4) emphasis on cognitive skills and achievement. As Kohn (1969) and Edwards (1979) have discussed, jobs at the lower levels of the occupational hierarchy presume that employees must be motivated and guided by work arrangements and supervision external to them such as rules, regulations, and extensive supervision. By contrast, jobs at the upper end of the occupational hierarchy require that employees be self-directed by internal norms that they have absorbed and that correspond to the overall needs of the work organization. Placing these traits in a schooling context, we anticipated that the preparation of students for working-class occupations would entail a great deal of attention to following rules and responding to externally imposed standards of teacher monitoring and supervision. Appropriate preparation of students for professional and managerial careers would stress the students' identifying and internalizing the norms and requirements of the school so that they could be self-directing and require minimal supervision.

A future as opposed to a present orientation also appears to be an important dimension for delineating jobs. Managerial and professional roles require an explicit concern with the future consequences of present actions, since decisions on whether to expand a facility, market a product, assign a patient to therapy, or pursue a legal strategy will all determine the extent of future success or failure. By contrast, clerks, technicians, machinists, and other nonprofessional workers need only follow the present work routine set out for their jobs, since there are few if any choices that will determine future outcomes. In educational terms, we observed the degree to which each first grade was characterized by tasks and teacher statements presented in terms of present versus future consequences.

Verbal self-presentation refers to the way individuals present themselves orally in responding to occupational situations. Professionals and managers need to participate in discussions as a part of group problem-solving; often when questions are asked of them, they must give a detailed, analytical response. By contrast, production and service workers are likely to be asked routine questions to which brief factual rather than analytical responses are expected. In this area we observed the development of verbal self-presentation skills when the teacher called upon children to respond to a question or to make a presentation. For children who are being prepared for working-class jobs, brief and routine answers and presentations would be adequate, whereas from those who are viewed as future managers and professionals greater analysis and detail would be sought.

It is commonly believed that high cognitive achievement is necessary to attain managerial and professional positions, whereas lower-level occupations require much less cognitive development (Hernstein 1973). Certainly, strong cognitive skills as reflected in test scores are required for access to classes for the gifted and honors courses in elementary and secondary schools, and they are a necessary condition for access to the best universities and postgraduate study. This cognitive-skill orientation is also evident in what economists call investment in human capital, where differences in earnings are assumed to result from differences in productivity that are largely attributable to educational effects on skills (Becker 1964). Thus, one would expect that there would be a greater emphasis on cognitive achievement in the classrooms of students who were being prepared for higher-level occupations than lower-level ones.

Data Gathering and Analysis

After acquiring a general familiarity with the neighborhoods, schools, and classrooms, we set out a systematic method of observation that would provide comparative data along the four dimensions of occupational orientation we had delineated. Both observers had received advanced training in ethnography, an anthropological approach to observation and data-gathering. Although other studies had observed classrooms and schools—for example, Leacock (1969) and Rist (1970)—none had developed techniques or observational instruments we could apply directly in this study. Accordingly, the approaches had to be developed independently.

After we had watched classroom activities for some time, we set out a detailed description for each classroom of both teacher and student behavior. Extensive notes were made on both teacher and student verbal presentations and activities, which were analyzed to delineate a working set of observational categories that could be used for classification. These were compared for consistency with a third-grade and a sixth-grade classroom in each school. Ultimately, we were to devote 56 hours of intensive observation to Mrs. Newman's class and a total of 73 hours in the Huntington School over the last four months of the 1974–75 school year. The comparable figures at the other site were 106 hours for Mrs. Jones's class and 122 hours total for the Smith School.

Heavy emphasis was placed on refining the coding instruments and on assuring that agreement among observers was high. Parallel coding by the two observers for the same classroom for a full day showed a reliability of .91 (Ebel 1951). In addition to written notes, audio recordings were made for many observation periods. The results were coded into data that were amenable to statistical analysis. The primary focus of the coding scheme was to take teacher-pupil interactions or verbal interchanges and categorize them in a meaningful way along the four dimensions of occupational relevance described above.

Each interaction was delineated according to its *strategy* and *message*. Strategy was viewed as the form or approach that the teacher used to communicate, whereas message involved the content of what was said, including the values inherent in that content.

Every teacher-student interaction that was observed was recorded in as much detail as possible in the time provided. These basic data were coded for each child and each type of interaction. This permitted computations of the number of interactions for each child for each coding as well as of the mean number of such interactions for each class. Essentially, these comparisons were based upon 20 children in Huntington and 25 in Smith, with transfers into Smith excluded from the data analysis. For these 45 children, a total of 1,080 interactions were recorded, 571 at Huntington and 509 at Smith. For purposes of normalizing the distribution of the means for statistical comparison, an arc-sine transformation of the data was employed (Hoyle 1973). Analyses were based upon comparing the average number of interactions of particular types between the two classrooms.

Statistical results reported in this chapter are based upon a two-way analysis of variance on these means, testing the relative effects of the classroom alone or when gender, ability group, and race of students are controlled for. In general, the criterion for statistical significance of a finding was set at the .05 level, although only a brief summary is provided here. Detailed presentations of the methodology and findings are reported in Wilcox (1977).

Relationship to Authority:
Internal Versus External Standards

As we noted, one of the important dimensions that tends to differentiate jobs is relationship to authority. Jobs in the lower portions of the work hierarchy are structured on the assumption that employees must be motivated and guided by work arrangements and supervision external to themselves, whereas in the upper parts of the hierarchy employees are expected to be motivated by internalized norms and values that correspond to the needs of the enterprise. Accordingly, we hypothesized that if children are socialized by the school for positions that are relatively similar to those of their parents, students in Smith would be more likely to be subject to teacher interactions that emphasize external controls and rules, whereas those at Huntington would be confronted with a relatively larger set of teacher interactions emphasizing the inculcation and expectation of internal norms for doing good work.

The internal-external distinction was evaluated through general observation as well as through the use of an elaborate scheme that was later subjected to statistical analysis. In general, an "internal" interaction was viewed as one in which the teacher treated the child as a self-directed person who was capable of handling a process in an independent way and of taking responsibility for the consequences of his or her activity. This was an interaction in which the teacher emphasized to the child his or her responsibility for shaping activities in a manner that promoted or relied upon internalized values, self-images, standards, or goals. By contrast, in an "external" interaction, the teacher emphasized that the child must follow certain standard rules, procedures, or directions to be set out by the teacher and made salient by authority and direct power. In the "internal" case the responsibility for compliance was placed on the child, whereas in the "external" case it was placed on the teacher.

Our observations confirmed that the overriding method of control in teacher-student interactions in Mrs. Jones's classroom was external. In fact, the most common strategy for getting the students to carry out the daily regimen was the use of teacher commands. Mrs. Jones would simply order, "I want that done now," or "You have an assignment; sit down and get busy," or some similar command. The second most common strategy was the use of direct praise and blame, such as "That's good," or "No, that's not right." There was also heavy emphasis on the repetition of rules such as "No fighting," "No running in the room," "Use quiet voices." But there were many others as well, such as "We don't hit or kick," "Come in right away when the recess bell rings," "You can't throw food in the cafeteria," "Stay off all fences and trees," and "No playing in the hall."

The external mode of authority was used to get the children to do their academic work as well, and it seemed only in certain cases where she was attempting to inculcate proper standards of behavior that Mrs. Jones resorted to internal approaches. For example, to a boy who came to her during art because he couldn't find the glue: "You've been in this classroom since September and you still can't handle that? You can solve that problem yourself" (internal). And to a girl in front of the class: "Good for you! You solved that problem" (getting a piece of paper out of the cupboard [internal]).

In summary, the vast majority of Mrs. Jones's attempts to control the activities of her students were through the use of commands and the repetition of rules. The responsibility was placed upon either a higher human authority or a set of mandates, rather than on the students themselves, for guiding and determining their own actions. These are external means of control, because they reinforce a pattern in which the impetus for behavior comes not from the children themselves, but from some external rule or authority figure who issues rules. In such a context, the children are not challenged to take initiative. This pattern of external control seemed to represent the overriding mode at Smith.

By contrast, the dominant form of control at Huntington was "internal." To the degree that external forms were used, they stressed the development of internal standards of performance, especially cognitive performance. The central focus of almost all of Mrs. Newman's statements was on academic work, even when she was using external approaches to correct "proscribed" deviant behavior. That is, rules or certain practices were expected to be followed because of their implications for academic work rather than for behavior per se. "Now you boys don't use good judgment when you come to the circle. Your legs are touching his, so pretty soon you're going to be kicking each other. See, the way you sit can help you study" (internal). "If you're talking to your neighbor, you're probably not looking at the clues and remembering what the answers are" (internal). "Jim, maybe it's because you're wiggling in your chair that you counted more" (internal).

A special emphasis was placed by Mrs. Newman on "using time wisely," which meant working quietly at one's desk during the independent work period. Students were expected to choose and pace their activities while avoiding the temptation of interacting with other students so that the minimum daily assignments would be completed. "Our fifteen minutes are up. Have you used them wisely?" (internal). "You really goofed off. Why do you do this to yourself?" (internal).

There were external standards imposed at Huntington, too, but they were generally explained to the students as being important for their learning. The children were expected to follow such rules as "think for yourself, listen to directions, don't bother your friends." The teacher told them the reasons behind the rules and made them take responsibility for failure to abide by them, calling to their attention the incomplete, incorrect, or sloppy work that resulted from student inattention to these regulations. When Johnny let Jimmy read to him, Mrs. Newman said: "You didn't really read. You were going to coast on him again. You've been doing that for a long time, and it won't work anymore. If you didn't have a friend here to do the reading, you would have been lost. From now on, you're going to be expected to complete an assignment. Being quiet and nice and sweet and cute won't help. You have a good brain, so use it" (both internal and external). When Tommy did not appear to be listening to a story, "No writing, Tommy. Play fair with yourself. Why is it so hard to follow directions, Tommy? You'll be a good football player, but no one will ask you to play. You really have to follow the rules" (both internal and external).

Even external modes of control such as repetition of rules were generally explained as a requirement for doing good work rather than just a limit or imposition on the activity of the child. The emphasis was on placing the locus of responsibility with the child through "play fair with yourself," "use good judgment," or "use your time wisely." The rules exist to help students do good work, and if they are violated poorer academic results will follow, for which the student will have to bear the consequences. Thus, Mrs. Newman attempted to inculcate and continually appeal to an internalized set of values, asking the children to think for themselves and decide what to do. We found such internally oriented control to be the dominant mode at Huntington, even though there were strong external controls as well.

In addition to this analysis of teacher verbal statements, we coded all the recorded interactions to do a statistical analysis of the patterns. Statistical results showed a much greater emphasis on external strategies and messages at Smith than at Huntington. For example, about 52 percent of the strategies at Huntington were coded as internal, versus fewer than 17 percent at Smith. The comparable figures for messages were about 67 percent internal at Huntington versus only 19 percent at Smith. On the basis of an analysis of covariance that controlled for differences in the race, sex, and ability group to which students were assigned, we found that the differences between these incidences of internal interactions were statistically significant at the .05 level. And, whereas external strategies were high in both classrooms (61 percent in Huntington and 83 percent in Smith), the external messages were twice as predominant in Smith (45 percent of interactions compared with 22 percent at Huntington). Thus, the general patterns that were observed were reflected in the statistical analyses. The data on internal versus external standards as reflected in teacher interactions with students therefore tend to support our initial expectations.

Present Versus Future Role Orientation

In looking at the degree to which the two classrooms were characterized by a present or a future orientation, we found the Huntington children being constantly reminded of the future consequences of their present activities. The teacher frequently referred to the future educational and professional implications of good classroom performance, and the mention of future occupational roles was common. "Good thinking. See, you're really thinking like a mathematician" (after a review of geometric shapes). "You'll be a good scientist" (writing fantasy stories). "You were good artists—now you're good authors." Students were also reminded regularly of the high standards they would have to meet to study at a prestigious university nearby as well as of the importance of preparing for the demanding work of second grade. "Eddie, this is going to be expected of you next year. You have to listen and follow through." After an independent work session writing stories for 35 minutes: "You have worked great. You are ready for second grade, because first graders can only work 15 minutes." The brightness of the future was emphasized with a "you can do it" attitude: "You just don't know how good you really are. Just keep trying, boys and girls." "If you don't get it, that's perfectly all right, Jimmy.

By Friday you'll get it without looking." The present and future were inextricably tied together at Huntington.

By contrast, the emphasis at Smith was on the present. The future consequences of present activities (educational or otherwise) were rarely mentioned. Smith children spent much of their time doing "fun" things, and there was little emphasis on preparing for the future. Essentially, they were expected to act like first graders rather than being pushed to be more mature for future roles. Though the teacher reinforced the progress that they had made while in first grade, she rarely extrapolated it beyond the first grade. References to the second grade tended to be negative and foreboding. For example, when the class failed to bring a seed from home, as Mrs. Jones had asked, she said: "We're not getting ready for second grade. This was homework." After struggling with several children about writing their letters properly, she warned: "In second grade they don't teach you printing. That's why you have to know it now."

References to role models in the more distant future were just as infrequent, although the teacher would sometimes tell the children to correct their own work, saying "Be your own teacher." There was no indication of an educational future beyond the upper grades, and the one mention of those grades came in the midst of a criticism: "This is important. You can't play an instrument when you get to the upper grades if you can't read these notes, if you can't read music. You need to know this stuff, and I'm really disappointed." The nearby university whose existence was talked about so often at Huntington was never mentioned at Smith. The constant reminder of a positive future and of moving toward it through academic achievement that was so prevalent at Huntington was simply lacking at Smith.

As with the observations on internal-external interactions, the observations of future and present status were coded for statistical analysis. We found that the Huntington teacher referred to future status and roles almost eight times as often as the Smith teacher did. Differences between the two classrooms were statistically significant after controlling for race, sex, and ability group factors. Thus, the overall emphasis on future roles and consequences of present activities was far greater in the upper-middle-class first grade than in the lower-middle-class one.

Verbal Self-Presentation

One school activity that offers an opportunity to observe the teacher's expectations about verbal self-presentation skills—and efforts to teach them—is the sharing session, a time for students to "show and tell" to fellow students an item they have brought to school or an idea they have. In both schools these sessions were characterized by the teacher asking for volunteers and selecting one from among those who raised their hands. The student would come to the front of the group, face his or her peers, and tell about something. The teacher would usually comment, and other students might ask questions. At some point the teacher would indicate that the presentation was over, and another volunteer would be chosen.

At Smith, sharing took place only about once every three days, and typically convened at the request of one of the students at no regular time. The feeling seemed to be that it was a nice activity, but not so important that it had to happen daily. The teacher commented on the presentations only about half the time; she seemed to view it less as a conscious learning period than as an enjoyable interlude. When she did comment, the two most frequent forms were a factual question requiring a specific answer or a simple positive closing remark such as "That's nice." Only 8 percent of the time (among the 102 presentations we observed over a six-week period) did she give any procedural instructions about how to make presentations, and then it was usually a cue about what else to say. For example, someone got up to say that her family had just bought a new car, and Mrs. Jones prompted, "Tell us the color." Another time a child brought in an old watch that his father had given him, and Mrs. Jones suggested, "Hold it up." The terse nature of the presentations and responses enabled her to include a large number of participants, averaging ten a session.

By contrast, at Huntington every day began with ten minutes of sharing. It provided time for the children to settle down in preparation for the independent work period. But it also gave Mrs. Newman an opportunity to improve the cognitive, grammatical, and presentation skills of the speakers through questions and suggestions. The length of the interaction allowed for fewer participants in each session than at Smith. After almost

90 percent of the 87 presentations Mrs. Newman responded, and in about a quarter of the cases she gave advice on speaking before a group: "What nice sentences you made! You told us so many things. We know exactly when and where and what." "I like the way Joanne shared yesterday. She called it a 'poster.' She was able to describe it more than 'this.'" "I really like the way Matt spoke so nice and loud. Although I was looking in my desk and rattling papers, I could hear every word he had to say. When we have something that's important to say, then we should say it so people can hear it."

Unlike Mrs. Jones's responses, Mrs. Newman's were often characterized by an open-ended (open cue) factual question or a thought-provoking positive closing remark. About 20 percent of the time she was able to tie the child's presentation to the subject matter of the previous day or use it as a basis for a discussion question directed to the class. The differences in teacher responses to sharings are summarized in the tabulation that follows:

	Huntington	Smith
No response	12.0%	50.7%
Factual question (open cue)	32.5	4.3
Factual question (closed cue)	4.8	21.4
Positive closing remark	27.2	17.9
Negative closing remark	1.2	.7
Extend presentation, throw questions to class	20.6	2.9
Other response	1.7	2.1

The content of the stories shared was usually happy and factual at both schools. At Huntington, children told primarily about experiences and only secondarily about material acquisitions, half of which were things like educational toys. At Smith, material acquisitions came up more frequently, with experiences in second place. Children at Smith rarely (one percent of the time) gave reasons for their thoughts; children at Huntington included reasons 12.6 percent of the time. Most stories talked about the present at both schools, but the percentage of future-oriented stories at Huntington (19 percent) was over twice that at Smith (9 percent).

In many respects, then, the patterns during sharing sessions paralleled patterns that we observed when the teachers were more directly in charge of the class and confirmed our sense of the differences between the schools that we documented in our systematic classroom observations.

Cognitive Achievement

As noted earlier, high occupational achievements are tied to strong cognitive skills; those with higher levels of knowledge and cognitive aptitude are more likely to make the most productive professionals and managers, whereas those with lower levels are necessarily relegated to more routinized work and inferior jobs. Certainly, high cognitive achievement is necessary for undertaking the substantial amounts of education required for professional and managerial roles, and it is crucial for obtaining entrance to the most prestigious educational institutions. Accordingly, the relative emphasis on cognitive achievement between Huntington and Smith represented an important focus for comparing the nature of socialization for work between the two settings.

At Huntington, cognitive schoolwork *mattered* in a way that it did not at Smith. Huntington children were expected to complete their assignments carefully and correctly. The teacher made her standards clear, and often spent time tutoring individual children and requiring them to do sloppy work over again while the others played at recess or watched a movie. Finishing the work was not enough in itself: "You're required to do more work than this. You have to tell yourself to go faster." Or again: "That's correct, but it's a pretty lousy A. Look at Jimmy's work. Isn't that a gorgeous A? You can work as well as he can. You just have to take a little pride in it. Your mother sends you to school with such nice neat clothes on. What if she gave you raggedy ones? That's a pretty raggedy A."

At Smith, the emphasis was more on completing the assignment and placing the finished work on the teacher's desk to be checked in. Mrs. Jones stressed the quality of the work less than the fact that it should be finished. Once papers were turned in, she allowed the children to play; this was something we never saw at Huntington, where children were constantly obliged to "use time wisely" by concentrating on schoolwork.

Huntington children learned that work for first graders was to master basic skills (especially reading) and to acquire the study habits that would permit them to learn independently. They received procedural directions and constant feedback on how to structure their study times and how to use classroom resources on their own: "This is first-grade boys' and girls' work—to learn to read. You didn't take time to look. Now don't do that to yourself, because you can be a good reader." "He didn't know the answer, but he knew the tool to help him. That's important." "That's what first grade is all about—we find ways to help us get the right answer." This is different from the learning style taught at Smith because it assumes that children should be held responsible for their own study habits and because it emphasizes the importance of those habits.

The difference in reinforcement for academic work could also be seen in the way the teacher responded to children's answers to her questions. At Huntington, of 142 responses coded, the majority were overwhelmingly positive (79.5 percent), with negative responses or neutral ones occurring less than a quarter of the time (9.2 percent negative and 11.3 percent neutral). By contrast, at Smith, of 256 teacher responses coded, only 29.3 percent were positive, and the majority were neutral (67.2 percent).

Besides giving affective feedback to children answering questions, the teachers incorporated children's answers into the discussion in different ways. We coded for three possible teacher response patterns. The teachers could give a response to *close off* the communication, such as a simple "okay" to indicate that the child or the subject discussed was finished. Or the teachers could *sustain* the question by asking for further information or another perspective from that same child. The third alternative was for the teachers to *extend* the answers given, asking for logical connections with further subjects not directly under discussion, or calling for class participation in response to a particular child's idea. For example, Mrs. Newman extended a child's answer in the following way while reading a story about the early bird catching the worm: "How do you know this is a worm instead of a mouse tail? Do you see something that the artist did when he was drawing the worm that we found out about from the movie yesterday?" (she points out the muscle ridges on the side of the worm).

At Huntington, the teacher sustained (40.1 percent) or extended (30.3 percent) the majority of the children's responses, whereas at Smith, the teacher closed most of them (83.2 percent), sustaining only 11.7 percent and extending a mere 5.1 percent. This has a limiting effect on the amount and kind of verbal practices called for in the two rooms. A tabulation of the length of children's responses shows that the Huntington children got much more opportunity to verbalize ideas, rather than just giving one-word answers. The teacher at Smith directed many of her questions to whole groups of children, so they answered simply and in unison. The tabulation that follows gives the results for length of response:

	Sound	*Word*	*Phrase*	*Sentence*	*Ave. No. of Sentences*
Huntington (n = 74)	–0–	14.9%	6.7%	78.4%	2.90
Smith (n = 138)	2.2%	47.1%	7.2%	43.5%	1.48

The content of cognitive presentations also varied between schools. Huntington stressed comprehension, with Mrs. Newman asking the children to repeat the reasoning behind an answer or to paraphrase what they had read. Both schools called for a high percentage of straight factual answers, although this happened proportionately more often at Smith. Percentages of interactions calling for the child to initiate his or her own reasoning were about the same at both schools. Interactions asking for feeling or fantasy responses were much more common at Smith; in fact, they almost never happened at Huntington. The tabulation that follows summarizes the kinds of responses requested by the teacher:

	Comprehension, repeat reasoning	*Straight factual answer*	*Initiate reasoning*	*Feeling or fantasy*
Huntington (n = 282)	28.4%	60.3%	10.9%	0.4%
Smith (n = 619)	2.4%	79.9%	12.9%	4.8%

Again, the data seem to support the expected types of differences. The emphasis on cognitive achievement seemed far greater at Huntington than at Smith. The overall classroom environment at Huntington underlines the view that academic work is the business of the class and other activities are secondary. At Smith academic work was treated as just another part of the daily regimen, and it was much more routine and unpressured. Even the question and answer sessions on particular subjects at the Huntington first grade were used to extend the discussion to other domains, whereas at the Smith first grade the sessions were more nearly self-contained, with little feedback and extension to other learning experiences. Teacher responses at Huntington emphasized a heuristic quality in which the responsibility for improving the answer was placed on the child through asking open questions, whereas the teacher at Smith emphasized a terse and closed response. Finally, the emphasis on the complexity and length of student response was greater at Huntington, as was the requirement for showing the rationale or reasoning behind the answer.

These patterns emphasize a difference in favor of preparation for a long path of schooling culminating in advanced university degrees for the first graders at Huntington, and a more applied and ultimately shorter educational experience for the Smith first graders. And these educational patterns are themselves likely to translate into more higher-level occupations for the pupils at Huntington than at Smith.

Summary of Classroom Observations

On all four occupational dimensions, the educational interactions in the two first-grade classrooms reflected a socialization pattern in which the Huntington students were being prepared for roles at the top of the work hierarchy and the Smith students for roles in the lower and middle portion of the job spectrum. This pattern seemed to hold despite the diversity of the dimensions themselves, and it supports our view that school practices are carried out in the context of a class structure. Schools differentiate the socialization of the young for work along lines that conform to parents' occupational roles.

Views of Teachers and Other School Staff

Part of the explanation for the different treatment of pupils in the two schools lies in the attitudes of school personnel and of parents themselves. Both before and during our detailed observations of the classrooms, we had opportunities to obtain the views of teachers and administrators in the two schools about the nature and consequences of the students' backgrounds and the expectations for their future success. In addition, we interviewed Mrs. Newman and Mrs. Jones in depth on these issues. From these interviews it became apparent that the teachers and administrators had views about the students and their families that differed systematically between the two neighborhoods.

One of the salient factors that was used to explain school practices again and again by both first-grade teachers and also by the other school personnel we interviewed was the nature of the neighborhoods the schools were serving. Mrs. Jones repeatedly emphasized the working-class character of the Smith neighborhood and how it compared unfavorably with a much wealthier neighborhood across town. In many of these conversations she emphasized that someone with her background would not want to live in the Smith area even though she had been raised there; indeed, only a few of the Smith staff lived in the immediate vicinity of the school.

When teachers referred to families in the Smith neighborhood, they presented them as a source of problems for the school. Staff members at the school would frequently make negative references about individual parents and their home lives, even though expressing sympathy for their situation: "All in all, I think that the parents are trying to give their kids the best home life they know. A lot of them are unaware, I think. They're so wrapped up in their own problems. I don't really feel that the parents, some of them, really realize what kind of a home life they are giving their kids, because they've got so many problems themselves that they can't solve. You get into a filtering down thing, too, from the parent to the child." Another teacher talked of her concern about parents who are not equipped to be good parents, and who do not care about their children.

I know kids that go home at 3 o'clock that are street kids until 6. Or, they go home to a babysitter, and the babysitter goes, "Sure, you know, [do whatever you want]." . . . There's families there that constantly give their kids money, "Go up to the 7-11, and get out of my hair. Go buy a popsicle or something." . . . I think there's a lot of parents, I know there are parents because I've called on 'em and said, "Hey, we've got a problem with your kid." "Well, I can't come tonight—there's bowling." The kid is the last thing on their minds. Kids just sort of happen. . . . I've seen kids with both parents working, who have timers on the TV, and when the timer clicks off, the kids know it's time to go to school, because they're too young to tell time. That's sort of pathetic, to my value system. I think that somebody ought to be there to comb their hair and feed 'em breakfast, and see them safely off to school.

This negativism and perceived status difference suggested that the problems that the Smith School faced were formidable in comparison with those in the wealthier neighborhood on the other side of the school district. It was clear that the teachers saw these factors as limits on what could be done with children in Smith. In other ways, though, the teachers saw the parents as being much more tolerant than the parents on the other side of town. In a school like Smith, the parents were "not on their back" all the time as they were believed to be in that school in the wealthier neighborhood. So, the combination of limited neighborhood resources and family problems in conjunction with the lack of parental pressure meant that teachers did what they were able to do in the schools, and there was little pressure to go beyond this. And according to the standards of expectation set out by the state's testing program, we were told that the school was doing better than expected for this type of situation.

The teachers and principal at Huntington expressed very different views about their neighborhood. Again and again they would allude to the income or power of the parents and their careers, and this seemed to reflect on the importance of the school. As the principal noted: "The population, the community is fascinating. You have so many college-educated people who have such high expectations of their children and of school. I think in this community, the school is a very significant institution." The parents were admired as successful professionals who knew what they were talking about in most instances, and the neighborhood was viewed as a desirable one to live in "if you could afford it." Just as at Smith, the Huntington staff seemed to generalize from the characteristics of the parents' achievements to a set of expectations for the children. Whereas this meant a relaxing of expectations at Smith, it meant a heightening of academic standards at Huntington. The principal demonstrated this in pointing to the high percentage of "gifted" children: "A lot of it is, of course, the way they come to us. I mean ability, of course, heredity and a few other things."

Not only was the home looked upon as a helpful adjunct in preparing the children for school and assisting them, but parental suggestions were taken seriously; most of the teachers referred to the parents as a valuable source of ideas, feedback, and support for school programs. The principal saw both the PTA and individual parents as being "very supportive" in assisting the school with outings and other voluntary tasks as well as in raising funds for special equipment and projects. Of course, the other side was that since the parents were highly educated and thought of themselves as well informed, they felt they had the right to challenge practices or policies they disagreed with. As one counselor put it:

> We have a really well-educated, articulate parent community here, and a lot of ladies with a lot of time on their hands, who just make a business of knowing everything that is going on in the school. . . . It's okay to be concerned, but sometimes it really gets overdone. . . . You can't be God, and if the parent wants to be critical, they can probably say, "You don't teach math very well," or "The way you approach punctuation in English is not correct." And, boy, in this community, they really do. They expect the teacher to be heaven-sent. That's more true in some of the schools. I would have to say that's almost a socioeconomic thing. In the parts of town where families are wealthier and more articulate, they tend to be pushier about that kind of thing.

Teachers in Huntington emphasized the view that parents expected their children to excel in all subjects and put pressure on the school and its staff if the students did not meet their high standards.

In summary, the teachers saw the parents as being successful and as expecting similar successes for their offspring. The students were also imbued with high expectations by both their parents and their teachers, and the parents were shown deference and admired by the school staff. Indeed, even the children were shown deference, as reflected in Mrs. Newman's views that Huntington was preparing the future leaders, "the first step to Stanford."

In contrast to Mrs. Newman, Mrs. Jones saw the Smith first graders as being average. When asked if she had any unusual children in her classroom, she replied:

I don't have any that are really (pause) . . . stand out as being (pause). . . . I have an awful lot of kids that are average everyday children. I don't have any outstanding artists this year. ——— is a good actor. There's a lot of children that have made an awful lot of growth, but I don't see that as being unusual. It's fun to sit back and say, is there anybody that's gonna be famous? I really think ——— is going to do something. [This was a child who was lowest academically in the class, but the teacher had praised his creative mechanical abilities.] I have an awful lot of average everyday Joe Smiths.

It was the "average" nature of the children that she emphasized, yet she had also described them to us as "smart, sharp kids," saying that this class was the best as far as cognitive knowledge that she had ever had. She evidently saw them as smart within the average range of talent.

The Parents' View

Efforts were made to interview all of the parents of students in the two first grades, even if it meant meeting the parent in the workplace. We were successful in obtaining interviews with at least one parent for 90 percent of the first graders in Mrs. Newman's class, and for 85 percent of the first graders in Mrs. Jones's class. Most of the interpretations that follow are based on interviews with the mothers—19 at Smith, and 18 at Huntington.

One of the major differences between the two sets of parents was the degree of involvement in the school. Whereas almost all of the Huntington parents participated in the activities of the school through the PTA or volunteer activities, or visited the school on occasion to deal with a school problem, only about a third of the Smith parents did. The uninvolved parents expressed a lack of knowledge about the school system and education generally, and felt the need to defer to the professionals. They had few opinions about the school and felt uncertain in making judgments. The school and its personnel were viewed as having a high level of status that was largely unassailable, and they had almost no criticisms of the school.

Part of this restraint stemmed from uneasiness about confronting the staff of the school to voice an opinion. One mother described the difficulty she had in getting herself to go to school to complain about the "rough, mean teacher" she felt was treating her child insensitively: "I wasn't going to go because I kept saying, well, you know, when I get over there I'll get upset and I'll cry. . . . I let quite a bit of time go by, I probably let six weeks go by, and then I lay awake so many nights I thought, well, this is ridiculous. I'm sure that I should do it, even if I do it wrong, I should do it anyway." Another theme that emerged from the interviews was the tendency of parents to blame themselves or their children for school problems, rather than the school. Either they thought that to blame the school would make no difference anyway, or they implied that the teachers and school staff were probably right and their child was wrong in some way. Of those parents who did express negative feelings about the education provided at Smith, the major focus seemed to be that their children were not being challenged sufficiently in an academic sense. Statements were made that children were being allowed to slide by without picking up basic skills, and that they were not challenged to deepen their knowledge and expand into more advanced skills. This perception was not shared by the school staff, who pointed to the fact that the Smith students were doing better than their "comparison range" on statewide tests.

Many of the differences between the two sets of parents were reflected in the answer to a question that we raised: "What would you do if the teacher told you that your child was having difficulty in learning to read?" Huntington parents indicated that the first thing they would do would be to go to the school to find out if the teacher was providing appropriate and adequate assistance to their child. If they were satisfied that this was the case, they would attempt to find out the reason for the deficiency. For example, was the problem due to a medical deficiency such as sight or hearing or emotional impairment? Based upon this analysis, they would take the child to the appropriate professional for further diagnosis and treatment, whether this meant eyeglasses, vitamins, psychological services, or tutoring. Essentially, they were optimistic that if they pulled the appropriate lever through challenging the school or purchasing various kinds of services for their child, the learning deficiency would probably be alleviated.

When the same question was asked of the Smith parents, few said that they would challenge the school or the teacher. They assumed that the inadequacies rested with the child or themselves. Though some said that they would go to school to find out what the problem was, they expected to hear that their child was "not listening" or "he goofs off" or "he seems to be a bit slow in understanding things." The typical answers to what they would do about it were that they would attempt to help the child to listen or work harder. They did not see the purchase of specialized services as the appropriate response. Many of them said that there might not be anything they could do if the child was just a slow learner.

The overall difference in views that emerged in the interviews was a kind of fatalism among the Smith parents about what could be done to help their children academically. The school seemed difficult to challenge, so the blame was turned back upon themselves and their children, and solutions became the traditional ones of trying harder or resigning themselves to the fact that their kids just "don't have it." By contrast, the Huntington parents expected that it was the responsibility of the school to educate their children properly, and they tended to challenge the school if they felt that their child was having problems. Once they were satisfied that little could be done to improve the school situation, they would look for solutions outside of the school through the purchase of professional services to help their children. Their view was essentially optimistic—in making the tacit assumption that in all likelihood their children had what it takes. It was only necessary to find out what was wrong and redress it if the child was not making adequate progress.

Some Answers to the Riddle of Class-Structure Reproduction

How could two schools operating under the same state laws and existing so close to each other show such different patterns? Why do they correspond so closely to the occupational situations of the parents in the two neighborhoods? Part of the answer lies in the attitudes of teachers and parents as expressed in our interviews. How do these attitudes fit into the larger picture? To answer this question, we reviewed some of the literature on the operation of schools in California and analyzed our teacher and parent interviews with an eye to gaining a larger view of the role of teachers and parents in a class-structured society. What we found is that a constellation of forces reinforces the differential transmission of parental status among schools.

Above all, differentiation is practiced and legitimized as part of differential expectations by parents, teachers, and administrators of how well children coming from different social backgrounds should do in school. Parents, school staff, and the state educational apparatus have different expectations for children from upper-middle-class families than for those from lower-middle-class ones. At the state level the evaluative mechanisms governing school performance set lower academic standards for schools enrolling children from the lower middle class than they do for schools with children from the upper middle class. The interviews with the teachers and school staff revealed a similar difference in expectations, as did the interviews with the parents of children in the two schools. Finally, even when parents try to intervene in the schools, the ability of lower-middle-class parents to obtain individual or group leverage over school policies is limited by their own education, their low sense of their own power and their tendency to attach too much importance to the professional expertise of school personnel.

Institutionalized Expectations of the State

California operates a statewide testing and assessment program to monitor the performance of its schools. Children are tested in basic skills, and the results are reported periodically on both a school district and an individual school basis. To prevent "unfair comparisons" between schools with differing student enrollments, the state Department of Education established a procedure for evaluating the test score results of schools and school districts that took account of the characteristics of the pupils themselves. Weighting factors included the test scores of the children at entry level (administered in October of the first grade), a socioeconomic indicator computed from teachers' estimates of parental occupations, the percentage of bilingual pupils, and the percentage of pupil mobility or turnover. Based on these factors, a prediction is made of how well each school will normally do on achievement tests, and this is used to establish a comparison range on which the school's actual performance is evaluated. A school is then given an A for scoring above its comparison range, a B for scoring below it, and a W for falling within it.

The following tabulation shows how the two schools we studied fared in the 1974–75 state-mandated achievement tests (the scores and comparison range are percentiles):

	Huntington			Smith		
	Compar-ison range	Score	Perfor-mance index	Compar-ison range	Score	Perfor-mance index
2d Grade reading	84–98	99	A	34–61	69	A
3d Grade reading	86–99	99	A	30–57	67	A
6th Grade reading	93–99	96	W	48–76	55	W
Written expression	91–98	97	W	49–75	48	B
Spelling	85–97	91	W	46–77	50	W
Mathematics	89–97	97	W	48–76	24	B

The implications of the comparison ranges are far-reaching: they indicate that the Department of Education expects and will accept a vastly different level of performance between schools like Smith and Huntington. A score of 55 is within the acceptable range for sixth-grade reading achievement at Smith, but it is far below the expectations for Huntington. All the factors used to determine the level of expectations are operating outside the classroom walls. The implication is, unavoidably, that what is important for school achievement is less the capability of the school than the characteristics a child brings from home.

As the state guide for the interpretation of test scores explains: "Those districts operating under what they consider constraining conditions feel that it is unfair to compare them with the more privileged districts in the state. . . . To compare a district with other districts without regard for the characteristics of the district is often meaningless and sometimes misleading. It is more useful to compare a district with similar districts in terms of social, financial, and educational problems and capabilities" (Calif. Dep't of Ed. 1975: 17, 23). Useful for whom? For a parent in a "disadvantaged" school district who wants the best education for his or her child, or for a school district that wants a minimum of complaints? Unfair to whom? To the parents who are seeking to ensure an equal educational opportunity for their children, or to those in the school system who would be forced to explain this structural denial of such opportunity?

Although the documents that outline the procedures suggest caution in applying the evaluations too narrowly, they assert that the expected performances are intrinsic to differences in student backgrounds: "The ranks in the column for predicted score ranges represent the test score range in which each district could be 'expected' to score based upon the pertinent characteristics of the pupils, the community, and the school district" (p. 25). To the degree that these results set lower expectations for children from lower-class backgrounds, they are probably a self-fulfilling prophecy: students whose comparison ranges are low are expected to do poorly, whereas those whose comparison ranges are high are expected to do well. In this way, the state's evaluation approach contributes to the differentiation of performance by social class by using statistical analysis to set higher expected ranges of performance for students in Huntington than for students in Smith. The self-fulfilling results of such differential expectations have been documented in a number of studies (R. Rosenthal & Jacobsen 1968; Rist 1970; Leacock 1969).

Even the use of entry-level scores contributes to this effect. To obtain entry-level scores, children are tested early in the first grade; the raw scores, or number of correct answers on a 35-item test, are converted to percentiles to provide rankings of schools. On the 1974 entry-level examinations, the Huntington first grade scored an average of about 30 correct answers, compared to 28 correct answers for Smith. But when these were converted into percentile scores for "standardized comparison," the Huntington first graders were ranked in the 90th percentile and the Smith ones in the 52d percentile. By getting an average of two more items correct on a 35-item test, the Huntington youngsters were given a percentile ranking 38 points greater than the Smith pupils. A relatively small difference in performance was given the trappings of a very large difference when expressed in percentile rankings. The rankings imply that pupils at the two schools have very different capabilities, whereas the actual scores suggest a far greater similarity. Thus the teachers and parents in each school were given a picture of different capabilities and expectations by the way the data were treated.

Both in the use of test score expectations based upon comparison ranges and in the artificial attempt to differentiate student performances through norming procedures (i.e. stating the score in relation to where the student would rank in a standard population) that conceal the "true" variations, the state sets the stage for educators and parents to differentiate their expectations according to the social class and neighborhood of the students. Few educators or parents are equipped to understand the nature of the statistical assumptions upon which such data are based, but all are able to comprehend the educational implications. As we found in both parent and teacher interviews at Smith, the "lower" entry scores and comparison ranges are used as a reason for justifying poorer performance and lower expectations for Smith's students.

The Role of Teachers

Teachers play an important role in legitimizing schools' allocation of knowledge and in preparing children's future social roles on a class basis. They do this through their willingness to accept the exigencies of preparing students for the workplace. Teachers are realistic about the characteristics that will be required for success, so it is little wonder that they have lower expectations for minorities, females, and the poor than for nonminorities, males, and the well-to-do. Their experiences tell them that students from certain backgrounds have a higher probability of access to and success in certain occupations than students from other backgrounds. They are merely accepting the nature of the world for which they are preparing youth. Even if they find these differences to be morally objectionable, they feel frustrated in their attempts to change them.

We have seen in the interviews with Mrs. Newman and Mrs. Jones that teachers accept the dominant ideology about the nature of the class structure—specifically that the characteristics of the lower-income, lower-educated families are to blame for the poor performance of their children in school. Thus, many teachers like Mrs. Jones conveniently blame their school's relatively lower test scores on the parents' social class, and limit their own potential effectiveness as teachers owing to their pupils' "poor" home background.

Giroux (1981) analyzes the formation of teacher attitudes in their education; he places that education in the context of an institutionalized (hegemonic) ideology and the ideological apparatuses of the State. Teachers at all levels, he argues, are important in legitimizing the categories and social practices of the dominant society; teacher-education programs attempt, through a "dominant rationality," to structure teaching methods so that teachers using them will reproduce the social relations of production (Giroux 1981: 150–55). Various forms of system-management pedagogy, or knowledge-based curriculum approaches, Giroux notes, are "but two examples of the so-called innovative approaches to classroom instruction that at heart are simply recycled and repackaged forms of the existing rationality that has dominated schools and teacher-education programs since their inception" (p. 150).

Such theories of technocratic rationality view teachers' roles as fixed and generalizable to any level of schooling. The teacher is characterized not as a creator of values, but simply as a receiver and transmitter of institutional norms. "Consequently, the teacher's own existential reality becomes lost amidst a form of socialization and the role theory that is blind to its own ideology" (p. 153). As a result, Giroux concludes, teachers tend to transmit a view of knowledge that is static and conservative, obscure in its ideological bases, and supportive of existing institutional arrangements. "Teacher-education programs have simply not given teachers the conceptual tools they need in order to view knowledge as problematic, as a historically conditioned, socially constructed phenomenon" (p. 155). This "objectified" view of knowledge objectifies the classroom social encounter, for knowledge and social relations are intimately related; it also allows teachers to classify students into those that "get it" and those that do not—a simple rationalization of the world that makes Mrs. Newman's and Mrs. Jones's view of their own actions perfectly acceptable in some objectively logical world order. Teachers are trained, as Giroux puts it (p. 155), "neither to recognize nor [to] use the cultural capital of others as a central category for dialogue and personal affirmation in their teaching. The result is a form of pedagogical violence that prevents teachers from establishing conditions which allow students to speak with an authentic voice."

The Socialized Family

The dominant American corporate capitalist ideology (in Gramsci's terms, bourgeois hegemony) is embedded in more than just State institutions, the workplace, and the media. It is everywhere, within the development process itself. This is a *contested* ideology, and when the social conflict inherent in American capitalist development breaks out into the open, as it did most recently in the 1930's and in the 1960's (and in a less pervasive way, with the women's movement in the 1970's), subordinate groups in the forefront of the conflict try to overthrow the roles the dominant ideology has them playing in the class-gender-race hierarchy. The result of such conflict has been to change these roles in material terms (the New Deal changed U.S. income distribution significantly and changed the nature of labor's participation in economic development) and in ideological terms (the trappings of class divisions changed after the New Deal and the Second World War; the social position of blacks was elevated significantly by the civil rights movement). Public education has been a major objective of all these recent social movements; its role in reproducing the relations of production and the division of labor makes it a key objective of subordinate group unrest.

Nevertheless, when the unrest has subsided, the underlying class-gender-race structure in America—despite a number of changes—reasserts itself because of the unrest's limited nature. Working-class families, over time, have come to have greatly increased educational expectations for their children, but—as our interviews with Smith parents suggest—they still remain "working class" in the eyes of the school and in their powerless attitudes toward State institutions. Of course, the school reinforces this self-perception: schools prefer parents not to interfere with professional decisions on curriculum and teaching methods. All parents, working-class or not, must overcome the barriers of expertise erected by school personnel. But the interaction between State institutions (legal, bureaucratic, educational) and individuals or families from different social classes constitutes one of the most important means of reinforcing or breaking down behavior rooted in class, race, and gender. Lower-class people's perceptions of their capacity to change the schools' treatment of their children are conditioned largely by the difficulty of making such change on an individual family basis, or even on the basis of a single school. But beyond this there is also an ideologically bound self-perception that makes it all the more difficult to convince isolated subordinate-group families that aggressiveness rather than passivity toward the schools is the only attitude that can yield change if it is to take place at all. Yet our interviews indicate that parents are aware of the lower scores and the lower expectations accorded their children. The interviews also show parents' frustration in getting a hearing with school personnel. The role of social movements historically has been to organize the isolated frustration of subordinate groups into collective action, increased political power, and changing self-perception.

Summary

The analysis of classroom processes in this chapter indicates that even as early as the first grade there are systematic differences in orientations toward work; each class is immersed in an educational context likely to prepare its members for the types of occupations held by their parents.

The reasons for these differences are not simple ones that can be dispelled by the judicious use of educational policy. Rather, they are embedded in the different social, economic, and political realities faced by families in different class positions. The official policies of the State, the attitudes of teachers and other school staff, and the assumptions of parents suggest different expectations between the two neighborhoods studied that tend to reinforce the differential class structure in preparing the young for future occupational roles.

As Kohn (1969) has shown, the occupational values and aspirations of the parents for their children tend to reflect the requirements for success of the occupations in which the parents find themselves, thus setting out different occupational orientations among children that mirror those of their parents. Similarly, Olim et al. (1967) have found class-related effects in maternal transmission of cognitive styles. All of these differences tend to be mirrored in the ways in which parents prepare their children for adult life. The schools build on this process of class differentiation rather than intervening to alter it. To a large degree, the operation of schools within a class structure contributes to the reproduction of classes from one generation to the next. We have obtained a glimpse of how complex and faithful that process is; it is both a conscious and an unconscious extension of differences in expectations and resources among different class groupings and the institutions that serve them.

As schooling expands, it does so in the context of the social conflict inherent in a society that is structured along lines of class, race, and gender. Schooling expands in response to subordinate-group demands, but as long as the class-race-gender structures are the underlying attributes of the society, only the form but not the substance of the reproductive role of schooling will change. Thus, the class-reproductive curriculum becomes more "hidden" when there are working-class demands, when the states are required to equalize access to education for blacks and Hispanics, or when schools alter the advising of young women so that they are not counseled out of sciences and mathematics. As we have shown, however, administrators, teachers, and parents still tend to reproduce capitalist relations of production and the division of knowledge associated with segmented-labor-market occupational roles. But the underlying social conflict between capitalist society and the social movements that challenge capitalist social relations also raises resistance to these schooling structures and practices. The historical expansion of schooling, even with its insidiously structured practices, has produced an institution that is more democratic and less biased than the workplace. Historically generated by these contending dynamics, the partial autonomy of schooling from the workplace has come to mean that the output of the educational system does not necessarily conform to the needs of the capitalist workplace, nor to the reproduction of capitalist relations of production. It also means that the amount of resources devoted to schooling may be inconsistent with capitalist reproduction.

The contradictions of educational expansion are as much a part of understanding the relationship between education and work as is the role of schooling in reproducing work relations. These contradictions are the subject of the next chapter.

6

Contradiction in Education

Education, we have argued, is set in the context of social conflict and is an integral part of such conflict. Public schools in America are an institution of the State, and like other State institutions are subject to the pull of two conflicting forces over their control, purpose, and operation. On the one hand, schools reproduce the unequal, hierarchical relations of the capitalist workplace; on the other, schooling represents the primary force in the United States for expanding economic opportunity for subordinate groups and the extension of democratic rights.

These forces are in structural opposition, creating contradictions—i.e. conflicts and internal incompatibilities—in education that result in a continuing struggle over direction. Although at any given time one of the forces may appear to dominate and achieve hegemony, the existence of underlying contradiction means that the struggle continues in various latent forms. Contradiction is at the heart of educational change by generating a series of continuing conflicts and accommodations that transform the shape of the schooling process. Changes generated by educational contradictions also induce changes in the workplace.

Schools are characterized by contradiction and conflict through their very function of serving American capitalist expansion and the democratic political system. These democratic and class-reproductive dynamics are conditioned by the larger social conflict outside the schools. To the extent that the democratic dynamic gains ground, the educational system diverges in certain respects from the structural exigencies of reproducing capitalist relations of production and the division of labor. This divergence, in turn, is capable of exacerbating or changing the character of social conflict. It is therefore not only conflict in production that can lead to crises in capitalist development, but also contradictions in reproduction. In the latter case, crisis emerges from the failure of one of the more important institutions of reproduction to reproduce properly the labor skills, the division of labor, and the social relations of production.

This chapter discusses contradictions in education. We argue that there are three types of contradictions associated with schooling, all of which result directly or indirectly from the tension that arises between the democratic thrust of schools and their role in reproducing the class and work structure. The first type of contradiction manifests itself in the political struggle over resources for schooling. Since schooling is "public," it has been the object of social and reform movements committed to increasing the social mobility of subordinate groups. These movements have usually sought to increase the resources going to schooling for school expansion generally and for the education of working-class and minority groups in particular. But such resource demands may reduce the capacity of the State to enhance the profitability of capital, with the result that conflict will occur over school expansion between capital and labor in times of declining or stagnant profits, slow economic growth, and declining real wages—as in the 1970's and early 1980's.

A second type of contradiction is internal to the educational process. The reproductive dynamic creates pressures in schools to produce a labor force with skills, attitudes, and values that fit into the hierarchical division of labor and to reproduce capitalist relations of production. At the same time, the democratic dynamic emphasizes individual liberty and democratic participation as well as equality of opportunity and occupational mobility through education. The student must be prepared to participate in an authoritarian and hierarchical system of work, but also be prepared to benefit from and contribute to a system of egalitarian democratic practices. To a large degree, establishing a curriculum, teaching process, and educational structure that support one set of requirements must be done at the expense of the other. As we will show below, one consequence of this type of contradiction is the development of workers who are overeducated for the types of jobs that will be available to them.

A third type of contradiction is imported into the educational process through the fact that the schools correspond with the workplace. Contradictions of this type arise out of the correspondence process itself. As the features of the workplace are embodied in schools, so are the contradictions of the workplace embodied in schooling practices. Especially important is the educational manifestation of the contradiction between capital and labor.

Contradictions in Resource Allocation

As we have stressed, the democratic capitalist State faces competing demands upon its resources. On one side are demands to use the resources of the State to increase the profitability of capital. On the other side are demands for greater opportunity and the expansion of democratic rights. Though some educational funding is clearly used to support the first of these objectives, considerable portions are also allocated to improve the opportunities of disadvantaged groups, including students from low-income families, the handicapped, minorities, and those from bilingual and immigrant backgrounds. Much of the growth of educational funding during the 1960's and 1970's was specifically devoted to these groups, especially in the form of the expansion of public higher education to accommodate the quest for social mobility of these and other "nontraditional" students.

But funding used to improve educational opportunities for subordinate groups may put a drain on the rate of capital accumulation by increasing taxes and reducing the types of assistance that benefit capital more directly. At a time of economic stagnation, the expansion of educational opportunities is particularly resisted by the representatives of capital, just as it is advanced by the advocates of labor. Additional resources for education must come either from increased taxation or from reduced services in other domains, including services to businesses.

There are also conflicts within capital and labor about school expansion. Some fractions of the capitalist class have an interest in a better-trained labor force, even when public resources are limited. These fractions line up with fractions of the working class that also want school expansion even if it means more taxes. Yet there are other fractions of the working class that resist school expansion during a fiscal crisis because they do not want to bear the tax burden of such an expansion. In Chapter 3 we discussed this contradiction and its recent political manifestations. As it is external to school organization, it can be generalized to the social struggle within the State as a whole, rather than just within schools. The particular nature of the current crisis is that social spending, which had traditionally expanded during recessions, is now resisted politically. The State's capacity to undertake deficit financing or increased taxation is limited by political resistance to inflation and to higher taxes. Growth in resources for the next wave of economic expansion is required during a recession. However, in the recent (1981–82) crisis the expansion of social spending by the State was severely constrained. The struggle over schooling resources became accentuated as unemployment and the competition for available jobs increased.

And though some employers may support the expansion of educational spending, their vision focuses on the resulting production of certain skills pertinent to their industries. For example, the high technology industry is pushing for increasing science and math education, but its demands do not discuss who is to get such training, how widespread the training should be, or how science and math should be taught. Middle-class-oriented science and math programs may be totally inconsistent with the needs of the poor for high-quality mass primary and secondary scientific education. In Chapter 9, we discuss in further detail how these present-day conflicts may play themselves out.

Contradictions Intrinsic to the Educational Process

Schools must produce workers who meet the needs of capitalist production. This means developing workers with appropriate cognitive and vocational skills for existing jobs or on-the-job training and with behaviors, habits, and values predisposing them to the organization of capitalist production. It also means establishing a system of socialization and certification for work roles according to class, race, and gender that systematically legitimates differences in life chances among those groups. Finally, it means promoting an ideology among youth that portrays capitalism as the embodiment of individual liberty and democracy and inculcates political loyalty to it as a system.

However, at the same time the schools are charged with producing citizens who know and care about democratic rights and equal opportunity and who are able to participate fully in the economic, social, and political life of society. The result is that schools generate a range of functions that contradict the efficient reproduction of capitalist workers. We have identified five of these functions that support the democratic side of schooling: (1) democratic participation; (2) social equality; (3) social mobility; (4) cultural development; and (5) independence of the educational bureaucracy. Each serves to divert the schools from the preparation of properly socialized workers by inculcating in students various traits that are in conflict with work requirements.

1. Democratic Participation

Since schools must prepare the young for democratic political participation, students are provided with considerable rights in the educational system that are absent in the work context. For example, students have wide latitude with respect to freedom of expression within the school—something that is neither guaranteed nor commonly found in the workplace (Kemerer & Deutsch 1979: Chap. 3). A student's constitutional rights to free speech are protected in virtually all schooling activities as long as he does not materially and substantially interfere with the operations of the school or the rights of others. Whereas workers can be fired at will unless they are able to negotiate contracts with other provisions, students cannot be summarily suspended from school (Kemerer & Deutsch 1979: Chaps. 5 & 6). The constitutional right to an education places far more stringent due process requirements on schools in expelling or suspending students than on the workplace in dismissing workers.

Even though schools are hierarchical and share many features with the workplace, there are far more opportunities for students to influence the educational process than for workers to influence the work process. These opportunities stem not only from the greater protections and guarantees of due process just mentioned but also from the fact that there are a range of educational decisions in which students and their families can have influence. For example, the student can participate in the choice of courses, teachers, and schedules, and family members can confer with school or school district authorities about particular educational needs for a child or group of children. School boards are usually elected, so educational decisions can be influenced through electoral politics as well. It is difficult to find any counterpart to these mechanisms for democratic participation in the workplace.

This is not to argue that the schools are always responsive to parent and student concerns—as the interviews in the previous chapter clearly showed. Participation by parents differs according to the occupational role of the parents, and some schools are more responsive to participation than others. Nevertheless, the very possibility of community control allows for greater democratic participation in decisions affecting schooling practices. Universities also allow for student and faculty influence over decision-making in areas such as investment and curriculum policy and hiring and firing. In both schools and universities, this participation is a source of contradiction. Participation can interfere with the reproduction of the relations of production; community, student, or faculty control can exacerbate contradictions in production rather than smooth the reproduction of social relations. Yet, these outcomes must be within the realm of possibility, since the schools—like other state apparatuses—are supposed to represent the will of the people and to reflect their needs in democratic societies.

Finally, an important part of the school curriculum is devoted to political socialization of the young. Students are introduced to the fact that we are a nation of laws with considerable rights and obligations. They are indoctrinated with the sense of justice built into a representative government with checks and balances. They are also provided a version of their history which stresses the fight against injustice (e.g. taxation without representation, slavery, prejudice, tyranny, and aggression). Yet the political rights and responsibilities of citizens and their constitutional protections—so heavily stressed in the schools—are largely absent from the work relation. Thus, an important part of the educational process challenges directly the very premises on which the employment relation is based.

2. Social Equality

In contrast to the ideology of the workplace, that of schooling has placed great emphasis on social equality. Historically, it was assumed that access to a uniform system of compulsory schooling would provide, in itself, equality of educational opportunity. But recent years have seen the interpretation of educational equality as turning more toward a quest for equal resources, equal educational processes, and equal educational results (Coleman 1968). Where inequalities are promoted, they are inequalities favoring those who need additional educational resources the most to compensate for some "undeserved" educational deficiency (Rawls 1971: 100–101). Examples of the quest for equal educational opportunity abound. Since the *Brown* decision of the U.S. Supreme Court in 1954 there have been numerous challenges to racial segregation in the schools. Inequalities arising from state systems of educational finance that have channeled more money to wealthy school districts than to poor ones have also been challenged and overturned (J. Pincus ed. 1974). Federal and state laws providing special programs for handicapped, low-income, and bilingual children also respond to this issue.

Attempts to provide greater equality of educational opportunity impart a dynamic to the school quite different from that of the workplace. There is an implicit tension between what schools are expected to do for the poor and discriminated against and what the economy is supposed to do for them. These expectations have been galvanized into the social movements that have challenged educational inequalities associated with race, gender, and family income, as well as other sources of what has been perceived as unequal treatment. These movements have pressured schools to pursue egalitarian outcomes, even when they are not consistent with the priorities of the workplace or of taxpayers. For example, testing and tracking patterns are constantly being challenged in the courts and by parent groups. Federal attempts to provide compensatory resources for low-income children have had to counter the attempts of local educational authorities to use such assistance to replace funding that would have otherwise been provided for the poor out of state and local sources.

Not all of these practices have created more equal educational outcomes, but they have raised expectations of more nearly evenhanded educational practices. For example, there is evidence of only modest improvements in the relative test scores of children from low-income backgrounds, despite almost two decades of compensatory programs (Levin 1977; Burton & Jones 1982); this suggests that the schools alone cannot compensate for substantial economic and other disadvantages. The evidence on the effects of school integration is also ambiguous. In fact, the previous chapter suggests that social class-related reproduction is sometimes subtle and independent of resource availability, and that certain forms of reproduction cannot be easily altered by educational policies. But the expectations of greater equality in the schools and the use of social movements and the courts to obtain it have contributed to a dynamic for the schools that undermines the strict preparation of workers.

3. Social Mobility

A related aspect of the drive for social equality in schooling is the quest for social mobility. Schools today are the most important institution for families seeking social mobility for their children, and their importance has grown over time as the availability of other routes has lessened. For example, the great decline in opportunities to enter or establish small businesses as large corporations have increasingly dominated the economy has left over 90 percent of the labor force consisting of employees working for wages and salaries. In most jobs, educational credentials are required for consideration for employment; and the higher the level of occupation and income, the greater the educational attainment required. Although the precise reasons for this relation are hotly debated (see Becker 1964; Berg 1970; Thurow 1975), the close relation between education and occupational opportunities is not.

The role of education in enabling individuals to improve their social position is not new. Even in colonial times, when status could be readily achieved through the amassing of property, education "was, together with wealth, essential for achieving the highest social rank" (Main 1965: 251). And as education began to be a requirement for industrial jobs in the latter part of the nineteenth century, there was a direct tie between a worker's level of education and his job. In fact, an important motivation for taking schooling was the improvement in vocational opportunities afforded to those with more education. The role of compulsory attendance laws in increasing school enrollments has probably been exaggerated, given the high economic returns to pursuing schooling from the late nineteenth century on (Landes & Solmon 1972).

Making education in effect a requirement for mobility creates contradictions in the workplace if the growth of skilled jobs does not keep pace with school expansion. As long as the economy grows rapidly and the demand for skilled labor increases, it is possible for the labor market to absorb the increases in educated labor. This has been the case in the United States until recently. The shift to manufacturing from agriculture established an initial demand for educated workers, and then the expansion of the work hierarchy required higher levels of education for managers and technical specialists. Following this transition there was a shift from manufacturing to services, with an attendant increase in the demand for white-collar workers, managers, and professionals. The expansion of the government sector in the postwar period also contributed to this increase.

But the ability of the economy to absorb educated workers has broken down in recent years. The expectation that education would lead to social mobility generated an expansion of educational enrollments and attainments that has exceeded the available number of jobs requiring those credentials (Berg 1970; Rumberger 1981). This has led to a serious underutilization of educated workers, a situation that may be creating a major force for change in the workplace as frustrated and overeducated workers behave in ways that are counterproductive to the requirements of existing work organizations. This phenomenon will be evaluated more fully later in this chapter.

4. Cultural Development

The popular view of schooling is that it addresses the cultural preparation of youth as well as their vocational preparation. This derives from the classical notion of education, with its emphasis on the humanities and liberal arts. Today's typical elementary school curriculum provides exposure to music, fine arts, literature, drama, and physical education, all in the interest of the full development of the young child. The standard fare at the secondary level includes these as well as even heavier doses of languages, history, and literature. In addition, there are optional or extracurricular activities in drama, chorus, and varsity sports. At the university level, it is possible to find cultural studies even farther removed from the concrete cognitive skills required in job markets.

This aspect of the school is relatively independent of the influence of the workplace, although it competes for school resources with more vocationally oriented programs. Certainly schools could prepare workers more efficiently for corporate production if cultural aspects were eliminated, but such an action would conflict directly with the social demand for such activities, especially by the middle class; moreover, the prominence of schooling in preparing people for the workplace would then no longer be hidden behind a patina of culture and citizenship.

Not only does the cultural aspect reduce the capacity of schools to develop workplace skills, but it may even create values and norms inconsistent with capitalist relations of production. The values that underlie the humanities, and literary and artistic criticism, create a critical approach to the acceptance of social institutions and customs. That this dynamic of the school is in conflict with the school's class-reproductive role is reflected in the relatively marginal nature of such subjects. During times of budgetary stringencies, the cultural courses are often referred to as "frills"—a term that makes them highly susceptible to cutting. Further, liberal arts graduates suffer most from poor economic conditions, since they cannot claim a specific job skill. Thus, the cultural autonomy of the school is monitored by the periodic downturns in the economy, and the long-run expansion of the educational system tends to emphasize the inculcation of vocational rather than cultural skills, as shown by the rise of community colleges and by the increasingly job-related nature of curricula in higher education. The cultural component in the curriculum has become less important as each level of schooling has become characterized by mass participation.

5. Independence of the Educational Bureaucracy

The fifth source of contradiction emerging from the schools' internal dynamics is the independence of the educational bureaucracy from the direct control of capitalist firms. There are limits to this independence, since the business community and its supporters can exert considerable influence, politically, on curriculum and schooling practices. Yet within those limits, educational personnel are not directly answerable to capitalist firms. Most educators have the protection of lifetime contracts that enable them to withstand obvious pressures by outside interests. Educators and their organizations can also pursue their own professional goals with relative impunity. Teacher organizations and other groups of educational professionals have developed effective political representation through their ability and willingness to contribute substantial sums to those candidates who support their goals. It should come as no surprise that much of the legislation governing the schools at both the federal and the state levels has been heavily influenced by organizations of professional educators.

Furthermore, through collective-bargaining agreements educational employees are able to exert pressures on educational practices in the directions of their own preferences, some of which may conflict with efficient preparation of the young for the workplace. For example, educators have generally been highly supportive of the democratic role of schooling. In addition, teachers are guaranteed broad latitude in their freedom of expression, and they are protected from arbitrary dismissal (D. Rubin 1972). The result is that educational professionals have substantial independence to address their own visions of schooling, rather than being highly accountable to a narrow set of vocational criteria. This relative independence on the part of the educational bureaucracy means that they may oppose many of the values and practices associated with a strict preparation of the young for jobs in existing work organizations.

Contradictions from the Reproductive Process

Another level of contradiction emerges from the very nature of schooling in a democratic capitalist society. As schools have come to correspond structurally to the workplace, they have also taken on many of the internal contradictions of the workplace. By corresponding to the relations of production and division of labor based on class, gender, and race, schools bring into the education process the key elements of the social conflict itself, so we find pupils alienated from their learning, and teachers fighting over pay and working conditions rather than over educational issues. There is often resistance by the working class or by minorities to a class- or race-biased curriculum and a schooling process that is blatantly dead-end for these groups. Thus we can identify three sources of contradiction associated with the correspondence of school functions to the needs of a class-, race-, and gender-structured workplace. These can be summarized under the headings of students as alienated labor; teachers as alienated labor; and class resistance to the school agenda.

1. Students as Alienated Labor

Just as most of the structure and content of the work process is set out by forces external to the worker, so there is a parallel situation facing the student. Although the student has greater freedom of expression than the worker and somewhat more choice in his or her activities, the overall educational agenda consists of course requirements and teaching methods formulated on the basis of state requirements and implemented by local school authorities. In this respect, students have little influence over the shape of their own educational activities, since they must work within a structure imposed without their influence or participation. Thus students pursue their schooling because it is compulsory and may lead to improved status and career prospects, not because it consists of activities that are freely chosen and intrinsically satisfying. In this context, schooling activities are undertaken by students in order to obtain external rewards—grades, promotions, and educational credentials. But this arrangement means that students are primarily interested in obtaining certification rather than knowledge, just as school authorities expect that students will learn what the institution is certifying at each level and for each type of education. Students therefore have an incentive to take shortcuts to credentials through short-term memorizing, giving the answers they think particular instructors want, and turning in work performed by others. It is little wonder that cheating is considered to be common in schools and that an entire "term paper industry" has developed around colleges and universities.

When students seek credentials rather than knowledge and skills, the role of schooling as a producer of trained labor will actually be undermined over time. That is, the schools will tend to provide workers whose actual skill levels are lower than their educational credentials imply. Since student effort is motivated by external payoffs such as the exchange value of those credentials in the marketplace, the content of the credentials will be further undermined by a fall in their value. For example, as the returns to college education have fallen (Freeman 1976; Rumberger 1981), students have begun taking fewer difficult courses (U.S. Dep't of Ed. 1981) and have done more poorly on test scores (Harnischfeger & Wiley 1975; Wirtz et al. 1977). The attempt by schools to reproduce capitalist relations of production creates an alienating experience for students, and the learning content of schooling diminishes over time for any particular credential—with the consequence for the firm being falling worker productivity.

The alienated student also affects school discipline. Many students are in school only because attendance is compulsory and future employment is tied to an educational credential, not because they are intrinsically involved in the educational process. Such students represent a constant potential for disruption. To the degree that they do comply with school authorities, it is from fear of punishment rather than from satisfaction with school activities. In this respect, students and workers are in a similar quandary. However, given students' greater constitutional rights to free expression and due process protections against expulsion, sanctions are much less effective against them than against workers. Accordingly, school discipline problems and disruption are inevitable, placing continual obstacles in the path of a smooth and ongoing process of educational reproduction. As youth unemployment has risen precipitously and remained at high levels (Levin 1983b)—especially for minority youth—the returns to compliance with the school regimen have fallen and discipline problems have increased.

2. *Teachers as Alienated Labor*

Although teachers are viewed as professionals, they do not have the autonomy of other professions. Teachers are charged with implementing educational laws and school policies without participating in the formulation or evaluation of such policies. In this respect, both the process and the outcomes of their activities are controlled by external forces, so that teachers are alienated like other workers. They lack the power to influence or control significant aspects of their working lives, since they operate within the detailed conditions of their jobs set out by school authorities (Levin 1980). Although they may aspire to greater control over their activities, they are dependent for employment on State schools that are based upon a restrictive work environment. In this respect, schools are largely characterized by capitalist relations of production, somewhat altered by particular characteristics of State employment in a capitalist society (Carnoy, Girling & Rumberger 1976). Thus, the fact that schools are employers—with relations of production between teachers and administrators that correspond roughly to those in capitalist private enterprises—means that labor conflicts in the schools will occur and will take approximately the same form as in the private sector.

Teachers have organized into unions that negotiate contracts with their government employers. If the negotiations are not successful, the teachers strike. In collective bargaining and teacher strikes, however, a community composed of families and their pupils—the raw material of the production process—indirectly employs the teachers, at least in theory. If the schools are viewed as *the* legitimate institution for preparing youth for both their work and their social obligations, their continued operation is vital to the community. The teachers negotiate and strike both against their immediate adversaries—State administrators—and against the community that they serve. Since parents pay teachers through taxes, it is against parents' interests to have higher teacher salaries or cuts in teacher services. Yet teachers work in a capitalist production unit and therefore behave like exploited workers. The fact that their service is vital to the community only makes their bargaining power greater.

In a sense, teachers have little choice, given the lack of alternatives for influencing the educational process and their own working conditions. They have to conduct their struggle for fundamental occupational rights as though they were private-sector workers in basic conflict with their employer. But demands for higher teacher wages create a dilemma for the State. If parents pay higher taxes, the dilemma is solved; but if, as is now the case, there is resistance to paying more, schooling services must be cut, with obvious implications for the capability of the schools to deliver properly prepared and socialized youth to the workplace.*

Teacher negotiations and strikes also affect the process of student ideological formation. School administrators take an active role in turning community sentiment—especially parent and pupil sentiment—against negotiating teachers with threats that students will sacrifice learning and potential employment and college eligibility if the strike is prolonged. Antiteacher sentiments may be further reinforced by an anti-union bias, which has been promoted by business interests and has become more prominent in recent years. Teachers are characterized as selfish and greedy rather than "pulling together" on behalf of the community as workers are supposed to do on behalf of the corporation. Demanding higher wages and striking against *the community* is characterized as "typical union activity." Yet even this antilabor sentiment contains contradictions, for these are the same teachers who are responsible for judging pupil performance and for inculcating pupils with values and skills once the negotiations and strikes are over. How can the teacher be at once selfish and also a source of inspiration for learning and dedication to knowledge?

3. Class Resistance to the School Agenda

Several major works on the schools in America (Sennett & Cobb 1972; Giroux 1981; Apple 1982a), in England (Willis 1977), and in France (Baudelot & Establet 1971) have discussed the school as a place of resistance by working-class

---

*O'Connor deals specifically with State workers' unions in the context of the "fiscal crisis of the State" (1974: 146–51).

youth to class domination. Since the school is a class-based institution, it must treat working-class children differently from those of managers and professionals, not to mention those of the capitalist class, even if these differences are less pronounced in schools than elsewhere. We have already suggested that this differential treatment starts early, and consists of signaling to lower-class children that they will not do well in school and that expectations for them are minimal. Sennett and Cobb show that this generates responses of overt defiance among some adolescents—those who seek to gain esteem and leadership among peers by acting out against authority. Doing well in school among lower-class youth may be considered as "giving in" or cooperating, particularly because it is so unusual for them to do well. They appear to be selected by the teacher for special consideration. Most adolescents, however, simply "drop out" in the classroom, resisting passively by not listening even though required to be in school until the age of sixteen.

Baudelot and Establet stress collective resistance. Schools are defaced and youth rebel openly in the classroom, even attacking teachers. The school is just one more dominating institution that has to be overthrown, a continuation of the class struggle in the workplace. Yet Baudelot and Establet stress that the struggle in the school is not the same as in the workplace. Students are not workers; they do not produce, and there is no surplus extraction on the part of schools. Thus the nature of the struggle is totally different: it is resistance to incorporation into production in a particular way, and resistance to the values and norms being pressed onto working-class youth—values that are alien and designed to dominate (Willis 1977).

For both Sennett and Cobb and Baudelot and Establet resistance is generated by the incorporation of class conflicts into the schools. The reproduction of the social structure generates resistance on the part of those who will occupy the lowest rungs in that structure—those designated to fail in school and therefore to fail in life. The fact that many pupils must do poorly (or just not well) in school to fill the ranks of subordinate labor markets creates the possibility of resistance to class-structured education. It is the reproduction of capitalist social relations and of racial divisions, therefore, that is the source of resistance; conflicts inherent in capitalist society, though different in nature from those of the schools, are carried over into the schools. Social conflict is thus also carried over into the educational system, even though its form may be different from that in the workplace and other social institutions.

Giroux (1981) and Apple (1982a) call on Gramsci's dialectical concept of hegemony and counterhegemony in arguing that schools reproduce class but that the practices of schooling—in attempting to expand and deepen capitalist hegemony—are resisted by counterhegemonic tendencies in working-class youth, young women, and minorities. However, counterhegemony as Gramsci defined it is necessarily rooted in social and political movements, as in 1968 in France and Mexico or in 1970 in the United States. The relation between movements and resistance to the hegemonic "hidden curriculum" in schools is not spelled out by Apple and Giroux. Our view is that resistance is embedded in social conflict, and social conflict outside the schools has historically shaped the class-structured schooling now being resisted by some subordinate groups. Our main argument in Chapter 4 was that though at any moment in time the schools are reproducing the underlying class structure of American capitalist society, changes in the structure of schooling and its practices are induced as part of class and social conflict inherent in that society. The constant struggle to expand democratic rights, both political and economic, also takes place within education, expanding the role of schools in the process of social mobility and in the more equitable treatment of subordinate groups. Therefore, social conflict shapes educational change over time. Resistance to ideologically based curricula and other schooling practices has to be set in the context of this conflict. Such resistance is not independent of the struggle going on outside the schools.

This interpretation is not meant to depreciate the contribution made by Apple, Giroux, and others writing about school practices from the ideological perspective. Their work is important to a fuller understanding of what takes place in schools and why. Yet we consider that resistance to schooling practices is a secondary rather than a primary contradiction. We agree that counterhegemony is often manifested as indirect resistance by pupils to the ideology imposed upon them by the schools. But we think that more important forms of counterhegemony inherent in social movements have historically influenced the very ideology that schools imposed. Thus, dominant ideology as reflected in schooling is continually shaped by social conflict both outside and inside the schools.

The Divergence of Education and Jobs

Now that we have reviewed the tension within an educational system charged both with reproducing a work force segmented along lines of class, race, and gender and with expanding social mobility, equity, and human rights, we turn to a specific example of one of the contradictions produced by this tension: the "overexpansion" of the educational system relative to the availability of "suitable" jobs in the labor market.

When the educational system begins to diverge from reproducing capitalist relations of production in a direction that results in failure to prepare labor skills corresponding to the needs of capitalist development, there will be pressures on the educational system to change. Changes in the workplace may also ensue to accommodate the problems created by the new labor force, and such work reforms may have educational consequences. In order to understand this process, it is useful to explore further the dynamic of educational expansion and its relationship to the expansion of appropriate job opportunities. Individuals and families demand schooling largely for social mobility. Higher levels of educational attainment are associated with better occupational opportunities and incomes, and the expectations of a better job and income are important factors that motivate students to obtain additional schooling.

In periods of rapid economic growth, a shortage of skilled labor creates pressure on firms to train and upgrade existing workers and labor-market entrants to fill needed positions for which there are not enough candidates with appropriate education and training. This is a relatively easy challenge to meet. But when economic growth is slow and creates relatively few positions for educated workers relative to their supply, the potential for conflict rises. Workers who pursued education to attain higher occupational positions will find their quest for social mobility frustrated by a lack of appropriate jobs. As we will argue below, such workers are likely to create problems for a smooth process of production and capital accumulation. This is the problem of overeducation or the underutilization of educated labor.

The "Overeducation" Phenomenon

Overeducation refers to the situation in which workers possess more education than can be utilized in available jobs. The reproduction of educated workers means that at each educational level appropriate skills, attitudes, behaviors, and expectations are inculcated that correspond to a particular level of occupations. Normally, workers expect to obtain jobs at a level commensurate with their educational attainments. We believe that a natural consequence of the democratic dynamic of the schools will be a tendency to produce far more people with higher educational attainments than can be absorbed by jobs requiring those credentials.

What, then, is the relationship between the jobs available for educated people and the numbers of people who are educated? This question can be divided into two parts. The first involves an analysis of historical increases in jobs that require educated workers, particularly those with a college degree. The second involves an analysis of the nature of increases in the number of people who have received college training. Taking the two parts together, we can compare the availability of appropriate opportunities for college graduates with the number of college graduates that are likely to be produced by the educational system.

Changes in Jobs for College Graduates

College training has been required mainly for professional and managerial positions. Three principal factors have determined the availability of such positions (Welch 1970). First, the overall growth of the economy has provided additional employment opportunities for graduates at all levels, including the college level. Second, changes in production technology have tended to increase the relative need for college graduates. And third, structural shifts in production from agriculture to manufacturing and from manufacturing to services have created increases in the number of positions requiring college-level skills. All these factors are responsible for the historical increases in career openings for college graduates, especially in managerial and professional positions.

Since the turn of the century, the United States has experienced relatively high levels of economic growth (Denison 1962). As the economy has expanded, so have openings for people with college-level training. After the Second World War, the annual real growth of the economy averaged 4 percent. This could have increased the size of real Gross National Product half again each decade if it could have been sustained, but by the 1970's real growth declined to only 2 percent annually.

The accord between capital, labor, and the State that had been struck during the Roosevelt Administration disintegrated in the late 1960's. Business investment patterns had changed from investing in increased labor productivity to investing in processes to reduce costs of energy and labor. The late 1970's were characterized by declines in real wages and profits, chronic inflation, *and* high unemployment (Carnoy, Shearer & Rumberger 1983). The economy has entered a new phase in which projections of growth and of new occupational positions for college graduates are much lower.*

A shift of the economy in the postwar period toward production demanding an increasingly educated labor force has also had substantial effects on increasing opportunities for college graduates. As noted above, the United States has experienced profound shifts from agriculture to manufacturing and in more recent years from manufacturing to services (Fuchs 1968). These shifts have been accompanied by occupational movements from farmwork to blue-collar work, and then from blue-collar to white-collar work, with an expanding managerial and professional component in the labor force. In 1900, about 10 percent of both the male and female labor force were found in managerial and professional occupations (M. Gordon 1974: 28). These proportions had risen to 14 percent for males and 16 percent for females by 1940 (Fuchs 1968) and to 30 percent and 24 percent, respectively, by 1980 (U.S. Dep't of Commerce, *Statistical Abstract 1982–83*: 386).

However, since 1970 the increases in these ratios have slowed

---

*Of course a number of unforeseen factors may upset these forecasts, e.g. a major war. For an excellent exposition of forecasting long-run economic growth and a comparison of alternative forecasting models, see G. Fromm 1976.

down. As Richard Freeman (1976: 64–69) has noted, the future growth of industries that utilize college-educated people will be especially sluggish in comparison with the unusually high-growth period of the 1960's. Such education-intensive activities include the educational sector itself, research and development, and government employment. All of these have fallen on hard times as the school population has stabilized or declined—and as fiscal crisis has hit the government, in turn reducing social welfare spending and university-based research. There will actually be declines in employment in some fields, notably in public education (M. Gordon 1974: 37).

Increasing Numbers of College Graduates

It is interesting to compare the pattern of changes in professional and managerial opportunities with the increases in the numbers of college graduates. The college-age population and college attendance burgeoned following the Second World War. From 1950 to 1977 the number of 17-year-olds doubled from about 2 million to over 4 million, and the number of high school graduates increased from about 1.2 million to over 3 million (Dearman & Plisko eds. 1982: 65). Whereas only about one-fourth of those 18 to 24 were enrolling in colleges in 1963, the proportion had reached over 40 percent by 1981 (*ibid.*: 92). In 1950 about 500,000 students enrolled for the first time in institutions of higher education, but by 1980 the figure had reached almost 2.6 million (Grant & Eiden 1982: 130). During the same period the numbers of bachelor's degrees awarded rose from 400,000 to 929,000 (U.S. Dep't of HEW 1976: 197; Dearman & Plisko eds. 1982: 116). The number of master's degrees awarded increased fivefold from 1950 to 1980, and doctoral as well as first professional degrees showed similar increases (U.S. Dep't of HEW 1976: 198; Dearman & Plisko eds. 1982: 116, 118). In 1967–74 alone, the number of bachelor's degrees awarded rose from 558,000 to 946,000.

Future increases in the number of college graduates will depend upon the rate of growth of the eligible population and their enrollment rates in higher educational institutions. We believe that projected declines in the growth rate of college-age youth (Cartter 1976: 45) will be offset by increasing enrollment rates and completion rates for college. Between 1970 and 1980 the proportion of 18- to 24-year-olds enrolled in college rose from about 35 percent to almost 42 percent (Grant & Eiden 1982: 92). As college graduates compete for jobs in a tight labor market, they will reduce the options available to high school graduates and increase the incentives to enroll in college. The most reasonable forecast seems to be for a more rapid increase in the number of college graduates than the modest rise in the population of 18-year-olds.

Evidence of Overeducation

This contrasting pattern of growth between job opportunities and the increase of college graduates suggests that in recent years there have not been enough positions requiring college-level skills and expectations to employ the available graduates. According to the Carnegie Commission on Higher Education (1973a: Chap. 3), there have been three phases in college demand. Prior to 1950, opportunities for college graduates seem to have kept pace with the supply except in periods of severe economic dislocation, such as the Depression and the Second World War. From 1950 to the mid-1960's, the expansion of opportunities outpaced the increase in college graduates. This represented a golden age for college graduates—their salaries rose more rapidly than those for other groups in the population (Welch 1970; Freeman 1976: Chap. 3). But since the late 1960's, the number of college-educated people has increased much more rapidly than the number of appropriate jobs.

There is general agreement among many analysts—despite their use of different assessment techniques—that from about 1968 there have been and in the foreseeable future there will be an inadequate number of jobs requiring college-level skills and training and challenging enough to be consonant with the expectations of college graduates (Berg 1970; Rumberger 1981a, 1983, 1984). This "oversupply" means that college graduates must settle increasingly for positions that have not required college training in the past, or that could be filled satisfactorily by persons with high school training or less.

Evidence of this trend is found in recent data on the educational attainments of workers in different occupations. Table 6.1 shows the percentage of employed graduates by occupational grouping, broken down into experienced and inexperi-

Table 6.1 Major Occupational Groups of Experienced and
Inexperienced College Graduates, 1960, 1970, and 1980

	1960	1970	1980[a]
Experienced workers (25–64)			
Professional and technical	61.9%	66.6%	56.8%
Managerial	14.3	18.0	19.9
Sales	6.7	5.3	6.7
Clerical	7.2	5.4	8.0
Other occupations	9.9	4.7	8.6
Total	100.0%	100.0%	100.0%
Inexperienced workers (under 27)[b]			
Professional and technical	66.3%	70.0%	47.5%
Managerial	4.8	5.9	14.4
Sales	9.9	6.2	7.8
Clerical	12.5	10.6	15.1
Other occupations	6.5	7.3	15.2
Total	100.0%	100.0%	100.0%

Sources: U.S. Dep't of Commerce, Bureau of the Census, *Educational Attainment in the United States: 1979 and 1978*, Current Population Reports, Series P-20, No. 356 (Washington, D.C.: G.P.O., 1980), Table 12; Russell Rumberger, "The Job Market and College Graduates, 1960–1990," *Journal of Higher Education*, 55, no. 4 (July–Aug. 1984), Tables 4, 6.

[a]Based on 1979 data.

[b]Workers with less than five years of labor market experience.

enced workers. From 1960 to 1970 the proportion of experienced college graduates employed in professional and managerial occupations increased, whereas the proportion in other occupations decreased. From 1970 to 1980 this trend was generally reversed, except for employment in managerial occupations. For young, inexperienced workers, the decline in employment opportunities during the 1970's—especially in professional areas—was even more severe: in 1970 more than two-thirds of all young college graduates found jobs in professional occupations, whereas in 1980 less than half did. The decline was especially hard on women, who are more dependent on public-sector expansion for employment opportunities (primarily in teaching). By 1980, one-fifth of all inexperienced white female graduates were employed in clerical occupations, almost twice the proportion in 1970 (Rumberger 1984: Table 5).

Are Jobs Changing?

One obvious possibility is that occupational titles do not adequately reflect changing educational requirements, and that the same occupations have come to require higher skill levels over time. Another possibility is that a more educated person will be more productive in virtually any job, because of his or her higher skill level. It is conceivable that the increasing number of college graduates who are relegated to jobs not previously requiring this level of education might not be "overeducated" for their jobs; rather, the attribution of overeducation would result from our not adjusting the data on occupations for other relevant factors.

Neoclassical human capital analysis argues that productivity is higher for people with more education within each job classification. There are two bases for this assertion. The first is that the more educated worker is able to be more productive within the narrow occupational role itself—higher sales for the sales clerk, more accurate and abundant paperwork processed for the clerical worker, and so on. But data indicate that workers with an "inappropriately high" level of education show no higher or lower productivity than "appropriately educated" workers (Berg 1970). The second basis for assuming that a higher level of education improves worker productivity within an occupation is that workers with more education are able to adjust to change or to situations of disequilibrium better and to make better allocative decisions in the use of their time and other resources.* Although such arguments have been made for the labor market as a whole, their empirical support is limited to data from small farms in less-developed societies (Jamison & Lau 1982). The contention therefore requires a heroic extrapolation to such highly industrialized societies as the United States, where only 4 percent of the labor force is in agriculture and many of these workers are employed on large corporate farms. Indeed, both the theory (Alchian & Demsetz 1972; Williamson 1975) and the reality (Braverman 1974; Edwards 1979) underlying modern corporate production techniques require that the vast majority of workers have well-defined and highly routinized jobs that can be easily supervised and that do not permit a large amount of discretion or decision-making on the part of the worker.

A more formidable argument against our assertion of over-

*See particularly Schultz (1975) and Welch (1970). There is a wishful quality about this argument for anyone who has visited a large office or production complex where the timing of work and resource allocation are often set out on the basis of rigid rules.

education is that the same occupational classifications require greater education and skills needs over time to accommodate new technologies. According to this view, clerical and sales workers, as well as workers in manufacturing and other occupations, have faced an increasingly complex set of job demands that have required successively higher levels of formal education. There are two methods of examining this hypothesis. The first is to review the nature of change in job content for particular occupations; the second is to examine the actual educational requirements of jobs at the present time and to compare these requirements with the educational attributes of jobholders.

Some of the most extensive studies of changing skill requirements associated with increased automation were carried out by James Bright (1958, 1966). Bright explored the implications of automating the production of both goods and services on an industry-by-industry basis. He found that in most cases the changes were in the direction of *reducing* the skills and training required of workers through increasing the routinization of tasks and decreasing the decision-making components. Braverman's (1974: Chaps. 15 & 20) historical analysis of office work and Greenbaum's (1979) study of data processing also suggest that the increasingly capital-intensive nature of clerical work has tended to reduce the scope of decision making and the complexity of skills necessary to perform in those jobs. The conclusions of these case studies are also supported by a recent analysis of changes in the skill requirements of jobs throughout the economy between 1960 and 1976 (Rumberger 1981b). Rumberger found little change in aggregate skill levels required.

The comparison of educational requirements for particular jobs and the educational characteristics of jobholders also supports the view that the rising educational attainments of workers cannot be linked to ostensible increases in job complexity. For example, Rawlins and Ulman (1974) have compared the educational requirements of jobs as determined by the U.S. Employment Service with the educational qualifications of jobholders. An analysis of 38 professional and technical occupations in the 1950–60 period showed that "much of the growth of education in the postwar period cannot be explained by job-related demand for academic skills" (p. 208). In independent studies using more recent data from the U.S. Employment Service's *Dictionary of Occupational Titles*, Miller (1971), Lucas (1972), and Rumberger (1981a) made detailed comparisons of educational requirements for jobs and the educational attainments of workers holding those jobs. They concluded that most jobs in the U.S. occupational structure require considerably less education than the average attainments of workers actually in those positions.

Our overeducation analysis is also reflected in the experiences of recent graduates themselves, especially those who were unable to attain entry to professional and technical occupations. A survey by the U.S. Department of Labor of recent college graduates in the fall of 1972 found that whereas almost 88 percent of those employed in professional and technical jobs indicated that their work was related to their field of study, only 39 percent so indicated among those employed as managers, sales workers, and clerical workers, and 32 percent among those in all other occupations (U.S. Dep't of Labor, Bureau of Labor Statistics 1974: Table A9). A 1974 survey of graduates who had entered college in 1961 found that only a minority felt that their skills were fully utilized in their work (Bisconti & Solomon, 1976: 7). Job satisfaction was particularly low for those in occupations that are not traditionally associated with college training, such as clerical and other nonprofessional work (*ibid.*: 8).

On balance, it appears that a large number of recent college graduates have found themselves in occupational positions for which they are overeducated. It is unlikely that the situation will improve in the foreseeable future. The college-eligible population is leveling off, but high unemployment and falling returns to high school education are stimulating an ever greater proportion of that population to obtain degrees. And in a period of relatively stagnant demand, each new graduate is competing with a large backlog of graduates from the recent past for each appropriate opening.*

*The U.S. Department of Labor already estimated in 1976 that in 1985 there would be one million more college graduates than jobs requiring a four-year-college degree (U.S. Dep't of Labor 1976: 20). Of course, even these estimates do not take account of the extent to which the *content* of future jobs requiring four years of college will utilize the skills of these graduates.

The longer-run outlook for economic growth is not only relatively gloomy, but the single most important employer of college graduates—the government—is likely to *reduce* significantly the number of new hirings in the 1980's. Further, the effects of high technologies on most existing jobs appear to be reducing the skill demands of such jobs rather than increasing them (Levin & Rumberger 1983a, 1983b). In particular, there has been and will continue to be a loss of autonomy in the professions. Health-care personnel, lawyers, accountants, and others increasingly find that their career options are primarily in corporate and government enterprises. The tradition of being one's own boss and choosing one's specialty and hours of work is becoming increasingly circumscribed. Many professionals will find themselves relegated to relatively repetitive, specialized roles in large organizations (U.S. Dep't of HEW 1973: 20–23).

Overeducation and Unfulfilled Expectations

Overall, then, the long-run picture is one in which college graduates are likely to have greater expectations than the labor market can fulfill. In the past, obtaining a certain level of education usually meant attaining an occupation that was consonant with that level of education—and such expectations still seem to characterize young people. A comparison of the occupational aspirations of a national sample of 1972 high school graduates with the labor force's occupational pattern in 1972 and 1985 supports this view. Even two and a half years after leaving high school, having been either in the labor market or in college or both, about one-half the respondents aspired to professional and technical careers. But such occupations accounted for only about 14 percent of positions in the labor force in 1972 and were projected to be about 17 percent by 1985. By contrast, far fewer respondents aspired to the lower-level occupations, although there were relatively more positions in these areas (U.S. Dep't of HEW, Nat'l Center for Ed. Statistics, *Nat'l Longitudinal Study of the High School Class of 1972*, prelim. data; U.S. Dep't of HEW 1976: 245).

With additional years of schooling, people increasingly expect that the jobs they obtain will correspond to their higher educational status. Not only are there prestige differences in terms of occupations that have required traditionally more education (Duncan, Featherman & Duncan 1972), but there are substantial income differences among occupations (Sewell & Hauser 1975) and in fringe benefits, employment stability, working conditions, and independence (Duncan 1976).

What will the consequences be if such expectations are left unfulfilled? Before discussing this question, it is important to note the context in which the job dissatisfaction of the young, overeducated worker takes place. In the past, economic insecurity was a dominant factor in workers' adapting to jobs that were below their expectations or were intrinsically distasteful. The possibility of future upward mobility gave at least some hope that things might become substantially better through conscientiousness and hard work. But recent surveys show distinct breaks from these past patterns, largely owing to youth's higher educational levels and to the social gains by labor in the New Deal and after—unemployment insurance, food stamps, and other kinds of economic cushions. A survey of college seniors suggests that they see themselves as being far less concerned than their fathers with earnings and security and much more concerned with the altruistic and intrinsic aspects of the job.* Comparing youth opinion polls in 1967 and 1973, Yankelovich (1974: 37) found that:

> Today's generation of young people is less fearful of economic insecurity than generations in the past. They want interesting and challenging work, but they assume that their employers cannot—or will not—provide it. By their own say-so, they are inclined to take "less crap" than older workers. They are not as automatically loyal to the organization as their fathers, and they are far more cognizant of their own needs and rights. Nor are they as awed by organizational and hierarchical authority. Being less fearful of "discipline" and the threat of losing their jobs, they feel free to express their discontent in myriad ways, from fooling around on the job to sabotage. They are better educated than their parents, even without a college degree. They want more freedom and opportunity and will struggle harder to achieve it.

These attitudes have probably changed again since the early 1970's, especially in the last two years of severe recession and

---

*U.S. Dep't of Labor 1974: 4. See the model of Flanagan et al. (1974) that attempts to illustrate the relationship between economic growth and the quest for nonpecuniary job rewards (p. 101).

reduction of social-welfare spending. There is undoubtedly more fear among young workers today than ten years ago, but the underlying divergence from earlier generations' attitudes toward authority on the job and aspirations for greater freedom and intrinsically more interesting jobs have probably remained.

In summary, the prospect of job dissatisfaction and its possible deleterious consequences for productivity seems to be increasingly related to the disparity between rising expectations for better jobs and the available job opportunities. Education has been found to be related to job dissatisfaction in a number of studies, the most thorough being one by Quinn and Baldi De Mandilovitch (1975). Using the extensive data from the 1973 Quality of Employment Survey as well as sophisticated statistical techniques to attempt to isolate the relations between education and job satisfaction, they found that "the most dissatisfied workers were those who were too highly educated for their jobs" (p. vii). In a related study, Kalleberg and Sorensen (1973) found that workers whose educational levels exceeded the estimated educational requirements for jobs showed higher levels of job dissatisfaction. The evidence points consistently to the probability that as the discrepancy grows between the job expectations of increasingly educated entrants to the labor force and the actual jobs available, the dissatisfaction of this group will increase.

Job Dissatisfaction and Implications for Production

Job dissatisfaction is a rising function of the discrepancy between the educational requirements of existing jobs and the rising levels of educational attainments and job expectations of the young. But what are the implications of such dissatisfaction for work organizations? There are few accurate indices on the extent to which such factors as employee turnover, alcoholism, absenteeism, drug problems, sabotage and related problems of quality control, or wildcat strikes have changed over time, and virtually no information on such changes for those occupations and industries whose labor force is characterized by increased percentages of young and overeducated workers.* It is therefore

---

*Berg (1976) has argued that the poor quality of such data is an indicator of the low priority that workers are given by managers; it may also reflect the fact that such

difficult to relate rises in overeducation to such costly problems as work stoppages, deterioration in quality control, and employee turnover or absenteeism (Henle 1974; Flanagan et al. 1974).

The problem of linking changes in the proportion of over-educated workers to longer-term changes in worker behavior is further compounded by the effects of the business cycle. During periods of recession, high rates of unemployment tend to discipline the work force. The lack of alternative employment tends to reduce worker disruption, turnover, and absenteeism. Whereas employee absentee rates rose from 1967 to 1970, they seem to have leveled off or even fallen during the recession of 1974–75 (Hedges 1973, 1975). For the overeducation issue, it is the longer-run changes that are interesting. A related problem is the lack of consistency in both concepts and operationalization of such terms as "employee turnover," "absenteeism," or other measures of worker dissatisfaction and behavior. Different studies on the subject have viewed the phenomenon and its measurement in different ways, and statistical studies that have looked for *relationships* have varied considerably in their rigor (Lyons 1972; Katzell & Yankelovitch 1975; Hedges 1973, 1975; Bureau of Nat'l Affairs 1970).

However, there is considerable support for the view that job dissatisfaction is directly related to both absenteeism and turn-over (see, e.g., White 1960; Newman 1974; and Schneider & Snyder 1975). The view is intuitively compelling, although the relationship is probably a complex one that requires an improved understanding of both the psychosociological dynamics of the workplace and the research operationalization of those concepts (Brayfield & Crockett 1955; Srivastva et al. 1975).

More direct ties between overeducation and indices of employee productivity, such as employee turnover, have been reviewed by Berg (1970). He concludes that overeducation may have deleterious consequences for production. The most ambitious study that explored the connection between hiring standards and actual job requirements (Diamond & Bedrosian 1970) was carried out for ten major "entry and near-entry" jobs

---

information may be interpreted as a criticism of poor management. In the latter case there is a disincentive for collecting and reporting accurate time series on the symptoms of worker dissatisfaction. See also Herrick (1975) for a discussion of these data and their formulation.

in each of five white-collar and four blue-collar occupations as well as one service occupation for 20 groups of firms. The authors found that hiring requirements were unrelated to job performance across cities, industries, or firms. In 17 of the 20 samples, there was little or no difference in job performance associated with the level of educational attainment of the worker. But the differences between the hiring standards and the actual requirements needed for the jobs "appeared to be an important cause of costly turnover in a major segment of virtually all of the 20 groups" (p. 7).

Other survey results suggest a relationship between job dissatisfaction and both industrial sabotage and drug use within the workplace. Quinn et al. (1973) investigated these linkages with data from the Quality of Employment Survey. They found that workers' reports of industrial sabotage were most common among dissatisfied workers, young workers, and men (p. 40; see also Quinn & Shepard 1974).

These findings are also consistent with the few case studies of work organizations characterized by rising numbers of young and more highly educated workers. Perhaps the most poignant of these is the experience of General Motors with its new Vega plant in Lordstown, Ohio. The relatively well educated and young work force responded to management's attempts to tighten worker discipline and increase production levels with wildcat strikes, sabotage, high absenteeism, drugs, and other disruptive activities (Aronowitz 1973: Chap. 1). Kremen (1972) describes a similar situation in a steel mill, and the *Work in America* report (U.S. Dep't of HEW 1973) indicates more generally the high potential losses in productivity for both business and government from the increasing disparity between worker aspirations and the reality of work organization.

We suggest, then, that rising levels of overeducation for the available jobs in conjunction with relatively high levels of material affluence are tending to create increasing problems for the production of goods and services in the United States. The higher levels of youth education are creating enhanced expectations for jobs that will confer high status, income, and responsibility. But the expansion of such occupational positions is falling far short of the increase of college-educated youth, and there also appears to be a tendency for existing professional and managerial jobs to become more routinized or proletarianized over time. We expect that these contradictory dynamics will create increasing dissatisfaction in the workplace, which will threaten productivity by increasing the level of disruptive behavior among workers.*

Implications for Reform of Education and Work

We have already emphasized that the tension between the democratic and class-reproductive dynamics of the educational system has implications for changing both work and education. As the educational system tends in a variety of ways to become a democratizing institution, it may exacerbate rather than mediate contradictions in production. The expansion of the system of education to satisfy the ideology of social mobility through educational mobility is an important example of a phenomenon that will disrupt production if permitted to continue. Of course, as the threats to productivity and the symptoms of worker unrest increase, there will be attempts to stem the potential disruptive effects of education's democratic dynamic through the reform of both the workplace and education. The most evident efforts to reorganize the conditions of work are the efforts by the federal government in the 1980's to reduce public assistance and other social expenditures, to pursue policies that have resulted in higher unemployment rates (in which 7 percent unemployment is tacitly defined as full employment), and to encourage anti-union policies. All of these efforts serve to make workers less choosy in terms of jobs and wages out of desperation. But there are also attempts by employers to humanize work and to increase worker participation at the various organizational levels to assimilate the "new" worker. On the educational side, the federal government has reduced its support for programs for improving the opportunities of disadvantaged, bilingual, and handicapped students and those in segregated

---

*For an analysis of this phenomenon within the overall framework of contemporary U.S. monopoly capitalism, see Wyco (1975). Herrick (1975) discusses ten aspects of counterproductive labor activity and suggests methods for estimating their magnitudes.

schools. The generosity of appropriations for student loans and grants at the college level is also being reduced, and there are attempts to change educational patterns by getting young people into the labor force at an earlier age. In the following chapters we review these reforms in the context of the larger social conflict in American society.

7

Reforms in the Workplace

The underlying conflicts between employers and labor in the American workplace changed in the 1970's and 1980's, and so did the reforms proposed to resolve these conflicts. As unions responded to demands for income security, the capital-labor relationship was altered. Unemployment in the 1970's was not the same as in the 1930's. With unemployment insurance and welfare, the unemployed were no longer compelled to work at any wage or in any job to avoid starvation. The long period of economic growth that began with the Second World War also raised real incomes of American workers by more than 60 percent—equal to the aggregate increase in productivity. The implicit capital-labor-State accord that enabled labor to capture its productivity increases left workers much better off in the 1970's than in the 1940's.

The economic crisis that began in the late 1960's thus involved the State as much as the private production sector. Capitalists blamed union demands and State spending on social services for inflation and declining profits. Middle-income earners joined the attack on social spending through a tax revolt. In response, government grew somewhat less rapidly in the 1970's. As important, the relatively rapid expansion of employment in private services and trade drew many married women into the labor force. And the transition from manufacturing to services continued. Real wages also fell sharply in all economic sectors and productivity increases slowed down.

Employers responded to the crisis by intensifying their struggle to exercise control over government policies, over the allocation of public resources, and over the workplace itself. Their response took two forms: (1) increased discipline of the labor force to place downward pressure on wages and to increase productivity; and (2) workplace reforms, to increase productivity by reducing conflict.

Because the State's social role has changed capital-labor relations, disciplining the labor force entails subjecting it to higher unemployment rates than before and reducing State spending on social welfare and public assistance (which increases the cost of being unemployed). It also means liberalizing immigration policies and using the State's legislative and enforcement apparatuses to reduce the bargaining and organizing power of labor unions.

An important reason for workplace reform is also related to keeping out unions. High-technology companies such as Hewlett-Packard and IBM have been successful in avoiding unionization because of enlightened management policies that make employees feel that they have something to say about the firm's policies and decisions. Furthermore, young workers with relatively high educational levels who have not experienced economic deprivation are more inclined to resist not only tedious, repetitive jobs, but also the undemocratic conditions of the work setting. Symptoms of malaise are rising worker turnover, absenteeism, sabotage, increased drug use, the deterioration of product quality, and challenges to discipline and existing work organization. Such threats to production and productivity are not resolved through normal collective bargaining with trade unions. Yet they have high potential costs and have put pressure on both managers and workers to reform the workplace.

As employers and sympathetic administrations attempt to discipline labor, social movements arise to resist such changes. The unions struggle to maintain their position in the face of onslaughts by corporations and the State. The organized working class focuses increasingly on national politics and less merely on collective-bargaining agreements. Solidarity marches and re-identification with the Democratic Party become official union activities. Women, minorities, labor, and the aged use their electoral strength to keep the State from reducing social-welfare spending; and students and their families lobby to maintain student grants and loans and low tuition in public colleges and universities. Even as neoconservatives attempt to bring school expansion and practices into line with the new disciplined labor force, the conflict over school reform continues. Average education among the young continues to rise, and there is increased competition for the educational careers leading to the small number of highly desirable jobs. The underutilization of education contributes to new conditions of worker-employer conflict. Schooling continues to prepare and orient most young people inappropriately for the jobs available to them. Dissatisfied workers create demands for change in the relations of production and the organization of work. Work reforms are likely to be a major response in assimilating these new workers into the workplace.

Which type of reforms will predominate—management reforms that restore discipline and raise productivity relative to wages, or worker reforms that give labor greater control over the production process? This is a political issue; it hinges on the level of worker consciousness and worker political power relative to the dominant groups. Contradictions existing in the State do influence conflict in production, but the results of such contradictions depend on the organization and political power of social movements relative to the political power of employers.

In this chapter we review workplace measures and reforms that emanate from this conflict in the production system. First, we analyze the traditional responses available to employers seeking to maintain and increase profits in the face of stagnating worker productivity and challenges to discipline and existing work organization. Second, we present a taxonomy of existing or proposed changes in the organization of work, including worker-initiated reforms. Third, we discuss criteria for determining which changes are most likely to succeed in the long run as a response to the problems of integrating young and highly educated workers into the workplace. Fourth, we discuss these promising reforms in detail, exploring the possible consequences of their adoption for the dialectic of education and work.

Traditional Responses

The most direct approach to combating increased conflict in the workplace is to make clear to workers that the alternative to cooperation is the loss of employment and income. The classic example is Henry Ford's method of disciplining his disgruntled skilled workers to force their acceptance of the newly invented automobile assembly line. Faced by a potential mutiny on the shop floor, Ford placed an advertisement in the Detroit newspapers offering five dollars a day (twice the going wage in 1912) to work in his plant. The following morning 10,000 job seekers showed up at the gates of the factory. He had made his point: the workers inside the plant were easily replaceable. He had to hire very few workers at five dollars a day; his workers stopped resisting the assembly line. They had been disciplined to higher productivity through fear of losing their jobs.

In Chapter 3 we discussed ways in which capitalist firms put pressure on workers' wages (downward) and on their productivity (upward). These are continuous efforts—they do not just occur in moments of increased conflict—but they are accentuated in periods of crisis. There are three major sources of change in these efforts. The first involves the capital-labor intensity of firms in particular sectors of economic activity, which generally increased until the 1970's (Denison 1979; Gollop & Jorgensen 1980), but began to decline in nonmanufacturing industry as a whole after 1973 (U.S. Dep't of Commerce, *Survey of Current Business* 1981: 59). The number of workers employed per unit of output decreased over time until the late 1970's, particularly as firms increased investment in the upswing from a recession. Unemployment levels at each stage of the business cycle have been rising.

Second, in the last ten years firms have tended to invest in lower wage production with short-term profits in mind rather than trying to raise labor productivity and wages with long-term capital investment (Bluestone & Harrison 1982). Productivity growth has slowed significantly in every sector since the early 1970's, and productivity remained constant between 1977 and 1982 (*Economic Report of the President* 1983: 208). Real wages have declined even more (Carnoy, Shearer & Rumberger

1983). The investment in lower wage production is reflected in the movement of capital from the United States to foreign countries, in the movement to better "business climates" (i.e. unfavorable conditions for labor organizing) in lower wage regions within the United States (Bluestone & Harrison 1982), and in the importing of cheap labor from abroad, since such labor is usually willing to work hard and not cause trouble, especially when in the country illegally.*

Third, the State has become increasingly involved in providing social support to labor and the poor and in employing the highly educated, especially women and minorities (Carnoy, Girling & Rumberger 1976; Carnoy, Shearer & Rumberger 1983). The conflict over the conditions of work has therefore shifted to the State and its allocative role. As social-welfare spending is reduced, the cost of unemployment to the unemployed increases, forcing them to take undesirable jobs at lower wages.

All of these measures, by increasing unemployment, the threat of unemployment, or the cost of being unemployed, keep downward pressure on wages and upward pressure on productivity among employed workers. If workers are causing problems, the existence of a large number of unemployed and the threat of a "runaway" shop convince those still holding jobs that they can be replaced quickly. There is also the fear that the plant will close unless they produce more for the same wages. Performing well or better is a logical response to such conditions. Yet there is always the danger that extracting more profit from labor—even well paid labor—could cause increased, not decreased, difficulties for employers. And since employers are attempting to change the structure of labor-capital relations by reducing State social-welfare spending and State–labor union cooperation, labor as a whole may be repoliticized to vote out neoconservatives and elect a prolabor government.

The outcome of the conservative policies is difficult to predict. The popular reaction to attempts to reduce social-welfare spending may place limits on State attempts to remove the un-

---

*It is estimated that there were more than six million illegal aliens in the United States in the early 1970's (Wachter 1974). They have probably replaced difficult-to-discipline minority youth in the labor force. Measured unemployment among minority youth in the early 1980's approached 50 percent.

derlying income guarantees for the unemployed, the poor, and the aged. Yet conservatives have weakened the union movement and real weekly earnings have continued to fall in many occupations (real earnings dropped by 16 percent between 1973 and 1982 [*Economic Report of the President* 1983: Table B-39]).

It is likely that the mobilization of labor, women, and minorities—not to mention environmentalists and antinuclear activists—will blunt efforts to redistribute income and reduce income security from the welfare system. Employers—especially oligopoly firms with long investment horizons—are likely, in the longer run, to turn to reforming the workplace even as they continue to threaten workers with plant closings and greater unemployment in order to lower wages. Furthermore, even as workers have to fight for higher wages, the higher level of education in the labor force and increased consciousness about the workplace have convinced workers that a higher wage is not the only issue over which they should be struggling. Conditions of work and control over jobs (preserving community and work in the face of runaway shops, dealing with the issue of illegal aliens, and combating high unemployment rates) have become important issues of the 1980's (Carnoy & Shearer 1980).

In the rest of this chapter, we analyze such nonwage reforms and their implications for wages, productivity, and profits.

Classifying Work Reforms

Although many people use the language of work reform and change to describe all alterations in the workplace, actual modifications vary from trivial to profound (Kelly 1982). It is useful, therefore, to classify existing or predicted work reforms in order to understand their scope and consequences. This section will provide that classification. The subsequent sections will evaluate the types of changes most likely to overcome the difficulties confronting both capitalist and government employers.

Table 7.1 presents a classification of work reforms in categories that are hierarchical in the sense that the first group (microtechnical changes) represents the most modest alterations

Table 7.1 Classification of Work Reforms

I. Microtechnical
    A. Job redesign
        1. job enlargement
        2. job rotation
        3. better equipment
        4. technical redesign of task
    B. Changes in physical work environment
II. Macrotechnical
    A. Organizational development
        1. new staff configuration
        2. regular meetings among staff
        3. open door personnel policies with respect to personnel grievances
        4. revitalization through seminars, educational and training
            opportunities and sabbaticals
    B. Profit sharing and other incentive payment schemes
    C. Redesign of organizations
    D. Flexible work schedules
III. Micropolitical
    A. Job enrichment and autonomous work groups
    B. Other forms of participative management (management consulting,
        workers' councils, etc.)
IV. Macropolitical
    A. Employee ownership
    B. Worker representation on corporate board
    C. Worker self-management
    D. Nationalization of industry

---

with the least departure from traditional practices, whereas the fourth (macropolitical) represents the most substantial and comprehensive changes, those in the governance of the work organization itself. Between these two poles are macrotechnical and micropolitical reforms. Each successive category also tends to be more comprehensive than the previous one and subsumes some of the changes in the previous category. For example, micropolitical alterations will generally require that there be macro- and microtechnical modifications in the work organization. However, the lower categories do not normally require changes in the higher ones. In this sense there may be some overlap among categories, even though they will be conceptually distinct.

Microtechnical Changes

At this level the focus is on changes in jobs or job situations within the organization as a response to an individual problem or set of problems. Such a problem might be high worker turnover in particular jobs or a quality control dilemma arising in a specific operation. The response is to provide a technical solution; such changes are generally designed by technical specialists (such as industrial psychologists, industrial sociologists, human factors engineers, and industrial engineers), and they generally can be adopted in piecemeal fashion according to where difficulties arise in the organization. Thus, a problem can be solved locally without affecting the overall operations of the plant, firm, or government agency. Most important, microtechnical changes are under the control of management and its technical advisers, and they are carried out at managerial discretion.

Of the two types of microtechnical changes in work, the more important are probably those that are included in job redesign (Davis & Taylor 1972; Rush 1971). To take a common example, if a difficulty has arisen with respect to productivity for a specific operation, it might be traced to problems of worker fatigue, boredom, or difficulty in staying alert. The response by the technical experts is to redesign the job to alleviate these conditions. Job enlargement refers to expanding the number of tasks performed by the worker to reduce the tediousness of repetition. Similarly, job rotation represents a way of rotating workers periodically among different jobs. Sometimes better equipment is provided so that the work can be more easily performed under the new conditions. For example, raising the height of a workbench, improving worker seating, or providing better tools and other equipment can reduce fatigue and improve the rate and quality of work. At the extreme, it may be necessary to redesign the task itself to conform more nearly to human factors that impinge on the work situation. In all of these cases, each job is considered individually to ascertain whether some redesign might be useful for improving productivity or alleviating difficulties.

The second type of microtechnical change involves alteration of the physical work environment—for example, removing hazards that impair the health, safety, or job performance of employees, changing the physical layout of the workspace, installing ventilation systems, and cutting down extraneous noises. Also, efforts might be made to make the work environment more pleasant by enhancing the appearance of the surroundings and providing such employee amenities as lounges and canteens. As with redesigning jobs, these modifications can be localized, and they derive from various technical analyses of how to raise productivity and reduce costs.

Macrotechnical Changes

Changes at this level share some of the characteristics of the microtechnical ones in that they are based upon technical alterations of various organizational operations, and are usually initiated by specialists working for management. The major difference is that the changes tend to be more pervasive. They embrace the entire organization—or at least are applicable to a large part of the work organization—in contrast to the more localized microtechnical changes.

Typical of the macrotechnical changes are those that go by the name of "organizational development."* These represent attempts to improve communications and human relations within the organization and to manage conflict. To a large degree, an attempt is made to find a shared perspective among conflicting groups, whether workers and supervisors or top executives and middle managers, so that the individual role and the organizational role can be more fully "integrated" (Argyris 1964). The Japanese model of consultation with workers on important decisions seems to fit within this framework, although the Japanese case is complicated by larger cultural issues and by job guarantees (to age 55) with an employer (Ouchi 1981). Presumably, if workers are listened to and if staffing patterns are deployed appropriately, worker dissatisfaction will diminish. Increases in opportunities for training and educational experiences, as well as sabbaticals, are also expected to contribute to worker satisfaction.

---

*This term is used very broadly to refer to a large variety of planned changes or interventions designed to improve the operation of an organization. Readers interested in learning more about organizational development should consult the *Journal of Applied Behavioral Science*, a regular publication of the National Training Lab, which has pioneered many of these techniques.

Representative of the organizational development types of reforms are methods for increasing communications among staff (such as holding regular meetings), open-door personnel policies, sessions among managers and workers emphasizing more productive group processes and dynamics for resolving conflicts, and reduced formality in communication (calling each other by first names) and attire. In some cases, staffing patterns are altered to improve lines of communication up and down the hierarchy. It is expected that such attempts at improving human relations and communications will improve the functioning of the organization and raise its productivity.

A second macrotechnical approach is the adoption of profit sharing or other types of work-incentive plans, based on the presumption that if workers have a stake in how well the firm does, they will tend to be more productive. Actual plans vary from the year-end division of a portion of the profits according to salary or seniority to more sophisticated methods that attempt to tie employee shares to productivity (Schwinger 1975). The effectiveness of such plans is unclear and depends on a large number of factors (U.S. Dep't of HEW 1973: 105–10). Other changes under this approach include altering payment from a salary to a commission or piecework basis, as well as providing monetary bonuses, vacations, and prizes for meeting particular work goals in sales and production (Lupton ed. 1972; Schwinger 1975). The principle underlying all these plans is that, by changing the structure of external rewards in ways consonant with the objectives of the organization, workers will come to support the organization's goals through self-interest.

A third macrotechnical strategy involves redesigning the production unit itself. The main difference between this approach and the job-redesign component of the microtechnical category is the matter of scope. Macrotechnical redesign refers to a much more comprehensive overhaul. Such a change might include new organizational and personnel configurations as well as modification or replacement of plant, equipment, and technology to create a new mode of operation. A notable example of redesign at this level is the case of automobile manufacture in Sweden. Both Volvo and Saab-Scandia have moved away from the traditional assembly line in some of their plants. At

Saab, the engine blocks and body assemblies are produced by teams of workers who organize and schedule production, provide training, and rotate particular tasks. Volvo has carried the team-assembly concept further by constructing a plant in which the assembly line has been eliminated; in its place are subassembly shops where teams of workers carry out functions similar to the engine assembly operation at Saab. Both firms claim improvements in productivity, quality control, and work-force stability (Logue 1981; Gyllenhammer 1977). These cases also required macropolitical changes in the workplace, as we will discuss in the next section.

A final category of macrotechnical change concerns flexible or alternative work schedules. There are two principal versions of this modification of the traditional work relationship: the compressed workweek, and flexible working hours ("flextime"). The former reduces the normal five-day workweek into three or four days of longer duration. Most typical is replacement of a five-day, 40-hour week with a four-day, 40-hour week (Poor 1973). Presumably, employees are more willing to tolerate adverse working conditions when they are given an extra day of leisure in each week.

The adoption of flexible working hours permits employees to choose their own work schedules within limits set by the firm. Depending upon the specific plan, the employee is given a choice of alternative work schedules or is free to vary the hours of work from day to day while fulfilling a total time obligation each day or week. In the latter case, employees must be present during a "core time" such as 10:00 a.m. to 3:00 p.m., but may adjust their other work hours to fit personal schedules (Wade 1973; Stein et al. 1976). It is claimed that such an innovation boosts employee motivation (Elbing, Gadon, & Gordon 1975), though there are limits to how extensively flextime approaches can be adopted without requiring other organizational changes.

Micropolitical Changes

Changes at this level alter the internal decision making of the work enterprise to increase the participation of workers in matters that affect the nature and organization of their work. The political aspect is reflected in the fact that here we encounter inherent change in the distribution of power over particular decisions included in the reform: some traditional managerial prerogatives are relinquished or shared with workers. Yet in this category such increases in worker participation are still limited to specific areas governing the execution of the work: only at the macropolitical level do we encounter political changes governing the operation of the organization itself.

The typical micropolitical modification will increase the participation of workers in determining such matters as production schedules, training regimens, work assignments, and work methods. However, such changes will not affect the overall control of the organization as reflected in decisions on the choice of products or services to be produced, pricing policies, investment plans, distribution of profits, or overall organizational structure.

A general term used to describe attempts to increase worker participation in what are traditionally thought of as managerial functions is "job enrichment" (Rush 1971: 13–14). This approach is based largely upon the work of Herzberg (1968) and Argyris (1957, 1964), who argue that the most important motivating factors in a job are intrinsic rewards such as feelings of achievement, personal recognition, control of the work process, and responsibility. The job-enrichment approach assumes that workers can be more highly motivated by increasing the vertical (or hierarchical) responsibility for the job—that is, by planning, organizing, and evaluating the work in addition to performing it.

One of the most important applications of this concept is the autonomous work group (Susman 1976). The assumption behind this approach is that most employees can relate much better to a small and identifiable group of which they are members than to a large impersonal organization. Attachment to the group and the high level of communication and interaction among its members foster the ability of the group to make internal decisions about how the work will be performed. Though the group is accountable to a higher level of management for its overall performance, internal assignments, scheduling, training, and consideration of new work practices are relegated to the work group itself. The development of this approach has been particularly associated with researchers at the

Tavistock Institute in London and at the Work Research Institute in Oslo (Herbst 1962; Emery & Thorsrud 1969; Emery & Trist 1960, 1969; Thorsrud et al. 1976).

Experiments in Swedish automobile manufacturing provide a good example of micropolitical changes in the work process. We have already described some of the macrotechnical changes, such as the shift from assembly lines to work teams, as based upon technical redesign of the organization; but substantial micropolitical changes are also involved, based upon the ability of the groups of workers to determine within reasonably broad limits the organization of their work. The Swedish example also shows the degree to which work reforms may fit into more than one subcategory of the classification scheme. In particular, the "political" types of reforms almost invariably have technical implications, although the opposite is not neccessarily true. Many technical changes in jobs can be carried out without affecting the pattern of decision making.

In addition to the approaches that increase the direct participation of workers in the decisions that affect their work, there are other, indirect forms of participative management. Perhaps the most important of these are worker councils or committees, which are either elected by workers or appointed by workers and managers, and which resolve jointly with management some of the major policy issues regarding the work setting (Jenkins 1974: 68–72). To a large degree, this is the *de facto* approach used in British industrial relations, where the shop stewards represent the interests of unionized workers in settling management-worker conflicts and negotiating changes in employment and work practices. This process has evolved in the British case as a part of normal industrial relations, and it is increasingly being considered in enterprises in the United States and Western Europe. However, it should be noted that there is clearly a difference when worker participation and consultation are established by law, as in West Germany (Svejnar 1982), and when they are established as voluntary practices on the part of management. In the former case there is a sharing of power in such areas as wages, working conditions, hiring and firing, new work methods, and so on. In the latter, though, worker participation is limited to those areas that management finds to be in its interest and can be withdrawn or modified unilaterally by management; moreover, consultation with workers on some issues may be a mere formality.

Macropolitical Changes

Changes at this level provide workers with greater input into the work enterprise as a whole, rather than just within their own work units. Whereas micropolitical changes only modify the internal distribution of decision-making roles, macropolitical alterations change the governance and direction of the total work organization. In principle, such reforms can increase the participation of workers in virtually all the policies of the firm, from internal work practices to the selection and marketing of products, and from determination of prices and investment policies to the allocation of profits or surpluses. In the West German case, worker councils appear to have macropolitical powers in such areas as job evaluation, employment policies, training, layoffs, and wage structure.

The specific form taken by any macropolitical reform is crucial in determining its results. This is evident in the case of employee ownership, the most far-reaching of the macropolitical changes. Employee ownership should vest in the workers the right to govern their own work organization and the nature of the work situation; but in fact employee ownership may have little to do with employee participation in management.

There are at least two general forms of employee ownership: (1) management-initiated, and (2) worker-initiated. Management-initiated employee ownership usually consists of a program in which part of the remuneration of employees is offered in the form of stock or options to purchase stock on the basis of seniority, salary, or position. In other cases the employees, acting as a group, purchase the firm by obtaining a loan that is repaid out of the profits. Perhaps the best-known plan for making such a transfer is that of the Employee Stock Ownership Plan, or ESOP, which will be discussed in greater detail in a subsequent section (Joint Econ. Comm. 1976).

Typically, management will choose the first of these plans as a means of supplementing wage and salary benefits while building a mechanism to increase employee motivation and productivity. The second plan is usually adopted primarily as a means of increasing the amount of capital in the firm, which is an intrinsic attribute of the ESOP approach. It is hardly surprising that management-initiated plans to increase employee ownership do not construct a mechanism for the employees to participate in the management of the firm. Indeed, it is probably safe to say that in a majority of these cases, the employees seem content to leave managerial decisions to traditional hierarchies with the tacit view that professional expertise is necessary to obtain maximum growth and returns to their stock ownership.

By contrast, employee-initiated ownership plans almost invariably involve workers in direct or representative participation in governing the work enterprise. The most typical approach here is the producers' cooperative, in which the members both own and manage the organization. Such cooperatives may be created from scratch, or they may derive from the conversion of conventional firms (Carnoy & Shearer 1980: Chap. 4; Jackall & Levin eds. 1984; Oakeshott 1978; Bernstein 1976; Thomas & Logan 1982). In either case, the workers exercise control over the internal organization of work, levels of remuneration, product planning and development, marketing, pricing, and other functions. In capitalist societies, the producer cooperative represents the most complete form of macropolitical reform of the traditional capitalist-worker relationship.

A second macropolitical reform is the inclusion of worker representation on corporate boards. This is especially prevalent in Western Europe. For example, in West Germany a policy of "co-determination" (*Mitbestimmung*) requires that one-third to one-half of the places on the governing boards of firms be delegated to workers (Jenkins 1974: Chap. 8; Carnoy & Shearer 1980: Chap. 6; Furstenberg 1977). The European Economic Community as a whole may adopt this pattern if a statute recommended in June 1976 that would require co-determination and workers' councils for companies operating in two or more countries is approved. In addition, a British Commission on Industrial Democracy recommended that the governing boards of all British firms employing more than 2,000 people be required to include elected worker representatives (Dep't of Trade 1977). Though worker representation on boards of directors is clearly on the rise in Western Europe, it is not clear that co-determination has had much of an impact on the nature of work and work organization; moreover, the policy is exceedingly controversial with respect to property rights and representation (Schauer 1972; Bastin 1976).

However, a broader initiative is reflected in the proposal of the trade unions in Sweden to create a system of "wage-earner funds" for purchasing Swedish industry (see Meidner & Andersson 1978 for the outline of this plan). Under this plan a percentage of company pretax profits and a percentage of workers' wages would be allocated to collective funds that would be used to buy shares in companies to make the workers the eventual owners. The plan being considered officially would create 24 such funds in 24 different local jurisdictions in Sweden. The boards governing the funds would consist of trade union officials and politicians. It is estimated that majority ownership and control of Swedish industry on behalf of workers would occur within five years of the start of such a plan. Needless to say, the idea is opposed by the Swedish Employers Federation and present owners of firms.

A third form of macropolitical work reform is worker self-management when the enterprise is not owned directly by the employees. This mode of control can take many forms; the Yugoslav version, which is the most highly developed, has workers' councils that make the major policy decisions for the firms. In small enterprises (fewer than 30 employees) all workers are members of such councils; in larger enterprises the councils are elected by the workforce. The council holds all formal power, and it makes decisions regarding hiring and firing, salaries, investment, and other operations of the firm (Jenkins 1974: Chap. 7; Adizes 1971; Vanek 1971; Horvat 1976; Blumberg 1968: Chaps. 8, 9; H. Wachtel 1973). Unlike some micropolitical forms of worker participation where workers and work councils are accountable to management, the Yugoslav arrangement makes the management accountable to the workers. Managers are appointed by the elected representatives of the central board of management. The personal income of the workers is dependent both upon the overall success of the enterprise and upon the contribution of the individual toward that success, although a minimum income is guaranteed to the individual independent of these criteria.

Versions of worker self-management are also found in China, Cuba, and Israel. In both China and Cuba there has been emphasis on direct participation in management and operation, rather than participation through representation. All members of the enterprise are expected to play active roles in contributing to the formation of the work process (Bettelheim 1975; MacEwan 1975). The Israeli kibbutz, or collective, is another well-known example of macropolitical worker control, where all decisions about production and the distribution and use of productive surpluses are made by the membership. The traditional work hierarchy is eliminated in favor of a democratic mechanism for making collective decisions regarding both production and consumption (Jenkins 1974: Chap. 6; Fine 1973).

A final category of macropolitical reform is the nationalization of industry, the transfer of a firm or industry from the private to the public sector. Such a transfer has obvious implications for altering how work is organized and how investment policies are controlled (Carnoy & Shearer 1980: Chap. 7). The exact forms of change will depend upon the nature of the transfer and the political context in which nationalization takes place. At one extreme (the usual case in Western Europe), a traditional corporate management is replaced by a traditional government bureaucracy, with no significant modifications in the organization of work. Indeed, it has been argued that from the viewpoint of the workers, nationalization can reduce the possibilities for change rather than increase them. Certainly, this has been one of the major criticisms of the state socialist societies of the Eastern Bloc. Nevertheless, it is possible to construct a scheme of nationalization that integrates worker participation in the decision-making apparatus—as the case of Yugoslavia shows. Again, the exact form and implications for modification of the workplace will depend on both the national and historical context.

In general, macropolitical organizational reforms represent the most far-reaching possibilities for changing the nature of organizations to increase the participation of workers in affecting the nature of their jobs and their work relationships. With changes in overall governance, corresponding modifications can take place in internal governance and in the technical arrangements of work organization. This hierarchical approach to describing work reforms from microtechnical ones to macropolitical changes tends to subsume the former categories under each successive classification, although there may be exceptions to this generalization. For example, employee ownership may change none of the characteristics of the work organization beyond who receives the dividends, and profit-sharing plans or co-determination may also have no effect on the nature of work.

Which Reforms Are Most Likely?

The classification scheme we have presented shows the variety of possible work reforms that might be considered as alternatives to the predominant ways of organizing work at present. This does not mean, however, that they are all equally likely to be adopted in the future. First, each form of work organization in this taxonomy arose under a concrete set of historical conditions and within a specific cultural, political, and economic context. The conditions supporting any approach will not necessarily be present as reforms are considered: for example, it is probable that the Yugoslav method of work organization in its existing form is only possible within a national system of decentralized socialism. Thus the classification represents a theoretical set of alternatives, whereas the actual alternatives will be constrained by the particular context.

Second, the attempt to change a basic social institution such as the workplace or the school is likely to encounter many problems, result in many errors, and elicit struggles among groups with different interests. This means that reforms may follow a pattern that is unstable in the short run—with failures and new reforms attempted—until a longer-run stability is achieved. For example, enterprises may attempt to provide micro- or macrotechnical reforms that do not include increasing worker participation, only to find that these types of changes then do not alleviate the problems they were intended to address. In that case, the next step might be an attempt at micropolitical change in an organization. Alternatively, an attempt at a micropolitical reform might create new problems in the work organization—for example, increased dissatisfaction on the part of middle managers, "squeezed" between worker decisions and executive decisions. In such a case, the firm may decide to seek a different participative approach that avoids this problem, or to step away from micropolitical reforms altogether.

That the process of change is not a linear and smooth one is evident from our dialectical approach. However, in the short run the types of changes that will be tried and the struggles that will ensue will depend upon a number of factors, particularly on who takes the initiative, management, workers (independent of trade unions), trade unions, or government. Each of these groups has different interests.

On the one hand, it is likely that management will prefer an incremental approach to change, beginning with those changes that will encroach least upon managerial prerogatives; on the other, the interests of workers will lead them to want those changes that maximize improvement in their situation. The following analysis is designed not so much to predict the precise nature and short-run outcomes of these conflicts of interest as to predict the types of changes that are consistent with a reduction of conflicts within the current social and political context. Of course, as we will emphasize at the end of this chapter, even an apparently stable social agreement between workers and employers will eventually decompose under the dynamics of the dialectic, as long as the internal contradictions of capitalism persist. This tendency was reflected in the breakdown of the postwar accord among capital, the State, and labor that has given rise to the present crisis. In that sense, today's solution will become tomorrow's problem.

Thus we must also ask what types of changes will contribute to alleviating the manifest conflict in the workplace given inherent differences in what employers and workers want at a particular historical moment. A useful way of answering this question might be to review the criteria of a good job currently set out by workers and potential workers and to contrast these with the apparent present requirements of firms. Following this, it is possible to review the actual role of trade unions and government as intermediaries of change. Finally, we will note the most likely work reforms consistent with this analysis, and we will discuss in greater depth a few of the possibilities.

The Workers' Criteria

Yankelovich (1974) found that among young people there were few differences in the criteria viewed as important in a good job, whether the respondents were blue-collar, white-collar, or college-trained professionals (p. 104). (See Table 7.2.) These criteria are similar to those set out by industrial psychologists and other specialists who have attempted to consider the most important dimensions for improving the quality of working life (Walton 1975; Davis & Cherns eds. 1975; Herzberg 1968; Robinson et al. eds. 1967; Blauner 1964). Further empirical support is provided by a study of over 1,500 American workers at all occupational levels who were asked to rank in importance some 25 aspects of work. The eight top-ranked categories were interesting work; enough help to get the job done; enough information to get the job done; enough authority to get the job done; good pay; opportunity to develop special abilities; job security; and seeing the results of one's work (U.S. Dep't of HEW 1973: 13). The overall conclusion seems to be that though issues of pay and mobility are still important, workers in general and young workers in particular are seeking "to become masters of their immediate environments and to feel that their work and they themselves are important—the twin ingredients of self-esteem" (*ibid.*).

The reforms suggested by these criteria are largely on the mi-

Table 7.2   Important Job Criteria Indicated
by a Majority of Young Workers

1. Friendly, helpful co-workers (70 percent)
2. Work that is interesting (70 percent)
3. Opportunity to use your mind (65 percent)
4. Work results that you can see (62 percent)
5. Pay that is good (61 percent)
6. Opportunity to develop skills and abilities (61 percent)
7. Participation in decisions regarding job (58 percent)
8. Getting help needed to do the job well (55 percent)
9. Respect for organization you work for (55 percent)
10. Recognition for a job well done (54 percent)

Source: Yankelovich 1974: 104.

cro- and macropolitical levels, for it appears that only an increase in the degree of participation and in cooperative decision making will accomplish many of the goals given in Table 7.2. In the U.S. context, a reform that would seem promising is the autonomous work group, with its emphasis on participation, cooperation with fellow workers, responsibility for a relatively large share of the work process and product, and flexibility from one work situation to another. Optimally, workers might wish to have the control implied by some of the macropolitical reforms, but it is important to consider additional constraints on the eventual determination of which types of reform will be adopted.

Management's Criteria

In most situations it will not be the workers who initiate work reforms. The owners of capital and their managerial representatives have the principal legal rights to determine the organization of work in private enterprises; and public administrators have these prerogatives in government agencies. This means that any changes will not only have to improve the situation of workers, but they will also have to be consistent with the criteria of public or private enterprises for initiating modifications of the workplace. Accordingly, it is necessary to set out the criteria for modifying the work organization from the point of view of owners and managers. One important criterion is to maintain or to increase productivity (Walton 1975; Herrick 1975; U.S. Dep't of HEW 1973; Work in America Inst. 1982). This means that any modification—whether new techniques to increase productivity, or new work procedures to reduce turnover, absenteeism, lateness, theft, sabotage, and work stoppages, and to develop closer identification with the work organization—must show promise of increasing labor productivity (Seashore 1975: 110).

Though the prospect of enhanced productivity (or an end to a decline in productivity) is a necessary condition for the adoption of a particular change, it is not a sufficient condition. Productivity is only of interest to a capitalist enterprise if it affects its profitability. Accordingly, improvements in productivity must also be captured in the form of increased profits. This is the second criterion that will govern the choice of workplace modification. Some changes will require immediate negotiations with workers and trade unions, who will want increased benefits because of the obvious increases in productivity. Other improvements in productivity will be more subtle, and the firm may be able to expropriate all or a large share of increased product into increased profits. Thus, although a direct impact on productivity is a necessary criterion for change, the indirect effect on profits represents a more important criterion.*

The final management criterion concerns control. The control of basic decisions about the use of property or capital in production is vested in the owners of that property, as reflected in the law. For obvious reasons, the history of work organization has been the development of managerial devices to consolidate the control of work and work force at the top of the organization (see Chapter 4 above; see also Edwards 1979; Marglin 1974; Braverman 1974).

Though technical changes in the organization of work do not necessarily require an erosion of this control, many political changes do encroach on the traditional prerogatives of management. Some may even make middle levels of management redundant, as workers make decisions that were usually relegated to those echelons (Kay 1974). Recent work (Alchian & Demsetz 1972; Jensen & Meckling 1976; Stiglitz 1975; Williamson 1975) that attempts to explain the high degree of monitoring and hierarchy of the corporate firm emphasizes that when work processes are interdependent, the separate contributions of each worker to the output of the firm cannot be identified. Accordingly, there will be a tendency for workers to shirk in the absence of a high degree of supervision and the establishment of meaningful sanctions. This challenge also would encourage the routinization of work tasks in order to reduce the costs of monitoring work effort. Some authors have argued that workers prefer such coercion because it raises the overall productivity of the firm and worker incomes (Stiglitz 1975). These same au-

---

*In the public sector this criterion might be the amount of resources controlled by the agency. If an increase in productivity results in a decrease in budget and personnel because of greater efficiency, there will be little managerial incentive to increase productivity (Niskanen 1971).

thors assert that a high degree of managerial control is crucial for maintaining productivity. But this explanation is in conflict with empirical studies showing that increases in worker participation tend to be associated with higher productivity (Levin 1983c; Jones & Svejnar 1982). Thus it appears reasonable to conclude that managerial control of the work process may be largely an end in itself rather than a requirement for productivity.

In summary, there are three criteria that management will use in assessing prospective changes in the organization of work: productivity, profitability, and control. The three are closely related; higher labor productivity is a general requirement for increasing profitability, and control of the organization is a necessary ingredient for developing ways of converting increased productivity into profits. Thus solutions most likely to meet these criteria will be more acceptable from the point of view of management, and there will not be a complete overlap between the preferences of workers and those of management.

The Trade Unions' Criteria

Before examining the reforms most consistent with worker and management preferences, we need to analyze briefly the role in work organization of the trade unions and the State. Trade unions, of course, represent organized labor in collective bargaining. Since the 1930's they have gradually taken on a capitalist structure, accepting the overall capitalist work relationship while bargaining on behalf of the workers on such issues as salaries and wages, hours of work, employment security, and safety conditions.

There are at least two reasons why trade unions in the United States are not likely to take the lead in altering the organization of work. The first is that the trade unions themselves have generally lacked an interest in highly decentralized (in the participative-democracy sense) solutions to the problems of work organization. The unions tend to be structured as a countervailing force to the oligopoly power of large corporations. Unions and corporations emphasize the same types of strong, centralized bargaining strategies. The focus on problems in the workplace and their solutions diverts energies from the larger struggle with capitalist employers and fragments worker solidarity by emphasizing local differences in worker needs. The emphasis on large, centralized trade unions rather than smaller ones dominated by grass-roots control tends to preclude a strong orientation toward initiating changes in the workplace (see Chapter 3 above; see also Aronowitz 1973: Chap. 4).

The second reason is that, historically, the alteration of the workplace has usually represented an effort to reduce labor costs or increase productivity with concomitant threats to employment security. Typically, attempts to alter the workplace have consisted of the replacement of men by machines and the further subdivision of labor. Given this historical pattern, it is not surprising that the unions are suspicious of a change in work roles and that the trade unions represent a fairly conservative element in this domain. The degree to which this attitude is held is reflected in the fact that some three-fourths of both union and management officials who were surveyed in 1974 agreed with the following statement: "Unions are suspicious of job enrichment, but they will support it once they are confident it isn't a productivity gimmick" (Katzell & Yankelovich 1975).

In addition, only about one-fifth of the labor force belongs to unions. Although unions are concerned about changes in the nature of work, they are not likely to be the prime initiators in most instances. Over the short run they are more likely to be a conservative force, especially in those industries where they have a strong bargaining position. But over the long run they may have to yield to other forces such as grass-root pressures for change (Aronowitz 1973; Hyman 1973, 1974).

Over the last four decades, unions have indeed responded to such pressures when it came to unemployment insurance, health care, and welfare. The indirect effect on work organization of such social legislation may be important, as we have argued. When employed labor's consumption is cushioned by social spending, the need to accept undesirable work conditions is reduced. When unions have worked as a social movement, the indirect effect on workplaces has been greater than when they operate as capitalist organizations bargaining directly with big business.

The State's Criteria

The role of the State in changing work organization is complex. In the United States, capitalist owners and managers rather than government still determine how most capital will be invested and how products should be produced. However, the State in democratic capitalist societies is not only responsible for protecting private property but has also had to make considerable concessions to worker interests. The State, as we have explained, is not merely an instrument of the business class; it is an arena of class conflict where social movements contest corporate hegemony. In theory, the State must represent both sets of interests; in assuming this role, however, it leaves itself open to conflict under a different set of rules than obtain in the private production system. Since the legitimacy of the State depends in large part on its apparent objectivity, State intervention must have the quality of being above the class struggle and being responsive to both labor and management. Since the State cannot represent the totality of management interests, it has not been in the interests of capitalists to have the State intervene in employer-labor conflicts except in situations where conflict moved beyond what management could handle on its own. By contrast, workers have not wanted the capitalist State to intervene if they felt they could win greater concessions without a State that carried the legitimacy of objective arbitrator but that always made more concessions to management (from the workers' point of view) than to workers. Given this history, we would expect the State to intervene only in cases where the manifestations of capital-labor contradiction are so severe that there is a serious challenge to the capitalist system itself.

Though there is little evidence of direct State intervention in work relations in the United States,* there is a strong State presence in such relations in Western Europe. In particular, the attempt to obtain widespread worker participation on the boards

---

*This is not to say that the U.S. State, through its increasing role in welfare payments, unemployment benefits, economic subsidies (primarily through defense contracts), and State employment, does not change the form of capitalist production and hence, indirectly, affect work relations. In this sense, the intervention of the State in work relations is increasing.

of firms at the level both of individual countries (e.g. West Germany and Holland) and the Common Market itself reflects an attempt to structure the mediation of the conflict in a particular direction—away from the demands of the leftist labor movements for nationalization of industry and worker self-management. The emphasis on co-determination reflects what Gorz (1968: 78) has called a "reformist-reform," a reform that defuses conflict by accepting the existing structure of capitalism while altering the composition of representatives on the boards. Thus it is no surprise to find that a British committee of inquiry report on Industrial Democracy in the United Kingdom concluded of the European experience with co-determination: "Worker directors have generally had little effect on anything, and secondly and consequently, they have certainly had no catastrophic effect on anything or anyone" (quoted in Wedderburn 1977: 166; original from Batstone & Davies 1976).

Sweden represents an important exception to this generalization. In that country there has been a long history of legislation supporting workers and trade unions (Schiller 1977). Under the Social Democrats there has existed a cooperative model between the government, the employers' association (SAF), and the major trade unions (LO and TCO). On one side the government has pushed for and achieved numerous work reforms: extensive health and safety regulations; strong employment security through protection from arbitrary dismissal; the right of workers to take leaves of absence for purposes of study; and most recently the rights of the workers to determine employment policies and the organization and distribution of work (T. Johnson 1962; Ministry of Labor 1975). On the other side, the government has insured the profitability of firms through relocation and training subsidies as well as a very active labor market policy (Rehn & Lundberg 1963; Meidner & Andersson 1973). The Swedish approach represents one of the most complete examples of government involvement in the work environment with the goal of avoiding conflict that might disrupt the normal functioning of its economic institutions. Though other Scandinavian countries have adopted some of these measures, none has gone as far as Sweden (Schiller 1977).

In summary, the State defends the rights of capital as private property and does not intervene in the organization of work except under conditions of rising and potentially disruptive class conflict, in which case it mediates the conflict first by pursuing established modes of state intervention (such as education and training patterns, public assistance, or public employment) and only then, if necessary, by intervening directly in the organization of work. To the degree that such intervention does occur, it is likely to take the form of creating reforms that reduce the overall conflict while maintaining the basic structures of capitalist control. The State performs a crucial role in averting the pressures by leftist groups to adopt more radical alternatives. The movements toward government support of co-determination in Western Europe represent an interesting example of this phenomenon.

In contrast with Europe, the lack of overt class conflict in the postwar United States has—at least until the current economic crisis—obviated such government action. But with the assault on social-welfare spending and real wages by corporations and the State, the potential for social conflict—expressed primarily as the struggle against conservative government policies—has increased. The protection of previous social gains is the first level of conflict, but even the election of a more prolabor government will not solve the crisis—which includes runaway shops, plant closings, and the decline in labor productivity and real wages. A future administration will have to be concerned about continued conflict in the workplace and possible State intervention there (U.S. Dep't of HEW 1973).

Strategies of Different Groups, and Specific Reforms

In the previous sections we suggested that different constituencies have different criteria for considering the adoption of work reforms. Workers will tend to emphasize those changes that increase their participation, autonomy, intrinsic interest in the job, and supportive relations with co-workers; they will also favor such traditional benefits as increased pecuniary rewards and fringe benefits. Managers will tend to seek those changes that increase productivity and profitability without a loss in control. Trade unions and the State will be much more conservative than either of the previous groups in seeking changes from the status quo, each initiating changes only under stress. Given these sets of priorities, it is possible to consider the reform strategies of the major constituencies.

Management-Initiated Reforms

By virtue of its legal rights and dominance in the ownership of capital, management will be the prime initiator of changes in work for the foreseeable future. This means that the majority of attempts to change work will follow the patterns set out by the needs of managers. On this basis, it is easy to rule out management-initiated changes that would encompass macropolitical reforms, since these would tend to reallocate power from managers and existing capitalist owners to workers or other groups. Such forms of change as the movement to producer cooperatives, nationalization, or complete worker control of the Yugoslav variety will not be candidates for managerially initiated changes in work.

At the opposite end of the taxonomy, many of the micro- and macrotechnical changes in the workplace will seem attractive to management if they are successful in increasing productivity and profitability. By definition, none of these types of reforms requires management to relinquish control. However, there are two reasons for believing that these types of changes in themselves will not be adequate to increase productivity over the long run unless they are accompanied by micro- or macropolitical alterations.

First, many of these changes are cosmetic; they do not make basic alterations in the structure of work and decision making. For example, improvements in management-worker communications and human relations do not solve the problem of uninteresting and routinized work with little or no worker influence over working conditions and low possibilities of advancement. Opening up lines of communication can only be successful in increasing productivity over the long run if there are adequate responses to the concerns expressed by workers. Yet many of these concerns reflect problems intrinsic to the existing organization of the workplace and production, and even a sympathetic and humane supervisor or manager will be unable to alter them without a structural mandate for change.

Second, the frustrations of the young and overeducated worker result in large measure from the lack of autonomy in, and low skill requirements for, the jobs that are available. In the past, it was possible to harness the hope of future advancement to supervisory positions as an incentive for working hard at lower-level positions (Doeringer & Piore 1971). But social mobility, both within and among firms, has declined over time as a period of slower economic growth has resulted in lower rates of expansion at the managerial level (Rumberger 1984). This means that the promise of obtaining promotion to a more autonomous and higher-status position in the future by showing good and stable job performance at a lower level will no longer serve as an incentive as powerfully as it did in the past. The implication is that at the lower levels of the firm, productivity will be maintained by placing an increasing emphasis on participation in the decisions that affect the work situation (Tannenbaum et al. 1974).

The most likely reforms for meeting the joint criteria of the various participants appear to be such micropolitical reforms as autonomous work groups and representative workers' councils. The record for improving productivity through these forms of participation is substantial (U.S. Dep't of HEW 1973: Chap. 4 and Appendix; Blumberg 1968; Jenkins 1974; Jones & Svejnar eds. 1982; B. Smith 1976; Guzzo & Bondy 1983; Levin 1983c). Further, the pressure by workers for upward mobility is somewhat blunted by the horizontal integration of tasks that would otherwise be organized hierarchically. The work group will tend to organize its own activities with respect to planning, training the members of the group for the various tasks, executing these tasks, and evaluating performance. Production bottlenecks that might have occurred by virtue of absences and a lack of coordination are reduced as workers are trained to do many tasks, and as they assist one another in the overall mission of the group. In some cases the focus will be on the production of a subassembly of a larger product, and in other cases the mission will correspond to the goals of a particular service department such as sales, accounting, or credit. Some spectacular productivity improvements have been reported for these types of changes (Kelly 1982; Logue 1981).

The shape of micropolitical reforms generally, and autonomous work groups specifically, will depend on the nature of the enterprise and its setting, varying according to the type of product or service, the internal organization for producing it, the ability to alter technology and capital to accommodate the new forms of participation, and so on. Initially, the changes will be determined by trial and error, although a mounting number of successful cases that have been documented and analyzed might be used as guidelines (Susman 1975; Thorsrud 1975; Emery & Thorsrud 1969; Thorsrud et al. 1976; Bernstein 1976; Davis & Trist 1976). It is reasonable to believe that aspects of some of these successes will become regular features of managerially initiated work reforms (Bernstein 1976; Greenberg 1975; Blumberg 1968).

One of the best-known cases in the United States involved the pet food division of General Foods. Before 1968, the manufacturing unit in Illinois had been increasingly plagued by problems of employee indifference and sabotage, resulting in product waste and plant shutdowns (Walton 1976; Ketchum 1975). In 1968, the company decided to construct a new plant in Topeka, Kansas, and to redesign the work process to avoid the problems of the Illinois plant. The solution encompassed organizing the 70 employees into six autonomous work groups of from seven to fourteen members, each with a team leader. During each shift, work groups were divided into processing and packaging units, the former group covering the tasks of unloading and storing new materials, drawing on existing stocks, and processing them into pet food, the latter responsible for packing, warehousing, and shipping. Assignments to specific tasks were made with team consensus, and substantial job sharing and rotation were built in—in contrast to the old plant, where tasks were permanently assigned to specific employees. In addition, the teams screen and select new employees, counsel those who are not meeting standards of performance or attendance, select representatives to serve on plantwide committees, and fulfill other decision-making functions.

The results have been dramatic from the standpoint both of the workers and of productivity and profits. A reduction in plant costs attributable to 92 percent fewer quality-rejects and an absentee rate considerably below the industry norm has generated an annual saving of $600,000 (Walton 1976: 238). From the perspective of the existing employees and management the plant is an overwhelming success; but it should be pointed out that from the perspective of the trade union movement, the reform tends to reinforce suspicions about innovation. The Topeka plant is a nonunionized plant that replaced a unionized one, and it produces with 70 workers what was estimated by industrial engineers to require 110 workers; indeed, the smaller number of employees is an important source of the cost savings (*ibid.*).

Important examples of micropolitical changes can be found in Swedish automobile manufacture, as noted earlier. In responding to the problems of high worker absenteeism, wildcat strikes, high turnover, and insufficient quality, Volvo decided to construct a new plant for some 500–600 workers in Kalmar built around the work-group concept. Each of the 25 work groups has its own area on the shop floor and its own rest area, each attends to a particular aspect of automobile assembly such as electrical systems, instrumentation, interiors, and so on; and each organizes the structure of the work, assignment of tasks, degree of specialization, and so on. The teams must deliver a certain number of subassemblies each day, but the scheduling of work, rest breaks, training, and other activities is determined by the groups. Each team takes responsibility for its work by conducting its own inspections for quality control (Gyllenhammer 1977).

An evaluation sponsored by the Swedish Productivity Council (a jointly sponsored body of the blue-collar trade union, LO, and the employers' federation, SAF) was generally positive with respect to worker acceptance and satisfaction, worker participation, reductions in personnel turnover and absenteeism, and productivity. The increased investment necessary for the special requirements of the plant appears likely to be more than compensated for by the long-run reduction in costs. Volvo now has several new plants designed along these lines.

In the Saab case (Logue 1981), management and the union initiated a team approach to door assembly with groups of seven workers, including a coordinator and six other members who worked in pairs. The coordinator position was rotated among workers on a weekly basis. The team did most of the quality control and maintenance of machinery, and, in consultation with management, hired new members and allocated a budget for equipment. Training was also done by the group. Workers were given a slight increase in wages for managing their own operations, and interviews with them suggested that they were more satisfied with their work situations.

Not only did the workers' situation improve, but so did productivity and profitability. Quality-control problems diminished, and the number of quality-control inspectors was reduced. In addition, worker turnover declined from over 50 percent to about 14 percent annually. Annual savings were estimated to be about nine times the annual costs, and Saab recovered its full investment for converting from repetitive assembly-line techniques to team assembly in only two and a half years. Both Ford and General Motors are pursuing similar kinds of team approaches to assembly. In fact, General Motors has initiated a joint study center aimed at the development of a new subcompact, Project Saturn (see "GM Car Project . . ." 1983). Seven joint subcommittees between management and labor will be set up on the principle of union and worker involvement in all aspects of manufacturing and assembly plans and processes.

The micropolitical approach has also been used successfully to improve productivity and quality control in the manufacture of semiconductors, or integrated circuits, by a major electronics firm, Zilog, Inc. (Gustavson & Taylor 1982). The use of work teams and decisions by consensus are at the heart of the new organization. The team approach has reduced the cost of "rework" and raised yields to 25 percent above those of comparable traditional facilities. Employee turnover is also considerably lower than at comparable firms.

Though a conflict between structural changes in the organization of work and employment security is inherent in the production process, this does not mean that such changes cannot be made. Trade unions will have to be involved, and employment security safeguarded to some extent. However, this will not be an important criterion for management in its quest to improve productivity and profitability. In at least one case in the United States, the use of work teams and increased worker participation in decision making have been initiated cooperatively by management and the union. The management of the automobile mirror plant of Harmon International in Bolivar, Tennessee, in conjunction with the United Auto Workers, agreed to work reforms that increased worker decision making over issues of job design, tools to be used, and the organization of work. Like other micropolitical reforms, there was no increase in worker participation in such areas as product choice, marketing, investment, or disposition of profits. Though productivity rose about 17 percent between 1972 and 1975 (*The Economist*, May 29, 1976: 87), the economic recession resulted in a reduction of plant employment from about 900 workers to 600 (*Business Week*, May 19, 1975: 52).

One approach that has been adopted by several dozen companies is the Scanlon Plan (Nat'l Comm. on Productivity and Work Quality 1975; Rush 1973: 42–50; Jenkins 1974: 222–24). The basic elements of the plan include (1) teamwork, with active employee participation; (2) a formal system for channeling employee recommendations for change to a production committee; and (3) a bonus system, which shares the results of productivity gains with the workers. According to systematic studies of one of the companies that adopted the Scanlon Plan, there were substantial reductions in the costs of production, increases in quality and employee satisfaction, and distributions of ample bonuses (Rush 1973: 49).

In summary, it appears likely that management-initiated changes in the organization of work will stabilize on micropolitical reforms, of which autonomous work groups, work councils, and extensive worker participation will be the core. To establish these modifications, it will be necessary to alter some of the technical aspects of the work environment, but micro- and macrotechnical changes in themselves may not resolve the productivity problems deriving from the dissatisfaction of an increasingly overeducated and underfulfilled workforce.

Worker-Initiated Reforms

Worker-initiated changes in the organization of the workplace are less likely than management-initiated ones, primarily because of the lack of worker ownership or control of the enterprises in which they work (Carnoy & Shearer 1980: Chap. 3).* There are, nevertheless, some circumstances under which such changes are probable. To illustrate the relative lack of

---

*It has been argued that workers actually control a vast amount of capital through union pension funds. However, whether workers really control this capital is open to serious question. Compare Drucker (1976) with Barber (1982).

ownership of the working class, it has been estimated by the staff of the Joint Economic Committee of the Congress that the wealthiest 20 percent of U.S. families own almost 80 percent of total personal wealth, and that the wealthiest 6 percent of the population own almost three-quarters of the corporate stock and almost 80 percent of bonds (Joint Econ. Comm. 1976: 7). This suggests that it will be difficult for workers to create significant changes in their work organizations.

However, there are ways that workers can acquire the capital that would enable them to determine the organization of work in their enterprises. First, they might purchase the firm through an Employee Stock Ownership Plan (ESOP). Second, they could gain control over union pension funds and use these to finance worker-controlled firms (either new firms or failing traditional capitalist enterprises) (Barber 1982). Third, they might start their own firms by raising the capital themselves. Fourth, they could pressure the State to take over firms through community economic development or nationalization programs and set up autonomous, worker- and community-controlled enterprises; or they could pressure the State to lend money to establish worker-controlled cooperatives.

Each of these has its disadvantages and advantages, and they are not mutually exclusive. They have been discussed in detail elsewhere (Carnoy & Shearer 1980), and we will not repeat that analysis here. However, it is worth pointing to some important features of each case. As we have already argued, ESOPs are generally organized by management to raise capital, not to give up ownership to employees. It is questionable whether employers would continue to make such plans available if they thought that employees would use them to gain control of the firm. However, in recent years a number of firms that had announced plans to close have been purchased by their workers. These include a large meatpacker (Rath Meatpacking Company), the eighth-largest U.S. steel producer (Weirton Steel), and a substantial former division of General Motors (Hyatt Clark Industries). Union pension funds are legally acceptable to firms and the State precisely because they are not controlled by workers. But where pension funds are invested by unions themselves (often they are controlled by banks as trustees), workers can democratize the decision making on pension funds by democratizing their unions. There is no legal reason why such pension funds cannot, for example, be invested in State development banks, which could then finance worker-controlled enterprises.

Starting up firms by workers themselves would be facilitated by greater availability of funds for producer cooperatives, which until now have not been a favored investment for private lending institutions (Jones 1977; Shirom 1972). The potential of producer co-ops is, therefore, intimately related to whether workers can gain control of pension funds or induce the State to use tax money for co-op promotion. Nevertheless, there are a number of privately financed co-ops in existence in the United States now, particularly small service-oriented establishments in most metropolitan areas (Jackall & Crain 1984). The largest and most successful cooperatives are in the Pacific Northwest in the plywood industry (Bernstein 1976; Greenberg 1984). And even though it lasted only a few years as a worker-run firm, Vermont Asbestos is yet another recent example of a privately financed worker-ownership effort. The demise of worker management at Vermont Asbestos points to another set of problems regarding worker participation and control in a capitalist society (Carnoy & Shearer 1980: Chap. 4).

The most successful example of self-financed cooperatives is in Mondragon, in the Basque region of northern Spain. Mondragon has an entire movement of industrial cooperatives, with sales in 1979 of about $700 million (Oakeshott 1978: Chap. 10; Caja Laboral Popular 1975; Thomas & Logan 1982). These firms manufacture products as diverse as home appliances, selenium rectifiers, semiconductors, miniaturized circuits, and hydraulic presses, and they include the largest refrigerator manufacturer in Spain. Total employment was about 18,000 workers in 1981, and comparisons with non-cooperative firms suggest that with only one-fourth of the capital investment per worker they are able to obtain an output per worker (value added) of over 80 percent of that for comparable firms (Levin 1983c).

To pressure the State to take action, either on the nationalization front or on the financial side, workers would have to turn to political action. Although a National Consumer Cooperative Bank was established in 1980 to lend money to consumer and producer cooperatives throughout the United States, it is already losing its government commitment as it becomes an independent agency. Similarly, the interest of the Commerce and Labor Departments in job preservation in the 1970's has waned under the Reagan Administration, even when plant closures mean the destruction of communities. It is possible that governments will become increasingly willing to provide loans and technical assistance to help workers save their jobs through the employee purchase of firms that are closing and the conversion of such firms to cooperatives. The reasons for such government support are not only the maintenance and creation of jobs under conditions of high unemployment, but the fact that available evidence suggests that productivity in cooperatives is high, and the capital required for each job created is relatively low (Carnoy & Shearer 1980: Chap. 4; Jones & Svejnar 1982).

In summary, the lack of worker ownership and control suggests that worker-initiated changes in the organization of work are not as likely to arise as management-initiated changes. However, the possible employment-generating aspects of worker-owned firms are likely to make them an increasingly attractive possibility from the point of view of government, particularly if conversion to worker ownership can salvage firms in high-unemployment areas that might otherwise close. Accordingly, various macropolitical forms of work organization in general, and the formation of producer cooperatives in particular, are likely to become more important over time (Jackall & Levin eds. 1984).

A Note on the Role of Trade Unions

The foregoing analysis illustrates an important dilemma for the trade unions. If workers behave in such a way as to take into their own hands the ability to modify their conditions of work through the costly pressures of absenteeism, turnover, sabotage, and wildcat strikes, then management will be pressed to provide changes in the workplace that alleviate these problems. But such modifications may undermine organized labor in two ways. First, to the degree that employed workers in any firm seek benefits only for themselves, they may settle for solutions that harm worker solidarity and gains for all workers in the long run. For example, they may accept workplace alterations that increase productivity while reducing the number of future jobs. Second, by coming to view the world as a set of decentralized work situations, workers undermine the centralized bargaining strength of the trade unions and make it easier for firms to come to agreements with particular groups of workers. This will be particularly true if the autonomous-work-groups approach creates a set of dynamics in which groups see themselves as competing against one another for benefits and power within the firm. The trade unions then will encounter worker animosity if they push for uniformity of benefits and job conditions across hierarchies of workers and among different firms and industries.

Most of the changes we have referred to will occur on a highly decentralized basis, and most will incorporate a reduction of hierarchy. The appeal of national and industry-wide trade unions may consequently diminish. Workers and managers may see the relevant arena of conflict as a local one, in which national or industry-wide agreements are unappealing or irrelevant. To the degree that managers are able to exploit this situation by shifting production activities to areas with weak unions or no unions and by undermining the formation of unions through emphasis on work teams and autonomous groups, the position of trade unions will become increasingly precarious. Certainly the illustration of the pet food plant in Topeka, Kansas, suggests this possibility.

Changes in Work over the Longer Run

Of course, erosion of trade unions does not necessarily have to occur. In Sweden, there is a central agreement on wages and salaries, as well as a national law that requires full co-determination by labor and management on employment decisions, the distribution and nature of work, health and safety issues, and a variety of other workplace concerns. However, although salaries and wages are determined through bargaining at the national level, other issues are negotiated at the local plant or firm level. In the Swedish context, it has proved possible to have a high degree of trade union solidarity over the basic conditions of work, while reserving the finer details of the employment situation to local bargaining with the participation of the workers who will be affected.

The analysis we have set out in this chapter represents an emerging phase of the dialectic of the workplace, and is not meant to represent a final stage or resting place. As long as the fundamental antagonism or contradiction of capitalism persists, it is to be expected that even these modifications will create the conditions of their own disintegration (Avineri 1971: Chap. 6). Thus, the question arises of what happens in the labor process as people work together to make decisions jointly about their work activities and working life. Does this lead to a higher level of class consciousness that will ultimately challenge capitalist control itself as in Sweden? To what degree do people who become accustomed to making scheduling, training, evaluation, and other types of decisions in the workplace begin to raise questions about employment, the types of equipment and investment, products, prices, and other aspects of the firm? How will such changes affect the strength and role of the trade unions?

Obviously, we see these as important components of a long-run analysis of work in capitalist society. Though we cannot provide precise answers to these questions, we will address the future dynamics that will determine the answers in the final chapter. Before proceeding to that level of analysis, however, it is necessary to review changes in education in a fashion that parallels our examination of the workplace.

8

Predicting Educational Reforms

The preceding chapter addressed workplace alterations likely to be adopted to overcome the increasing difficulties of absorbing the overeducated and inappropriately socialized worker. Not only has the educational system become more and more unsuccessful in preparing the young for existing work opportunities, but, as Chapter 6 suggested, the democratic dynamic of the schools tends to create a work force that increases disruption and conflict in the hierarchical and unequal workplace. Both private and State employers are being compelled either to discipline labor more forcefully or to alter the work situation. These actions are geared to reducing the emerging threats to profits and managerial control. Though the future will bring a variety of attempts to change the organization of work on a trial-and-error basis (with resulting conflicts among the different constituencies), we have predicted several long-run changes based on analyses of the principal contending interests.

Our approach suggests that employers will move to create new work forms to integrate the "new" worker. School reforms that attempt to bring schooling into line with the workplace (the reproductive dynamic) will be heavily influenced by changes in the workplace. Part of the need for educational reform may be taken care of through labor discipline: as unemployment increases, especially of the educated, information about difficulties in the labor market reaches students, increasing competition for fewer "good" places in the schools themselves. Students become more concerned about grades, about getting into the best colleges, and, once in college, about being admitted to professional and graduate schools. Thus, increased unemployment and competition for jobs discipline students as well as workers.

Yet even with increased student discipline, the forces behind the reproductive dynamic will need reforms to make schools more effective producers of socialized labor. This means that there will have to be changes in the workplace *and* alterations in the patterns by which the young are prepared for work. In the 1970's and 1980's we have witnessed attempts to reform education in such a way that it will provide the labor requirements of the production system and a new and relatively stable pattern of mutual interaction between labor and capital. But if these attempts confront the democratic dynamic head-on, they will have difficulty succeeding. Indeed, they may even mobilize social movements to act politically on a whole set of issues, including education, as minority groups and women see their previously won gains threatened by attempted "reproductive" reforms.

In this chapter we discuss educational reforms and their relation to the reproductive and democratic dynamics in schools and the workplace. First, we will organize a taxonomy of existing or proposed educational reforms to parallel the classification of changes in the organization of work. Second, we will suggest principles that determine which educational reforms are likely to be successfully implemented. Finally, we will discuss these reforms in detail with attention to their consequences.

Classifying Educational Reforms

It is often difficult to identify precisely the changes implied by educational reforms because the rhetoric is often more salient than substantive innovation. Recent studies of educational change suggest that the results are more limited than the language of the alteration, and descriptions of educational reforms usually lack rigor and mean different things to different people. Beyond the problem of definition, there is an enormous heterogeneity of implementation, so that the identical concept varies widely in practice (Berman & McLaughlin 1975; Gross et al. 1971; Charters 1973).

A perceptive study of school settings has argued that educational change is so nebulous that rarely can one even find accurate descriptions of what has taken place (Sarason 1971). Our approach is to list illustrative changes that have been suggested for education. The descriptions are intended to differentiate them from other proposed changes. Whether the reforms have the effects that their advocates predict is open to empirical inquiry; we will not draw firm conclusions on these matters, except to suggest that both the structure and the content of certain of these reforms tend to correspond to particular changes in the workplace, and that some are more likely to be adopted than others.

Table 8.1 presents a classification of educational reforms. The microtechnical label refers to those relatively small technical changes in the educational process that do not require organizational modifications of schools and that can be localized within the educational system without having a larger impact. The macrotechnical category includes a more comprehensive set of alterations that affect the organization and the content of schooling. Micropolitical reforms entail changes in the internal governance of schools with respect to who makes decisions about curriculum, personnel, resource allocation, and instruction. Finally, macropolitical reforms involve major changes in the governance and political control of education.

As in the previous chapter, these categories are hierarchical in the sense that change in each successive category requires supporting modifications in the previous category. For example, micropolitical reforms would be likely to result in changes of a macro- and microtechnical character as well. Each of the four categories includes reforms that respond to both the democratic and the workplace dynamics. It is the specific nature of each of the reforms and its application that will determine the type of dynamic with which it is most consistent.

Microtechnical Educational Reforms

A good example of microtechnical changes would be new courses or subjects, which can be implemented with little impact on the overall structure of education. Though conceptually

Table 8.1   Classification of Educational Reforms

I. Microtechnical
   A. New subjects
   B. Changes in instructional materials (e.g., different approaches to
      teaching reading, purging sexist textbooks)
   C. Teacher retraining
   D. Multi-cultural and bilingual programs
   E. Educational technology (specific application)
II. Macrotechnical
   A. Differentiated staffing
   B. Team teaching
   C. Open classrooms
   D. Flexible modular scheduling
   E. Mastery learning
   F. Educational technology (generalized use)
   G. Desegregation and integrated education
   H. Changes in financing education
   I. Minimum curriculum or graduation standards
   J. Career education
   K. Recurrent education
   L. "Back-to-Basics"
III. Micropolitical
   A. Changes in internal governance of classroom or school with respect to
      students, teachers, and administrators
   B. Greater responsibilities for students in instructional process (e.g., peer
      teaching)
IV. Macropolitical
   A. Community control
   B. Educational vouchers and tuition tax credits
   C. Deschooling policies
   D. Factory-run schools
   E. Shifts in governance structure and representation

---

this category is parallel to that of microtechnical changes in the
work process, there may be no necessary link between the two.
The addition of a subject such as sex education, or a new approach to teaching such as the "new math," has only nominal
implications for microtechnical changes in work. However,
when vocational subjects are added to the offerings of community colleges, the connection between demands in the workplace and the new subject may be quite direct.

Other microtechnical educational reforms include the adoption of different instructional materials based upon (1) alter-

native approaches to teaching or (2) changed social values (e.g., new attitudes toward women and minorities). New approaches to teacher training and retraining may also fit this category when they are dedicated to the preparation of teachers in specific areas or for particular subjects. Similarly, the adoption of specific forms of instructional technology—such as audio cassettes for language training, programmed instructional texts, or computer-assisted instruction for a particular subject—will tend to be microtechnical in nature. Finally, the hiring of bilingual teachers and the adoption of multicultural curriculum units in the social studies represent other alterations of the traditional approach that are consistent with this classification. Though there are many other examples, the overriding principle common to all of them is that such changes tend to be compartmentalized within specific boundaries so that there is little impact on the organization of schooling.

Macrotechnical Educational Reforms

Macrotechnical changes are distinguished by their widespread implications, but they are technical because they do not entail changes in the governance or political control of education. They can be initiated by professional educators and related specialists. Just as changes in the governance of the workplace usually lead to alterations of technical operations as well, the same is probably true of changes in the governance of education; so the distinction between political and technical educational reforms may be blurred in practice, a factor we should keep in mind in reviewing this and the subsequent political categories of change. Many of the macrotechnical reforms represent major changes in school organization that cannot be readily achieved without an accompanying change in governance. Perhaps this explains the poor record of macrotechnical reforms in the past when they have not been supported by existing political forces (Berman & McLaughlin 1975; Carnoy & Levin 1976a).

One typical macrotechnical reform is differentiated staffing, which creates greater hierarchical specialization of labor for pupil instruction (Allen & Bush 1964). This approach is based upon a technical analysis of instructional tasks, a determination of duties and personnel requirements for each task, and an appropriate schedule of remuneration that reflects differences in responsibilities. A career ladder is created to increase opportunities for advancement beyond what is possible in the more traditional educational staffing model. Evaluations of differentiated staffing suggest that it has been both short-lived and ineffective in altering the educational environment (Charters 1973; Pelligrin 1973; Wacaster 1973).

Another staffing reform is team-teaching, generally defined as an arrangement whereby teachers cooperate in the instructional process, each drawing upon special competencies. The actual use of the approach is much more ambiguous (Beggs ed. 1964: 16; Goodlad & Rehage 1965: 10). In practice, team-teaching may simply mean that more than one teacher instructs a group of children or that teachers rotate among classes. Depending upon the application, team-teaching could increase the amount of teacher interaction through joint planning and implementation of instruction, or it could reduce it through the emphasis on greater specialization. Obviously, the outcome will depend upon the specific application, and there is little empirical evidence on the phenomenon.

A macrotechnical reform that received substantial publicity in the early 1970's is that of the "open classroom," which was based upon the changes that have taken place in many British primary schools (Featherstone 1971; Silberman 1970: Chaps. 6 and 7; Eisner 1973). These schools discard the more formal classroom and curriculum structures and replace them with a variety of activities from which children can choose. The emphasis is on promoting an environment in which individual students can pursue independently their own perceived needs, while teachers and other personnel assist students in assessing their needs and selecting appropriate activities. The substantial independence that is encouraged among students enables the instructional staff to spend much of its time working with pupils who have difficulties or designing new instructional approaches and projects. Individual student choice guides the selection of activities and participation in the school environment. This reform requires modifications of the physical structure of the classroom as well as changes in teacher training, curriculum, and materials.

A more structured macrotechnical attempt to individualize

secondary school instruction is flexible modular scheduling. Where the traditional secondary school relies upon uniform time segments and organizational arrangements for each course, the school using flexible modular scheduling designs classes and other educational experiences in which the amount of time and mode of presentation vary according to subject matter, student needs, and available facilities (Petrequin 1968). In general, a set of offerings is listed among which students choose and set priorities. A computer is used to coordinate student choices with time requirements and scheduling possibilities, subject to the availability of particular facilities, so that most of the students will be able to obtain the combination of activities they desire.

Whereas the two reforms just discussed emphasize heterogeneity in student activities and outcomes, mastery learning represents an attempt to improve the homogeneity of student outcomes (J. Block 1973; J. Block ed. 1974; Bloom 1976). The objective of mastery learning is to organize instruction to maximize the number of students who meet a predetermined level of mastery in each subject within the time limit set for the task. This is attempted through individualized instruction to differentiate the approach according to the aptitudes of the learner, a sequential assignment of resources from those students who have achieved mastery to those who have not, and the use of students to tutor other students. If mastery learning is successful, there should be greater equality in cognitive outcomes. The implications are obvious for work reforms that require cooperation and teamwork based upon relatively equal skill levels (Levin 1974a).

Although educational technology can be a microtechnical modification when applied to a specific subject or portion of the curriculum, educational technologies also have been adopted as a basis for pervasive reforms (Arnove ed. 1976). The most important of these are educational radio and television (Schramm et al. 1967; Mayo et al. 1976). In some school systems, such as that of Hagerstown, Maryland, educational television has been used for a substantial part of the instructional program. The same is true in higher education, as seen in the Open University in Great Britain and the Mid-American University in the United States. In Samoa, Colombia, El Salvador, Niger, South Korea,

Ivory Coast, Mexico, and Brazil there exist nationwide or regional systems of educational television or radio that serve as the principal media for classroom instruction.

In most cases the programming is developed centrally and transmitted to all classrooms at a particular grade level. Though the motivation for constructing such systems is ostensibly to cut costs (Carnoy & Levin 1975), compensate for teacher shortages, and improve the quality of instruction, the use of the medium influences student socialization (Leifer et al. 1974). For example, because most educational television and radio instructional systems are constructed to provide instruction to a passive audience, they are more likely to develop youngsters for relatively nonparticipative social and work roles.

Another macrotechnical reform, the attempt to desegregate schools, can also have profound effects on the organization and operation of schools. Schools may have to change many of their policies to adapt to the mixture of races and social backgrounds (Orfield 1974). These alterations may extend from changes in tracking policies to new curricula, instructional materials, and teacher-training approaches. If these attempts are successful in providing fully integrated schooling experiences, then the changing attitudes of different races and social classes toward one another could have strong implications for work reforms that would reduce hierarchy and worker stratification.

Recent reforms in financing elementary and secondary education to more nearly equalize spending among school districts also have macrotechnical implications (J. Pincus ed. 1974; Coons, Clune & Sugarman 1970). In principle, such a redistribution of funding can be expected to reallocate resources among districts with a concomitant tendency to equalize educational results. If an equalization of student outcomes were achieved, the reform would have implications for the distribution of skills and other attributes that prepare the young for work and other aspects of adult life. Whether school finance equalization will more nearly equalize educational outcomes and life chances has been challenged (Jencks et al. 1972; Levin 1974b).

From the late 1970's, there have been attempts both to improve the quality of secondary education and to assume minimum graduation standards by imposing minimum curriculum requirements and test standards for graduating students. The majority of the states are considering or have implemented legislation requiring specific high school courses and/or a passing score on a competency examination for high school graduation. These policies have created great controversy, particularly over the arbitrary nature of the tests and their lack of predictive value for occupational success and citizen responsibilities (Levin 1978).

Finally, there are three closely related attempts to reform the schools at the present time that are macrotechnical in nature. These reforms are direct attempts to make the educational system more responsive to the immediate needs of the workplace. They are career education, recurrent education, and the "back-to-basics" movement. Each emerged in the 1970's with the aim of tightening the link between schools and the requirements of work organizations. Career education refers to a diverse set of traditional reforms for more closely integrating the worlds of education and work; recurrent education is designed to increase the number and variety of educational opportunities that are available during working life, and the "back-to-basics" movement refers to the attempt to return the schools to a traditional learning environment with substantial structure and tightened discipline. Each of these will be discussed in detail in a later section.

Micropolitical Educational Reforms

Micropolitical educational reforms refer to changes in the internal governance of education that alter traditional decision-making power over the educational process. Though such reforms may increase the influence of teachers in relation to administrators, or vice versa, the most notable type of micropolitical reform would be a shift in decision-making power to students. In recent years there has been some movement in the direction of greater student and teacher input into the decision-making process, especially at the secondary and postsecondary levels. In the universities these changes have taken the form of student-initiated course offerings and subject majors as well as decline of the *in loco parentis* regulations that enabled higher educational institutions to dominate the private lives of their students.

In many cases there exist formal ways to increase student involvement in the governance of educational institutions. Though the changes are often cosmetic—for example, the typically ineffectual role of student councils and student associations—there have been many attempts to increase student representation on official committees and governing boards. In some cases the student members do not have voting rights, although they are permitted to present the student viewpoint in discussions and to place items on the agenda. Even when students do have voting power, they generally constitute a small minority of the membership of committees. They do not represent a potent force in themselves; but it is possible to build coalitions between students and some faculty members or administrators on particular issues, so student representation can influence the outcome of some deliberations. Depending on the actual arrangements for student representation, the device can parallel that of internal worker participation in an advisory capacity.

The modest outcomes of student participation in the governance of educational institutions is in marked contrast with historical proposals on this subject. John Dewey noted in the early part of this century that a democratic adult society required democratic principles of organization and consensus in the school (Dewey 1966). More than a century before, the concept of a self-governing school had been outlined and applied by Joseph Neef, who saw the school as a democracy in which the entering children would first receive a course in ethics and the rights and duties of citizens in a free society. Following this preparation, the students would form a Republic by setting out a constitution and laws as well as the elements of their government. They would then be self-governing in both the process and the content of their education. Because of the influence of the Swiss educator Pestalozzi reflected in Neef's approach, he was called to Robert Owen's utopian community of New Harmony to establish the educational system. The short life of that community does not permit a detailed analysis of Neef's attempt to create a self-governing educational process.* But it is

---

*Neef's educational principles and experiences are reported in two volumes that he wrote: *Education* (1808), and *Neef's Method of Teaching* (1813). The account reported here is taken from one of the major works on the Owenite community of New Harmony, Indiana—Lockwood 1971 (orig. ed. 1905).

interesting that the famous utopian community, with its egalitarian and democratic tenets, was seen as requiring an educational approach with a corresponding set of principles.

Though micropolitical reforms have not been prominent in the United States, they have been in Western Europe. Especially in West Germany, there have been nationwide demands for increased participation of teachers, parents, and students in the internal decision making of the school (H. Weiler 1973: 52–56). Similar changes have taken place in both the macro- and microgovernance of the West German universities.

One final version of an educational reform that has micropolitical implications is peer teaching or tutoring (Melaragno & Newmark 1971; Ehly & Larsen 1980). The concept behind this approach is to enlist the assistance of students in teaching other students in order to provide more individualized instruction or to create supportive student "communities."* The particular forms of peer teaching can entail drawing on high-achieving students to assist slower ones or older children to assist younger ones. There is a parallel between this educational reform and peer training and cooperation in the work enterprise.

Macropolitical Educational Reforms

The most comprehensive educational reforms are macropolitical in that they represent alterations of the governance and control of schooling. Whereas micropolitical changes refer to modifications in decision-making roles among those groups internal to the schooling process—students, teachers, and administrators—the macropolitical ones address the overall control of the educational enterprise. The all-embracing nature of these changes means that they are likely to have profound effects upon the micropolitical and the technical characteristics of education. Macropolitical reforms include changes in the control of the existing school organization as well as shifts in the provision of education from the existing schools to educational marketplaces and to workplaces.

---

*For example, mastery learning methods may use student tutoring to assist in meeting the mastery criterion for more students and to enable teachers to focus on those students who need their help. The supportive community orientation tends to view cooperation between students as useful for creating democratic and equal societies as well. Both views are reflected in Dewey 1966.

The most obvious shift in control is from one constituency to another. For example, in the early 1970's the French government imposed a reform increasing the power of the business community and its representatives to govern the structure and content of French higher education (Patterson 1976). This modification of political control was apparently a concession to certain interests to make the French universities responsive to business needs. In West Germany, university reforms have altered the power of students, faculty, and administrators to appoint faculty and make other decisions. Interestingly, much of the call for greater autonomy of schools and greater participation of teachers, parents, and students in their internal operations has been attributed to the corresponding "controversy over co-determination (*Mitbestimmung*) in industrial management" (H. Weiler 1973: 53).

One form of macropolitical change is the movement for community control of schools. During the last two decades there have been demands by black and other minority citizens in large cities for a shift to neighborhood school boards with responsibility for personnel, budget allocation, curriculum, and other school policies (Levin ed. 1970). These reforms are based on the premise that school bureaucracies and educational professionals have little concern for the needs of children from low-income and minority families. Reformers have argued that if the people most affected by school policies were to take responsibility for the schools in their neighborhoods, educational results could be drastically improved.*

Though many big-city school districts have responded by proclaiming administrative decentralization and forming citizen advisory boards, actual control of decisions has not been altered in most cases. In New York City a more extensive plan has been adopted, but the size of the subdistricts (many as big

*However, consider the causes of differential socialization suggested in Chapters 4 and 5 and the degree to which neighborhood-based school boards and parental participation might reinforce or alter these results. At best it could be argued that a local school board with increased parental participation could create a learning process in which the "natural" tendencies toward a class-based system of reproduction are altered and challenged by a rising class consciousness. At worst, the approach could further the present system of class-based reproduction by isolating neighborhood schools even further from the broader vantage point of professional control.

as medium-sized or large cities) and the concessions necessary to the teacher organizations resulted in little added power to neighborhoods. It would appear that community control of schools could have profound effects on the participation of students, parents, and educational staff at the school level if such plans were fully adopted.

In contrast to the collective orientation of community control, educational vouchers and tuition tax credits represent a focus on individual choice, shifting the control of education to student and family by establishing a market for educational services. Parents would be given a tuition voucher that could be used for schooling at any approved educational institution (Friedman 1962: Chap. 6; Coons & Sugarman 1978). The State would set out eligibility requirements for participation of schools, and educational enterprises would be encouraged to enter the marketplace to compete for students, whose vouchers would be redeemable from the State. In principle, the profit motive would operate to make schools responsive to the wishes of parents and students, with a resulting increase in educational diversity. The educational clientele would be able to exercise control over their education by selecting the schools that best fit their personal needs. Schools unable to attract enough vouchers would not survive.

Critics of the voucher approach have argued that the marketplace has always provided better results for upper-income groups than for lower ones and that a system of market choice would lead to increased segregation by race and social class among schools as well as an increase in the intergenerational reproduction of social class (Levin 1980). Nevertheless, the federal government has initiated voucher demonstration projects to test their feasibility (D. Weiler et al. 1974).

Tuition tax credits represent a mechanism to subsidize families for the tuition paid at private schools through a specified reduction of income tax liability. In the late 1970's and early 1980's a number of bills were proposed that would provide tax credits of up to $500, and President Reagan made tuition tax credits a central goal of his educational program. To the degree that tax credits encourage individual choice in the educational marketplace, they would have some of the same impacts as educational vouchers. A number of analyses have been carried out to ascertain their probable consequences on equity, choice, and educational quality (James & Levin 1983).

A different approach to macropolitical educational reform is the deschooling proposal (Illich 1971), which would reduce the dependency on formal schooling and substitute educational opportunities in other forms such as access to libraries, informational and educational technologies, on-the-job training, peer training, and other "nonformal" educational alternatives. Since the institution of formal schooling would decline, the control of education and its effects on youth would be determined by the availability of nonformal opportunities that arose.

The evidence suggests that such opportunities and the ability to take advantage of them are directly related to the connections and social class of the family. Traditionally, when children from poor and minority families have "deschooled" themselves by dropping out, few training alternatives have arisen to replace the role of formal schooling. By contrast, middle-class and upper-middle-class youngsters have had only to rely upon their parents' contacts or the "free" schools that have arisen to serve their needs. The emphasis on individual choice and options through deschooling would be likely to create patterns of opportunities similar to those that would result from educational vouchers; both are ways of adopting an educational marketplace to replace the existing schools.*

A final macropolitical reform of education is shifting control from the schools to the workplace. This change can take the form of increased on-the-job training as a substitute for formal schooling, or it can encompass a more profound shift in which literacy and other basic components of socialization are organized and transmitted in the work setting. In such revolution-

---

*Since people from the middle and upper classes are more experienced in choice situations than people from the lower classes, who face fewer options in virtually all aspects of their lives, it is reasonable to believe that the deschooling approach of Illich would create more unequal results than the present system. This is especially likely when one considers that a nonformal system of educational opportunities must necessarily rely heavily upon information and social or business connections. Evidence on the unequal effects of such a reform are reflected in the following studies that explore noncompulsory educational offerings: Harnqvist 1978 (a general view on the determinants of the individual demand for education); Cook 1975 (evaluation of the equity aspects of the preschool television program "Sesame Street"); and E. Rosenthal 1977 (a report on some results of participation in programs of adult education).

ary societies as Cuba, China, and Tanzania there have been attempts to bring schooling to the fields and factories (for Cuba, see Carnoy & Werthein 1977, Fagen 1969, and Leiner 1973; for China see Fraser 1972, Hawkins 1974, and *Prospects* 1975: 480–504). Though most formal and institutionalized educational experiences in such societies still take place in schools, there appears to be an increasing focus on the provision of basic literacy skills, cultural experience, and scientific and technical training in the workplace. In the United States, various proposals have been advanced for increasing the exposure of the student to the workplace and reducing the length of time in formal schooling (Coleman et al. 1974). These will be reviewed in a subsequent section of this chapter.

In general, macropolitical reforms represent the most extensive types of changes in education. As with the macropolitical work reforms, changes in the overall governance of education would be likely to stimulate corresponding modifications in the internal governance and technical organization of the educational system.

Which Educational Reforms Are Most Likely?

The classification of educational reforms in Table 8.1, like that of workplace reforms, is a catalog rather than a prediction. All of these changes are not equally likely in the attempt to tighten the correspondence between education and work. In this section we will suggest which educational reforms are most likely to be adopted.

In setting out these structural changes in education, we must differentiate between the immediate responses and the ultimate results. The fact that a reform is attempted does not mean that it will succeed. The history of planned change in education is replete with failure (Berman & McLaughlin 1975). Such failure is especially likely when reforms are viewed as changes that are recommended and implemented by outside experts according to a mechanical formula. Almost never will any reform be successfully achieved in this way.

Clearly, reforms arise through political action. The conventional politics of education represents an analysis of how interest groups such as parents, teachers, taxpayers, or religious groups perceive and act upon issues, forming coalitions and molding strategies to obtain particular educational goals (Wirt & Kirst 1982). This analysis is important in explaining how particular reforms are adopted at specific times and in specific settings. Accordingly, it is important to show how interest group politics fits into the analytical framework we have set out.

According to our thesis, there are two major forces that mold the agenda of the schools: one presses for an education that will provide opportunity, mobility, equality, democratic participation, and the expansion of rights; the other presses for an education that will provide appropriately trained workers with the required skills, attitudes, and behavior for efficient production and capital accumulation. The struggle between these forces sets the larger framework within which the conventional politics of education is found. The struggle over democratic versus capitalist reforms must always be worked out at a concrete level by the dynamics of political interest groups and social movements.

For this reason, specific reforms should be analyzed not only for their overall importance for the democracy-capitalism schism, but also with regard to which class fractions they appeal to among both popular and capitalist interests. For example, some fractions of capital have an interest in educational expansion and the production of workers with specific vocational skills that will serve their industries; other fractions seek workers with a strong basic education that will provide a foundation for on-the-job training; yet others have few requirements for educated labor and will prefer to minimize the tax burden from education.

Similarly, different groups in the population have different priorities. Minorities and lower-income groups have an interest in obtaining strong basic education for their children that will provide them with options for further study as well as a sound foundation for job training. Middle- and upper-middle-class groups are likely to be more interested in the quality of academic training in secondary schools and in higher education, since they normally assume that their children will receive a solid basic education. Different religious and political groups will have different preferences with regard to curriculum content and even the role of public versus private schools.

The educational professionals themselves will reflect in their own actions not only both the democratic and the capitalist perspectives, but their own goals as well. Beyond their educational goals, they will have occupational objectives concerning salaries and working conditions. Indeed, in many educational settings they are considered the most powerful single educational interest group (Wirt & Kirst 1982: 15–17). Beyond the educational consequences of reforms, teachers and other professionals also have considerable self-interest in the decisions.

For these reasons, the specific forms of educational change will be heavily conditioned by the conventional politics of education. However, the factors that frame the debate and that determine the longer-term directions of education will be shaped by the larger struggle taking place between the pressures for a more efficient work force and those for a more egalitarian and democratic educational process.

Like workplace reforms, educational reforms represent a response to concrete organizational pressures—in this case, on the schools. One or more aspects of schools are viewed as problematic so that pressures build up from certain constituencies for change. Though these constituencies can often be viewed as those interested in greater "equality" versus those interested in greater "efficiency," the existence of class fractions as interest groups makes the scenario more complex on any specific issue. Low student achievement, disciplinary problems, pressure on the schools to make students more "realistic" about the nature of available jobs, and the dilemmas of rising educational costs have all created the setting for present educational reforms. The schools must respond to these and other emerging problems by doing something that will reduce conflicts among constituencies that have different priorities for the schools.

For example, state systems of elementary and secondary education have been challenged in the courts as being unconstitutional because they provide more educational support in wealthy school districts than in poorer ones (Coons, Clune & Sugarman 1970; Wise 1968). In many states these claims have been upheld by the courts (J. Pincus ed. 1974). But the court battles have not resolved the underlying issue; not only does the legal maneuvering among different constituencies continue, but so does the conflict at the levels of the state legislature and the school district. Reforms that increase the revenues collected from wealthy jurisdictions and distribute them to poorer ones, thus narrowing the disparities in educational expenditures between school districts, have been resisted by wealthy jurisdictions and by constituencies who view equality as a threat to diversity, to innovation, and to special treatment for gifted students. Teacher organizations and other professional groups are concerned about the effects of new financing approaches on the salaries and collective-bargaining positions of their members. All of these constituencies have joined in the struggle to mold the new legislation and its implementation in ways that favor their interests or at least minimize the damage to them. These conflicts will continue at legal and legislative levels as well as in school districts during implementation.

These conflicts are part of the semiautonomous nature of public education. Like the State of which it is a part, education's separateness from production puts it in the political arena, where workers ostensibly have rights equal to those of capitalists, and students' parents to those of school administrators and teachers. Though this equality may not exist in fact, opponents usually assume that it does exist, and the political process by which educational reform takes place must behave as if there were political equality. But in a capitalist society, educational reform is different from work reform because the struggle over reform is carried out in the two arenas under different rules. Educational reform must take place as if it were conforming to the demands of the interest groups involved in education; this is not true of the workplace, where it is clear that workers have a totally different set of rights from capitalists.*

The struggles over reform are also conditioned by the historical context in which they take place. For example, it is no mere coincidence that the major victories for greater equality in schooling coincided with the tight labor markets and economic

---

*We should also note that it is not obvious that all participants in the educational reform struggle believe that reforms will be adopted, or that if adopted they will actually change the life chances of young people significantly. For many, political struggle over education is the only meaningful political issue available, and/or one of the few issues where their influence can be felt at all. A good example is school busing, whose effect on black children's success is ambiguous, but whose political impact in bringing out blacks' economic and social plight is important in and of itself to the black community (Tyack & Hansot 1981).

growth of the 1960's. Advocates of rapid school expansion—especially in higher education—were able to draw upon the support of employers who needed more trained workers and taxpayers who could afford to support education from their rapidly rising incomes at a time of relatively stable prices. Under good economic conditions it was relatively easy to yield to demands for increased schooling opportunities for children from minority and low-income backgrounds as well as for females. Furthermore, it was possible to draw upon the momentum and general support of political coalitions, courts, and legislatures that were generally favorable to the expansion of social services for the disadvantaged. Finally, with high proportions of families with school-age children, there was strong support for education.

But with the economic downturn of the 1970's and a reduction in families with school-age offspring, a new economic and political reality was created that began to undermine such programs. Emphasis was placed on fitting the young more closely to available work opportunities and on cutting back funds for schooling, while barely maintaining existing programs designed to equalize educational opportunities. Finally, with the beginnings of recovery from worldwide recession in 1983 and the increasing economic competition with other nations, the emphasis on educational equity has largely disappeared from the national educational agenda. Rather, the national calls for reform have stressed raising educational standards to meet the economic challenge of the future (Education Comm. of the States 1983; Nat'l Comm. on Excellence in Ed. 1983). That is, the economic and political conditions of the 1980's have created demands for once again focusing on schooling for workplace efficiency. This movement is supported by employers who have seen profits fall over the 1970's, parents worried about the economic futures of their children under high unemployment, and taxpayers concerned with "efficiency" in government.

Through trial and error, through strategy and counterstrategy, groups competing over educational reform reach a new position that compromises the interests of all contending parties in roughly inverse proportion to their political strengths, their abilities to forge coalitions with other groups, and their success at winning over the support of "noncombatants" who influence the process. It is within this context that present work-oriented educational reforms should be perceived. The mere attempt by one group—whether educational professionals, businessmen, administrators, or parents—to push for changes in the educational system does not mean that such changes will succeed. This can be seen clearly by reviewing three reforms of the 1970's that have strong implications for the workplace: career education, recurrent education, and the "back-to-basics" movement.

Since the origins of overeducation and its consequences for frustrated and recalcitrant young workers were reviewed in detail in Chapter 6, here we want only to repeat the important point that the lack of employment opportunities for both high-school- and college-educated youth has created pressures on the school to reconsider and improve career preparation. The expectations for career success through education have been confronted with the hard fact that good jobs are in short supply. Despite the high rates of youth unemployment and underemployment, many students, young adults, their families, and social commentators have placed the blame for the lack of appropriate jobs on the failure of the educational system to provide appropriate skills and attitudes among youth that would lead to employability.

Career Education

The most widespread response to the difficulties of finding employment for the young has been the attempt to initiate career education. Though this reform movement is ambiguous enough to provide a large number of amorphous goals, including appropriate preparation for the "career of life" itself, it has generally taken the form of a concentrated effort to articulate and integrate more closely the worlds of schooling and work (Marland 1974; Hoyt et al. 1972). Ways of doing this include attempts to improve career guidance on existing job positions, to increase the career content of curricula, to intersperse periods of work and schooling as part of the regular educational cycle, and to provide a more realistic understanding of work and its innate dignity.

Each of these palliatives attempts to reduce the divergence between the school and the workplace, with the assumption that it is the school that must make the accommodation. Tacitly, it is assumed that the workplace will not change, nor will available employment opportunities; rather, it is the values, attitudes, expectations, choices, and skills of the young that must adapt to the disjunction between the world of schooling and the world of work. Through better counseling and career guidance, the students will learn more about themselves and their potential opportunities. Curricula will be modified to make them more appropriate to existing jobs, so that students are better prepared for the types of employment that they are likely to find.

Further, students are to be provided with opportunities to become more familiar with the workplace at an earlier age by combining school with work. In some cases the student will alternate time between study and work as part of a daily, weekly, or other periodic pattern. In other cases, students will be exposed to various types of jobs and workplaces through field trips, readings, films, and other classroom activities. Work-study programs have existed for a considerable time for students in vocational areas at the secondary level and for those attending postsecondary institutions that have sponsored cooperative educational programs (Knowles et al. 1972). However, it has been proposed that such offerings be expanded to include virtually all youngsters at the secondary level to ease their transition from school to work (Coleman et al. 1974; Nat'l Manpower Inst. 1977).

Finally, though some curriculum change would provide more vocational courses such as typing and accounting for students who were pursuing liberal studies, there is also a more pervasive aspect of career education that would attempt to reestablish the work ethic and inculcate the view that even the lowest-status job has dignity. Just how this would be accomplished is not clear; the literature on career education encourages the formation of these values through the schooling process, but there is little evidence that young people are becoming as a result more realistic or accepting of the available career opportunities, or more productive in their careers. As noted in Chapter 6, a national sample of high school graduates in 1972 was not found to be more "realistic" about careers (as reflected by their career aspirations) even after being out of high school for two years and having worked. The expectations for social and occupational mobility through the educational system are major reasons that students obtain as much schooling as they do, so it seems ironic that the educational system should be proposed as a vehicle for reducing the expectations of the young for high job status, pay, and working conditions. The career education approach must inevitably fail as long as there are not accommodations in the workplace that provide other incentives for students to modify their expectations and behavior.

Knowledge of available jobs does not alter the fact that good jobs will be in short supply for the foreseeable future and that most young people will be disappointed with their work status. Nor does an exposure to available jobs create the impression that work is creative, useful, and characterized by dignity.* An earlier familiarity with the world of work and its routinized tasks, repetition, and supervisory control may have an effect quite opposite to what was intended. To the degree that the schools provide an image of the workplace as providing self-fulfillment, opportunities for advancement, and constructive activity, the reverie may be interrupted at an earlier age than at present, only to be replaced by cynicism and hopelessness (Steinberg et al. 1981).

Recurrent Education

Though recurrent education seems to be more an intellectual concern than one that is evident in practice, it too is a work-oriented reform now being advocated. Recurrent education refers to the attempt to distribute learning opportunities over the entire life span rather than concentrating them at the beginning. By contrast to the present approach, which requires substantial formal education and training prior to the initiation of a career, recurrent approaches would make it possible to spread out one's educational experiences according to emerging needs at different times of one's working life (Mushkin ed. 1974; Levin & Schutze 1983b).

The support for recurrent education tends to be fragile when

---

*For an elaboration of these criticisms see Behn et al. 1974. Terkel 1974 provides interesting insights on the dignity issue. This assumes that students will be employed as supermarket baggers, "fast food" outlet cooks and cashiers, waiters or waitresses, and stock clerks, rather than as writers, lawyers, brain surgeons, or journeyman crafts workers. Also see Grubb & Lazerson 1975.

one compares the implicitly divergent motives of educational institutions and social policymakers (Levin & Schutze 1983a). One important effect of recurrent education would be to reduce the demand for traditional educational credentials as people redistribute their educational experiences over their lifetimes and substitute more training experiences for traditional college study. With an increase in the opportunities for later study, the high current demand for college credentials by young people would probably drop, alleviating pressure on job markets by the college-educated. Instead, young people would seek jobs at lower levels and would undertake training and further education later in response to personal and job needs. Clearly, this would tend to reduce some of the consequences of "overeducation."

One reason the education industry is so supportive of the recurrent education concept is that it hopes to capture a new clientele at a time when enrollments are threatened by a declining population of the traditional college ages. However, if the young are able to find career opportunities that satisfy them with little need for more education, it does not seem likely that they will undertake college at a later date. Though new audiences might be obtained for the educational institutions by creating greater flexibility in age and admissions requirements, it is not clear that these new enrollees would compensate for those who postponed their further education.

Even more important, without changes in the nature and availability of jobs, the recurrent educational approach must necessarily have a minimal effect on reducing immediate enrollments of the young in colleges and universities (Levin & Schutze 1983a). First, the lack of jobs will create an incentive to obtain more schooling, since the opportunities foregone will be minimal. Without the temptation of good jobs, it is simply a better decision to get more schooling to improve one's chance for the future. Second, the structure of job markets tends to limit career mobility to a largely disparate set of career miniladders. Without a college certificate, a young person will have difficulty gaining access to the occupational positions that require more training, for the routinized and lower-level manufacturing, clerical, and service positions require no additional training, nor do they offer a route to a different occupational ladder with greater educational or training requirements. Job incumbents will find that their potential occupational mobility will depend on entering the firm at the highest possible entry level so as to have access to better career opportunities, rather than working their way up from the bottom through recurrent education. The janitor or stock clerk will have little chance of getting into management, even with recurrent educational accomplishments, whereas the college-educated youth who is able to begin in a higher position will have a much greater probability of moving into middle or upper management.

As in the case of career education, the premises of recurrent education are not likely to be met under the existing conditions and organization of the workplace. Even when educational sabbaticals are provided by firms as part of a collective-bargaining agreement, they have not been taken advantage of except by those who were already among the most highly educated and those occupying the higher occupational positions (Levin & Schutze 1983b: Part III).

Back-to-Basics

Another response to the present crisis is the "back-to-basics" movement. In apparent reaction to both the job picture and the decline in test scores (Wirtz et al. 1977), many educators and parents have called for more structured schools that would place greater emphasis on discipline and basic skills. Though there is little research on the extent of the movement, it does appear to be on the upswing.* But if the decline of school discipline and student achievement is in large measure owing to the declining exchange or commodity value of those attributes in the workplace, then an attempt to improve the career possibilities of youth through such devices may not make any difference. If much of the desire among students and parents for proficiency in such skill areas as reading, writing, and arithmetic is driven by the rewards in the marketplace for those skills, then the depressed condition of the job market provides little incentive for putting energies into studies to improve skills.

When the job market was more buoyant, and when good jobs and admission to the best colleges were available only to stu-

---

*In a national survey in 1977, 83 percent of respondents approved this trend (Gallup 1977: 36).

dents who showed evidence of such skills, there was a strong incentive for students and teachers to take these subjects seriously. Grading practices were more severe, students took more of the traditional courses in high school and college (U.S. Dep't of Ed. 1981), college entrance examinations were studied for, and so on. When it became obvious to the majority of young people that entrance to a good college was no longer highly competitive (College Entrance Exam. Bd. 1980) and that few good job opportunities were available for college graduates anyway, only a small body of highly dedicated students (such as premedical students) focused on such skills. Again, the argument is that there is a connection between the success of educational reforms that attempt to reduce the increasing divergencies between schools, the workplace, and supportive changes in the workplace itself.

There is yet another factor to take into account. Crisis in the economy and the need to cover private-sector injustices with public funds (including expanded employment for highly educated minority and women professionals in the public sector itself) create fiscal problems that affect the schools directly. Reduced funding for education makes it difficult, if not impossible, to develop creative reforms that address both the reproduction of workers and the democratic functions of schools. The flexibility of educational reforms is reduced as class sizes become larger and programs are cut. Furthermore, the capacity for the schools to employ minority professionals—consistently one of the most important demands of minority groups on the educational system—is also reduced.

It is not just that educational reforms designed to respond to the needs of the workplace are confronted by contradictions in the workplace itself. Such reform efforts are also faced by continued contradictions in education, both because of the semi-autonomous nature of schools and because of the structural correspondence of schools with workplaces that was stressed in Chapter 6. The three attempts at educational reforms that characterized the 1970's and early 1980's have not succeeded at this point because they are inconsistent with labor-market conditions and confront the democratic dynamic of the schools. Each would dampen educational opportunities that had been expanded by popular movements in previous decades without providing supportive incentives in the workplace that would encourage the desired educational behavior.

Conditions for Successful Educational Reforms

Above all we have asserted that there is a continuous struggle within both the capitalist State generally and education specifically between forces pressing for greater democracy and equality in education and those pushing for greater efficiency in reproducing the skills and personalities required by capitalism. In any historical phase, one of these movements generally gets the upper hand in achieving its ends, only to be undermined by its own success. For example, the first half of this century saw the primacy of the influence of the capitalist workplace on schools, whereas the next quarter century witnessed an unprecedented shift toward democratic and egalitarian reforms. But the high cost of these reforms in combination with a serious economic crisis have reinforced the demands of the workplace once again. Low rates of capital accumulation and low productivity increases in the 1970's prompted reformers to focus on the need for improving the reproduction of efficient workers.

Under these conditions we believe that educational reforms will in the 1980's proceed largely from the reproductive dynamic, and therefore will be rooted in workplace reforms. Basic changes in schooling have traditionally followed change in the workplace at times of shifts from the democratic to the worker-reproduction focus. Under such a shift, the workplace is viewed as what must influence educational decisions at both personal and institutional levels. We noted that when the workplace lacks opportunities for advancement, students and teachers will take the schooling tasks less seriously and test scores will fall. Attainment of the traditional objectives no longer ensures success or justifies the efforts when their value declines in the labor market.

Yet even when historical conditions are such that the reproductive dynamic is dominant, attempts to impose school reforms that reproduce unequal and hierarchical work conditions will have difficulty succeeding. Those reforms will be challenged by social movements trying to defend social gains. Only if the organization of work changes in other directions and sets out new incentives for workers can there exist supportive conditions for change in educational institutions. For it is only under those changes in the workplace that school reforms will speak at all to democratic demands.

First, such changes will create an image of progress that will be transmitted to the schools through both official and unofficial channels. Witness the rapid adoption by schools of computers during the 1980's. Schools that adapt quickly to the new requirements will have greater success in placing their graduates than those that do not. Second, employees in occupations that will be affected by changes will tend to embody the new requirements in their child-rearing practices and in their expectations for the schools. Parents transmit to their children the values that create success in their own occupations; this has been shown both in our study of occupational socialization in Chapter 5 and in other studies on the subject (Kohn 1969). Further, as changes in the nature of work become obvious to students and teachers, they too have a shared incentive to modify their behavior. Through both formal and informal means, basic changes in the structure and content of work tend to alter the consciousness of workers and managers. As citizens, voters, parents, and businessmen change, the new attitudes are transmitted to students, teachers, administrators, school boards, and legislatures. Essentially, the schools become engulfed in a new, politically acceptable social reality that creates powerful incentives and pressures for altering their functions to conform with the changes in the workplace.

Specific Educational Reforms

Given this process of educational change, the stage is set for suggesting educational reforms that are likely to be adopted in the future under the conditions of struggle in the workplace and the schools. In the previous chapter we suggested that because of the configuration of power between workers and management and the need to improve productivity and profits, likely workplace reforms were those of a micropolitical nature, altering the internal governance of work around the use of teams. In general, these would increase the participation of workers in determining the nature, supervision, allocation, and scheduling of work tasks, as well as training. We have argued here that given the present popular configuration of political power between popular social movements and capitalist interests, the kind of school reforms that can be implemented even in a period where the forces of reproduction dominate would tend to be those associated with improved work conditions and increased equality. At least four changes in workplace behavior are associated with team work, and each has important educational implications.

1. Educational Decision Making

A major shift reflected in the use of work teams is the emphasis on group decisions by those who will actually perform the work. The more traditional approach separates the planning and evaluation of work from its execution, with the former done by managers and technicians and the latter by operatives. But under the team approach, workers must carry out all of these functions as well as select, train, and counsel members of the group and make decisions on the selection and maintenance of equipment. In contrast with the present educational system, where the emphasis is on functioning as an individual in competition with fellow students, a corresponding shift in education would emphasize functioning as a member of a cooperating group.

There are many potential educational reforms that would support these changes in socialization. They would include a greater emphasis on democracy in the school setting with greater student participation in selecting personnel and curriculum, determining resource allocation, and engaging in the process of conflict resolution. Through both representative and participatory democracy, the fuller involvement of groups of students (and perhaps teachers as well) would become part of the educational decision process. There would also be greater emphasis on group projects and assignments and on group awards—in place of the present focus on strictly individual performance and accountability. Emphasis would also be on integrating student teams by race and social class, for a reduction of hierarchy in production would reduce the need for student stratification and hierarchy in education.

The emphasis on group decision making would also increase

the use of cooperative modes of interaction in schools, both among teachers and among students. Cooperative work among small groups and training in group dynamics would become appropriate (Sharan 1980). Cooperative problem solving would also become more prominent in the school curriculum as work teams are faced with particular challenges that require a collective response (Slavin 1983).

2. Individual Decision Making

Under existing forms of work, most workers need make few individual decisions because to a very large extent the nature of the work tasks and the pace of work are determined by the equipment, technology, and organization of production. With a high level of specialization of tasks, it is only necessary to master relatively few and simple job components and perform them on cue. But under a team assembly approach, individuals will have a much wider range of potential tasks and decisions. For example, each coordinator will have to make decisions regarding the availability of supplies and the allocation of team members to avoid bottlenecks. Accordingly, it is likely that schools will shift their emphasis to a much greater extent than at present from memorization and routinization of learning to individual decision making and problem solving. The fact that individuals will have to make more workplace decisions both as individuals and as members of a small collectivity will mean that they will have to be able to use information to provide insights to the work team as well as to intervene when needed in the production process.

3. Minimum Competencies

At every educational level, existing schools tend to produce a wide range of competencies that are functional to production as long as there is a substantial hierarchy of skill needs. But as the organization of production shifts to team assembly and a flatter hierarchy, large differences in skill levels are dysfunctional. That is, team assembly will require that all members of the team have skills and knowledge that are more nearly equal in order to share tasks and participate fully.

These needs suggest two reforms in educational testing and curriculum. First, educational testing will tend to shift from an emphasis on normative tests to criterion-based ones. Normative tests represent an attempt to rank students on a distribution of performance without concern for what is good or poor performance in an absolute sense. That is, norm-based tests can only indicate who is better or who is worse in a particular domain. They cannot indicate whether one meets a particular standard of performance set out by an external criterion. By contrast, criterion-based tests set out particular guidelines of performance and measure proficiencies of students according to whether they meet those standards (Popham 1978). Given the importance of assuring that members of the work teams have the proficiencies to function in all phases of their work, it is the latter that are more important. Accordingly, it would appear that minimal-competency approaches using criterion-based tests will become more prominent.

In a related way, a curriculum based upon mastery learning approaches is likely to rise in importance (J. Block 1973; J. Block ed. 1974; Bloom 1976). Mastery learning begins with the assumption that all students can meet minimal proficiencies if given the appropriate instruction and adequate time to meet those standards. The educational challenge underlying mastery learning is to organize the curriculum and instruction to bring all students up to mastery levels—as measured by criterion-based tests—in all of the relevant skill domains. Although mastery learning is not a dominant medium of instruction under a school organization predicated upon producing educational outcomes that are highly unequal and that rank students according to who is best rather than what is known, the mastery learning approach would seem to correspond more closely to producing the skills needed by work teams.

4. Peer Training

Finally, under the team assembly approach workers would be trained by fellow workers as new members were added to the teams. In this sense, all workers will have to have the capabilities of training their peers on the various tasks that the team performs. Under the more traditional forms of work, training is generally relegated to a few specialists or supervisors who are given responsibilities for initiating new workers into their roles. Similarly, in existing schools the instruction is the delegated responsibility of teachers and other instructional personnel.

The widespread shift to team production is likely to stimulate a much greater emphasis on peer tutoring in the schools. Though there have been many demonstrations and experiments with students teaching students, the practice is not widespread in education (Ehly & Larsen 1980; Newmark 1976; Verduin et al. 1977). Experiments have shown that peer tutoring improves the performance and sense of efficacy of the tutor as well as the performance of the tutee (Allen ed. 1976). Thus there appear to be significant educational payoffs in themselves from this approach. But, even more important, a proliferation of peer tutoring in the schools will make every individual both a teacher and a learner. This is a central premise of the team approach, and it is also a more general feature of a democratic organization.

Other Trends

In addition to the particular dimensions of socialization and their associated educational reforms that would be likely to emerge under more participative work reforms, two general changes are important. Although recurrent education is not likely to be adopted widely at present for the reasons that were discussed in a previous section, the concepts of recurrent education may become much more practicable under a system of worker participation. The reasons for this are that the increased flexibility of work roles and the tendency toward horizontal mobility implied by the flattening of the job hierarchy will emphasize career progress in terms of service on different teams over the life cycle. Though a substantial amount of training can probably take place on the job itself through peer teaching, some job changes may require additional formal education and training in the classroom. Accordingly, the recurrent education approach will become more functional, and the use of "educational sabbaticals" will probably become more common as employers provide continuation of salary and other benefits while workers retool their skills or learn new ones. Educational entitlements might also be provided by the government for such purposes (Kurland ed. 1977).

Finally, there will probably be an overall shift from formal programs in educational institutions to formal and informal training on the job. To a large degree, the kinds of competencies that will be needed to work in groups—to cooperate, to rotate tasks, to adapt to new techniques—will be ones that can be attained more readily on the job than in an educational context removed from the workplace. It seems reasonable to believe that there will be some long-run substitution of training on the job for formal education, though the extent of this shift is difficult to predict.

9

The Potential and Limits
of School Struggles

The schools are an arena of conflict because they have the dual role of preparing workers and citizens. The preparation required for citizenship in a democratic society based on equal opportunity and human rights is often incompatible with the preparation needed for job performance in a corporate system of work. On the one hand, schools must train citizens to know their rights under the law as well as their obligations to exercise these rights through political participation. On the other, schools must train workers with the skills and personality characteristics that enable them to function in an authoritarian work regime. This requires a negation of the very political rights that make for good citizens.

That the educational system is charged with both these responsibilities creates within it the seeds of conflict and contradiction. The ensuing struggle between the advocates of two different principles for their objectives and operations tends to fashion schools that must necessarily meet the demands of both masters imperfectly.

Historically, tensions between these two dynamics have been set in the context of wider social conflict. Schools are part of a State that is both democratic and capitalist, and this dichotomy creates a major struggle in its own right. Since schools are situated within the State, they reflect that struggle. However, this is not to say that the influences of the two opposing forces are always in balance. To the contrary, in any historical period there is a tendency for one dynamic to gain primacy over the other. This can fuel a new round of opposition in which the opposing dynamic gains primacy, in a continuous and periodic cycle.

Schools are conservative institutions. In the absence of external pressures for change, they tend to preserve existing social relations. But external pressures for change constantly impinge on schools even in the form of popular tastes. In historical periods when social movements are weak and business ideology is strong, schools tend to strengthen their function of reproducing workers for capitalist workplace relations and the unequal division of labor. When social movements arise to challenge these relations, schools move in the other direction to equalize opportunity and expand human rights.

Such shifts in primacy are not a coincidence. Strong pressure in one direction creates contradictions that activate powerful social forces to shift the momentum in the other direction. For example, the gains of big business over labor in production and in the State (including education) during the first three decades of this century fostered social and educational inequalities that were contrary to the precepts of a democratic society. In the next four decades strong social movements were unleashed to address the educational needs of the economically disadvantaged, blacks, females, the handicapped, and linguistic minorities. Laws were passed providing these groups access to national resources, programs, and schools not available to them in the past.

Much of this shift took place, however, in a period of economic expansion during which personal income was rising. The State—because of its highly visible and positive role during the Depression and the Second World War—was able to get an increasing share of national resources after the war. Under the New Deal accords, labor and business could both see gain from economic growth and State arbitration of the growth process, and as long as the economy grew steadily, rising levels of taxation were viewed as a necessary cost of prosperity.

With the onset of lower growth rates, inflation, and falling real wages in the 1970's, however, this delicate arrangement began to deteriorate. A fiscal crisis of the State further constrained educational expansion. Social commitments to increased equity and equality became the subject of intense conflict, which was further exacerbated by the decline in school-age populations, especially among the middle class. Education seemed to lose its high priority as an increasing proportion of students came from minority and working-class backgrounds and as more older families had no children of school age (Kirst & Garms 1980).

Moreover, many of the educational programs and commitments to greater equality and democratic participation incurred high economic costs, and others, such as busing for racial balance, were socially disruptive. The result was that public educational spending per pupil rose dramatically, but—faced by fiscal constraints—government had to curtail educational choices once taken for granted by most families. In that sense, the legal victories and legislation of the 1950's, 1960's, and early 1970's, in which democratic and egalitarian ideals prevailed, contributed to and even stimulated the political backlash of spending cutbacks. The larger struggle between capital and labor over the resources controlled by the State during this period of economic crisis resulted in reductions of social spending on education, health, and other social services. The democratic dynamic so strong during the postwar period had been in part undermined by its own success: social problems had appeared soluble by expenditure of what for a time was a constantly growing source of public revenues generated by steady, seemingly unending economic growth. Once the economy stopped growing, however, the coalition that supported expanding social services broke down. The egalitarian dynamic thrives on a coalition of diverse groups. When the available resources for democratic reforms were curtailed, that coalition decomposed into divisive groups fighting for the shrinking pie. This conflict enabled opponents of the social, racial, and gender gains in education to begin to assert their agenda.

Social Policies in the Early 1980's

The U.S. economy in the 1970's was marked by business efforts to raise profits back to the "normal" levels of the mid-

1960's and by labor's attempt to maintain real wages. In the arena of liberal government policy in which these demands competed, neither met with success. Growth and profit rates remained low, real wages continued to decline, unemployment rates and prices rose, and with inflation of nominal incomes, effective income tax rates increased.

This period witnessed a transformation in the structure of production, through four major changes that further contributed to economic difficulties. It appears that in the late 1960's and early 1970's, the implicit New Deal accord among capital, labor unions, and government to equate real wage increases to productivity increases began to disintegrate. With this breakdown, employers in manufacturing, where unionized labor is most prevalent, changed their investment policy from capital investment to raise productivity to attempts to reduce wages (Carnoy, Shearer & Rumberger 1983: Chap. 4). This tendency to invest in plant relocations in regions with lower labor costs and without unions (both inside and outside the United States) was not totally new, but it was sharply accentuated during the early 1970's. Although capital investment per worker in manufacturing increased rapidly after 1973, employment remained almost unchanged at 20 million wage and salary workers. Despite this increased capital per employee, productivity increases slowed and real wages fell. Outside of manufacturing, productivity increases and real wages also fell, but capital per employee fell and employment rose rapidly.

In both sectors, employers appear to have pushed for reduced wages rather than for higher productivity. In part, this effort shifted investment overseas and to nonunionized regions of the United States (Bluestone & Harrison 1982). Another effect was to accelerate the already rapid incorporation of women into the labor force, as employers took advantage of the major untapped domestic source of low-paid workers.* The new investment pattern contributed to a slowdown in the growth of domestic employment in manufacturing and a gradual shift of that employment to the Third World, both through direct investment by

*Between 1960 and 1980, the total labor force grew by less than 50 percent, but the number of women in the labor force almost doubled (U.S. Dep't of Commerce 1982: 376).

U.S. manufacturers and through loans by U.S. banks to Third World governments and producers.*

The second major change that transformed the structure of production was the separation of capital accumulation from job creation. With the oil price increases of 1973 and 1979, profits from manufacturing, commerce, and services shifted to oil and gas companies and—as petrodollars reentered the United States—to banks. By 1980, about 45 percent of gross domestic private investment came from these two sectors, compared to 26 percent in 1966 (see *Economic Report of the President* 1983: Table B-83; *Business Week*, June 1, 1980). Yet these sectors accounted for less than 10 percent of employment. In contrast, the share of total domestic profits in commerce and private services remained approximately constant in the 1970's whereas the share of labor in those sectors rose slowly but steadily (*Economic Report of the President* 1983: Tables B-83 and B-37). This change in the structure of production has persisted and characterizes the American economy today. It suggests that those sectors where employment is expanding most rapidly will have to turn increasingly for their investment capital to other sectors. The current period is historically distinct from others in that the economy no longer generates capital and employment in the same sectors as it did when agriculture and then manufacturing were dominant. The effect is to put much more emphasis on finance than on production itself.

The third major change was the rapid growth of high technology industry. Besides the employment and capital accumulation effects within the industry, its products could have significant effects—through robotization, computers, and automation—on productivity and employment in other industries, especially commerce and services. The effect would be to reduce employment in those other areas.

The fourth major change was increased foreign competition in markets traditionally dominated by goods produced domes-

*Direct investment abroad by U.S. investors rose 12 percent annually between 1972 and 1980, but U.S. bank loans increased by 43 percent annually in those same years (*Economic Report of the President* 1983: Table B-105). U.S. foreign investment in manufacturing increased from $61.2 billion to $90.7 billion (current dollars), or 48 percent, between 1976 and 1982 (U.S. Dep't of Commerce, *Survey of Current Business* 1981).

tically. Part of this competition came from foreign branches of U.S. firms, and another part was stimulated by U.S. banks and industries lending to foreign firms. But much of the competition also came from Japan and newly industrializing countries that were generating their own capital and competing directly against U.S. producers in the U.S. market. Technology transfer, both legal and illegal, accelerated, so that newer products such as microchips and video games were being produced by imitators in Asia only a year or two after being introduced in the United States.

One major effect of these changes in production has been the increased role of the State. The State is responsible for softening the impact of capital movements by providing unemployment insurance and welfare payments to the unemployed. It is the State that is called upon to retrain workers who are displaced by foreign competition and to expand formal schooling in times—such as the 1970's—of increasing youth unemployment (which has hovered at the 20 percent level or even higher in recent years). It is the State that helps stimulate high technology growth through military procurement and through research and development funding—primarily military and NASA. It is also the State that is called upon to come up with solutions to the low rate of growth, to inflation, and to the increasing rate of unemployment. Already in the 1950's and 1960's, the State, more than private employers, was the object of social movements' demands for reform. Even in their demands for equal wages, the civil rights and women's movements focused on the State rather than on private employers.

It is not surprising, then, that when growth rates slowed down, it was the State that became the site and focus of conflict. The structural changes that occurred in private production precipitated social conflicts that the State has been unable to resolve. In turn, those conflicts expanded the State role as the arena in which they were played out. By the mid-1970's, as we argued in Chapter 3, middle-income families had become increasingly reluctant to pay the rising public costs associated with the changes in production that had increased the numbers of poor as real wages fell, that had increased unemployment as capital moved, and that had increased early retirement as fewer older workers were able to find jobs that paid well. Yet the victims of changes in production, the poor and unions, also contributed to the crisis. They seemed locked into demanding higher benefits from government and higher wages from employers—actions that were opposed by the middle class, and even by many employed, lowpaid, non-unionized workers because of the inflationary consequences of such demands. With such divisions among working people, the historic coalition that had been established in the 1930's began to founder, unable to respond cohesively to the new situation.

The election of a Republican government in 1980 was the logical answer to the Democrats' failure in 1976–80 to slow inflation, raise real wages (real wages did rise in 1976–79 but declined sharply in 1980), or meet increased foreign competition in both domestic and foreign markets. The 1980 election represented, by and large, not so much a rejection of the democratic and egalitarian gains of the previous decades as a demand for respite from their costs and a quest for economic growth and jobs with stable prices. The two are coupled because Americans seem to believe that economic growth is still the single biggest contributor to solving social problems.

After the Reagan victory, the majority of the population appeared willing to undergo a major austerity program if it would lead to the end of inflation and to economic recovery. The heart of the neoconservative appeal was its position against government spending and for individual initiative. There are deep roots in the American character that resonate to such an appeal. Deepest of all is the conviction that democracy and laissez-faire capitalism are inexorably linked—so linked, in fact, that we can measure the health of democratic ideals by how little government interferes in the economy. Thus, for many who voted for conservatives, democracy was very much an issue. But the Reagan Administration's response to this mandate was not a populist, democratic, conservative program. Instead it aimed almost exclusively at increasing profit rates and the income of the rich, on the assumption that only by income redistribution toward greater inequality could rapid growth be achieved—precisely the inverse of Keynes's view in the 1930's. According to the Congressional Budget Office (U.S. Congress 1982), income earners in the lowest income categories suffered net losses as a result of the 1981 tax and benefit cuts, whereas those in higher income categories received large gains. As part of this redistribution and as a way of cutting government spending, social programs—from government employment to welfare spending to health care and education—were all cut significantly in real terms. Yet, simultaneously, real military spending was increased.

Budget cutting was intended to reduce consumption, thereby reducing inflationary pressure and pressure on interest rates, to allow the Federal Reserve Bank to reach its goals early so that the economy could begin expanding on the crest of an investment boom to be stimulated by supply-side tax cuts. Once inflation and the expectations of inflation were curbed, capital investment and economic growth were to revive robustly.

This is the "economics" side of Reaganomics. But the investment stimulation was accompanied by attacks on social spending that had distributional and ideological purposes. The logic of the argument against social spending was as follows. If investment was to be stimulated, profit rates had to increase. Average corporate profit rates had fallen from the high rates sustained in the 1950's and mid-1960's, and this had presumably deterred productive investment. American industry was also suffering increasingly at the hands of foreign competition because of relatively high wages in the United States. Finally, the argument continued that one of the most important components of inflation had been wage settlements that had exceeded the slow growth of productivity. Both the market power of unions and the political power of labor had served to raise wages and improve working conditions, including workplace health and safety, beyond the capacity of the State and industry to support them.

To the Reagan Administration, the solution to all these problems seemed to lie in a two-pronged attack on labor. First came reductions in income-maintenance programs, the main intention being to reduce the rise in government spending, but another aim being to force increased numbers of people into the labor market. This in turn created additional unemployment and—especially among minimum-wage occupations—downward pressure on wages. The second, and more direct, attack on labor involved reducing the power of labor unions both through legislation and through support of legal challenges to the unions because non-unionized labor means less upward pressure on wages, less interference in the profit-making capability of private enterprise, and the undermining of a traditional source of support for the Democrats as well.

The major anomaly in Reaganomics occurs because of another aspect of its social program: militarism couched in virulent anti-Communism. This anomaly cannot be separated from Reagan's overall political economy—it is the sine qua non of postwar neoconservatism. And rightly so. If a Republican administration is going to increase average unemployment rates and also redistribute income to corporations and the rich, it must have an ideological stance that plays to mass political support. Making America the great military power it was back in the early 1960's is intended to do that.

Military spending is scheduled to climb from about 25 to more than 30 percent of a growing federal budget, from a total authority of $214 billion in 1982 to $400 billion in 1987. This includes building the B-1 bomber and the MX missile and refitting the Navy with new aircraft carriers and submarines. It does not include the booming U.S. arms export industry, like the AWACS Saudi-Boeing contract, now canceled because of falling oil prices. If our economy still had technology and production organization that were far ahead of the competition, and our only problem were underutilized capacity, military spending could serve to stimulate production, much as it did in the Second World War and Korea. But the conditions in the U.S. economy today are totally different: although industry is operating considerably below capacity, its two main problems are declining ability to compete effectively against imports and the high cost of credit.

Defense spending aggravates both these problems. Some years ago, in his book *Pentagon Capitalism* (1970), Columbia University professor Seymour Melman suggested that Defense Department contracting promoted built-in inefficiencies at the production end and built-in cost overruns. Melman also noted that military spending accounted for most of American industry's research and development and that the military-industrial sector employed many of the country's most able engineers and scientists. The utilization of these resources on military products means that they are *not* available to strengthen the civilian economy. These arguments have been largely confirmed in recent years (DeGrasse 1983).

The enormous increase in military spending also has its financial impact in contributing to growing federal deficits. Deficits, in turn, create increased competition for private capital and put upward pressure on interest rates. This would not be so bad for America if the deficit were invested in new consumer goods technologies, in saving energy, or even in longer-range programs for reorganizing our transportation, health, and education systems. All these investments could create a healthier basis for the future long-term development of our economy and society.

The faith of conservatives in military spending can best be viewed as a social investment policy. In the main, this explains why the Reagan Administration is so wedded to it despite the "short-run" impediments it poses for the rest of Reagan's economic package. As a social investment policy, military spending rates Communist expansion as the single greatest threat to America's way of life. A precondition of such an economic/social policy has to be military preparedness and aggressive steps overseas to halt Soviet imperialism. Such steps can only be effective if the United States is clearly the world's strongest military power, willing to use that power whenever and wherever necessary to protect America's interests. Economic growth is meaningless if there is no security against the Communist threat. The revival of American capitalism does not make much sense if capitalism cannot protect itself on a world scale. In these terms, military spending is social investment. Within this framework, it is the very basis for ensuring the continuation of American institutions and therefore cannot be subject to compromise.

Military spending tends to keep interest rates high because of its contribution to large federal deficits without producing usable consumer and producer goods. It therefore hurts small businesses. It competes for engineers, technicians, and many other skilled labor categories, driving up the price of those types of employees. Many small businesses in technology-related industries are forced to pay higher wages for a whole range of skilled workers whose job alternatives lie in defense industry.

There are, however, two countervailing effects. Military spending also strengthens certain unions—such as the Machinists Union—that politically oppose Reaganomics and are powerful actors in the union movement as a whole. But, at the same time, military spending combined with cuts in government employment are a boon to small businesses, which are seeking qualified, non-technical, college-educated personnel—precisely the personnel not demanded by military contractors and released by government cuts. The Reagan Administration claims that the planned elimination of 300,000 Federal jobs will be offset by 1984 through an increase in defense industry employment. Yet the people who stand to lose their jobs from these cutbacks are not the ones being hired by defense contractors. Government employment primarily benefits professional women (both white and black) college graduates and professional minority men (about 50 percent of these two groups worked at all levels of government in the 1970's) (Carnoy, Shearer & Rumberger 1983: Chap. 6). Military contractors will hire some women and minorities, but few at the professional level. Large corporations have a dismal record on this score. It will be smaller, more competitive businesses that will have to employ these highly educated minorities and women, and at much lower wages than government paid them. Businesses in certain nonengineering industries and services could therefore benefit by the shift from direct government employment to military contracting.

The implications of shifting federal spending from social welfare to military contracts are clear for social mobility of women and minorities: much of this portion of the labor force is being forced into unemployment or into lower-paying, lower-skilled jobs. Military production tends to favor white, male, higher-skilled labor. The militarization of the economy relative to the expansion of other government services or even other private goods and services means greater discrimination in the labor force. In short, it represents increased sexism and racism. The principal employment for minorities in the military is as soldiers, although for low-skilled whites and minorities, military service is the single most important form of post-secondary-school vocational training.

The bottom line of Reaganomics is that it favors a small, already well-off minority of Americans at the expense of the bottom 60 percent of families on the income scale. The Reagan Administration has also put enormous resources at the disposal of large corporations in the form of accelerated depreciation, and has changed the conditions of using those resources by cutting enforcement of pollution controls, rolling back health and safety regulations, and siding with business against organized labor. Women, blacks, and Hispanics are losing the economic and cultural gains they made in the last two decades. Labor unions are more on the defensive than at any time since the 1920's. Reaganomics hopes to change the social conditions of U.S. production in order to raise profits and promote investment. All these sacrifices, it is argued, will result in higher growth and—in the long run—a trickle down of higher incomes and better jobs now going increasingly to the white upper-middle class.

By the summer of 1982, the results of combining supply-side tax cuts with monetarist high interest rates had important fractions of the business community moving against supply-siders. From the Wall Street point of view, the potential of huge federal budget deficits until 1989 or beyond portended either continued high interest rates or new rounds of inflation. Opposition in the business community aimed at increasing certain business and excise taxes and cutting military spending. Certain business groups also began opposing the Administration's severe attack on the public education budget. The specter of declining growth of engineers and scientists in an age of high-technology expansion brought businesses associated with that sector into the education-spending arena.

But the most important reaction to Reaganomics occurred among the groups most affected by its social policies. The coalition that had disintegrated in the 1970's came back together to elect liberal Democrats in the 1982 elections. Political resistance prevented cuts in Social Security and Medicare/Medicaid, and created a backlash against military spending increases. In the spring of 1983, despite signs of economic recovery, blacks and liberal whites elected a reformist black mayor in Chicago. As early as September 1981, the AFL-CIO—historically not the most militant of labor organizations—organized a mass demonstration against the antilabor, antipoor aspects of the Reagan program. Women's groups became increasingly anti-Reagan as the extent of the Administration's social policy's effects on women became clear. The increased politicization of labor, minorities, and women is a direct response to the Administration's attempts to reinforce the reproductive dynamic and permanently weaken the principal social organizations supporting the democratic dynamic. The political struggle we observe is one in which the two forces are vying for the power to develop society in a particular way, each exploiting the weaknesses and divisions in the other.

Educational Reforms of the 1980's

Nowhere is this struggle better reflected than in education. The educational thrust of the 1950's and 1960's was toward equality, but the economic crisis of the later 1970's and early 1980's served to shift the momentum to the efficient production of a work force that would respond to the needs of employers. Especially prominent was the charge to the schools to make U.S. industry competitive again through increasing the rigor of education and training. In 1983 and 1984 more than a dozen reports were issued by national commissions, business groups, political groups, educators, and citizen organizations (Griesemer & Butler 1983). The two most important in terms of national sponsorship and dissemination were *A Nation at Risk* of the National Commission on Excellence in Education (1983), a report to the U.S. Secretary of Education, and *Action for Excellence* of the Task Force on Education for Economic Growth of the Education Commission of the States (1983). Both reports argued that much of the economic malaise of the nation was attributable to its educational weaknesses and recommended specific reforms for raising educational standards. This emphasis was in sharp contrast to the preoccupation of the previous three decades with educational equity, equality, and access.

The emphasis in most of the reports was on more required courses at the high school level, especially in sciences, mathematics, English, and computers, although one of the major reports (Boyer 1983) stressed writing and communications skills. Other recommendations included better teacher selection and retention through improved teacher training, evaluation, dismissal, and systems of merit pay; more time on instruction through longer annual school sessions and school days, the assignment of more homework, and more effective use of instructional time; and higher standards for high school graduation and college admissions.

These reports reflected the shift of commitment away from equity for bilingual, economically disadvantaged, racially isolated, and handicapped students in favor of a work force that would be more highly qualified to meet the needs of U.S. industry. Indeed, the reports make a point of justifying their recommendations on the basis of the crucial role that the schools must play in making the work force internationally competitive in a world of high technology. This movement away from equity was also reinforced by the reductions in federal grants for students with special needs and the shift to block grants, which permitted the states to determine how the funds would be used rather than targeting them to specific equity programs. At the same time, many conservatives, with the support of the Reagan Administration, pressed the case for public support of private schools through both educational vouchers and tuition tax credits. Educational vouchers would provide state-subsidized certificates that could be used to pay private school tuition. Tuition tax credits would enable parents to reduce their tax burden by some portion of tuition for each child enrolled in a private school (James & Levin 1983). The arguments were that such arrangements would improve educational standards through market competition for students (Coons & Sugarman 1978) and that student achievement would be higher in private schools than in public ones (Coleman, Hoffer & Kilgore 1982). Both of these arguments were challenged by other researchers (Levin 1980; *Sociology of Education* 1982; Willms 1983).

The educational response to the economic crisis was to reject the pattern of equality and democratization of education that had characterized the three previous decades in favor of shifting support to private schools and to the more advantaged students who were preparing themselves for college careers. This pattern was rationalized on two grounds. First, it would permit reductions in public expenditures by cutting commitments to the less-advantaged, thus freeing up resources for tax reductions and expansion of the military budget. Second, it would focus on the presumed needs for high skill levels in a high-technology work force to meet the new demands of a competitive international climate. There is a tacit assumption here that disadvantaged, handicapped, and minority students are less likely to be central to filling the educational needs associated with a high-technology economy. Rather, the focus on educational standards, computer skills, and assisting private-school constituencies took precedence over the democratic aspirations of education.

It is noteworthy that similar types of reforms have been recommended in times of earlier economic crisis. In the last three decades of the nineteenth century and the first decade of the twentieth, one of the most important educational reformers was Charles Eliot, president of Harvard University. In the depths of the serious economic crisis of 1893, Eliot issued his noted *Committee of Ten Report*. In comparing *A Nation at Risk* with the Eliot report of some 90 years earlier, Edson (1984) found that their attitudes and the circumstances surrounding them were almost identical. Both recommend that high schools require four years of English, three years of history or social studies, three years of science, and three years of mathematics. The earlier report recommended four years of a foreign language, whereas the more recent one pushed for only two years of a foreign language, and a half year of computer science. Both reports recommended longer school hours and improvements in teacher selection, justifying their recommendations by dwelling on the superiority of schools among our main economic competitors in Western Europe and, in the case of the recent report, in Japan.

Edson concludes that the social, political, and economic upheavals that preceded each of the reports led to a climate in which "individualism" and "survival of the fittest" were viewed as the path to stability and excellence. In both cases, such arguments were translated into educational terms that would simply ignore the needs of those who had to be "coddled" to be successfully integrated into the mainstream of American life. If the schools were to dawdle to assist the less fortunate, the nation would be threatened "by a rising tide of mediocrity that threatens our very future as a nation and a people" (Nat'l Comm. on Excellence in Ed. 1983: 5).

The states have also been pursuing the national agenda for reforms. Whereas the federal share of expenditures had risen from less than 5 percent of total expenditures on elementary and secondary schools in 1960 to almost 10 percent by 1980, the percentage dropped again to about 7 percent by 1984. Thus, the responsibilities for reforms have fallen on the states, many of which had established tax- or revenue-limitation measures. This meant that the states were seeking to implement the national recommendations for reform, often in the form of legislation, without adequate appropriations for satisfying the new requirements. For example, lengthening the school year and school day, alleviating teacher shortages, and retaining better teachers require hefty increases in school spending. But many of the states adopted the recommendations of the national reports without considering the costs of carrying out the changes. These costs were estimated at about $20 billion by Alan Wagner and Frances Kemerer at the State University of New York in Albany.

California is an important case in point, having passed Senate Bill 813 in 1983 without providing the necessary revenues to fund most of the new programs. Among the provisions called for in SB 813 were a longer school day and school year, improved classroom teaching, more demanding graduation requirements, increased teacher salaries and the establishment of a higher-paying category of "mentor teachers," and improved administration. Although these and other changes were expected to cost at least $1.5 billion to implement, less than $500 million in new funding was provided for the 1983–84 school year. Even with significant increases promised for 1984–85 as the state's economy improved, funding was not expected to meet the costs of the changes. California has over 4 million students in public elementary and secondary schools. The incentives to provide modest increases in the length of the school day and school year alone were estimated to cost over $250 million.

Hence, the reforms of the 1980's thus far are largely in the direction of greater efficiency in the educational system with respect to the particular outcomes considered important for economic vitality. The implicit message was that better education was a question not of more spending per pupil but of better "management," better teaching promoted by competition, and greater student discipline. Emphasis was placed on higher standards for preparing students for what was perceived as a workplace requiring higher and higher levels of skills for high technologies. Resources for funding the reforms were not adequate to the task, and the concern for equality in education and the democratic goals of schooling were relegated to a "benign neglect."

In this decade, the pressures for using the schools for reproduction of the work force have achieved primacy over those on the side of democratic and egalitarian reforms. Though much is said about the economy, little is said about democracy in pursuing educational change. What we wish to emphasize is that the struggle between the two forces is still very much alive, even though the present policy seems to favor capital accumulation rather than equity and popular participation. It is therefore instructive to point out the factors that will undermine the present strategies, ultimately reinforcing what we have called the democratic dynamic of schooling. These factors include the false promises of high technology; high unemployment; neglect of minorities and the poor; and the general trend toward participation in the workplace.

The advent of high technology has been held out as the driving force of our future economy. Although there is no single definition of high technology, the term is generally associated with computers, microelectronic devices, biotechnology, robots, and telecommunications. Firms involved in high technology are considered to have large investments in research and development and to employ relatively large numbers of persons with technical skills (Riche et al. 1983). One of the assumptions of the national educational reforms is that traditional entry-level jobs in the economy will diminish, whereas highly skilled technical positions will increase to meet the expanding needs associated with microcomputers and other high-technology applications. Indeed, the view of many of the educational reports is that a lack of trained personnel for skilled positions is likely to place the nation at risk with respect to its competitive position in the world economy. At the same time it is assumed that low-skill jobs will disappear as the new laborsaving technologies make them redundant. The implications for students are that those with minimal education (such as completing high school) will face fewer job possibilities, whereas those with computer knowledge and other forms of scientific and technical training will have virtually unlimited opportunities.

Both the popular media and the schools have stressed this scenario, with the schools benefiting from the greater willingness of state treasuries to loosen the purse strings to finance education for a high-technology future. But the available evidence does not support this optimistic view of job development. Although jobs in many high-technology occupations are growing at a very rapid rate, the absolute number of increased jobs in these occupations is very small because they begin with a very small base. For example, the Bureau of Labor Statistics (BLS) of the U.S. Department of Labor estimated that between 1982 and 1995 the fastest-growing job category would be computer service technicians, with an increase of almost 100 percent in numbers of jobs over that period (Silvestri et al. 1983: 46). But since there were only about 55,000 such jobs in 1982, the increase would amount to only about 53,000 jobs. Although jobs for building custodians are expected to grow by less than 28 percent over that period, almost 800,000 new jobs are forecast for that occupation, or about 15 times as many jobs as for computer service technicians.

In fact, the occupations likely to experience the largest growth in terms of absolute numbers of jobs are heavily dominated by such low-level service occupations as building custodians, cashiers, office clerks, sales clerks, waiters and waitresses, and nurses' aides and orderlies (Silvestri et al. 1983: 45). Different studies of the job market are consistent in finding that relatively few new jobs will be created in high-technology occupations, and that most job growth will occur in service occupations that pay relatively low wages and require little education (Riche et al. 1983; Rumberger & Levin 1984). The BLS has estimated that only about 6 percent of all jobs will be in technologically oriented occupations in 1995 (Riche et al. 1983), and that of the 40 occupations expected to contribute the most jobs to the economy, only about 25 percent will require college degrees (Silvestri et al. 1983: 44). Not only does job growth favor low-skill jobs rather than the highly skilled ones that are the object of the educational reforms, but even many existing jobs are being transformed by technology into ones that require fewer skills. Traditionally, typists were required to have knowledge of document formats, letter-perfect typing skills, and strong spelling skills. However, word processors can correct typing and spelling errors automatically and provide appropriate document formats from memory, enabling operation by persons who have only the most rudimentary typing skills. Increasingly, powerful software packages permit highly sophisticated applications to broad classes of problems with only minimal programming skills. Many highly automated offices have no programmer at all, since all computerized tasks can be done through "user-friendly menus" of options. Similar stories can be told for computer and computerized-machine repair, data processing, auto repair, design, drafting, and many other occupations (Levin & Rumberger 1983a, 1983b). Whereas earlier forms of automation allowed the replacement of physical labor, the newer technologies displace mental labor, enabling jobs to be eliminated and reduced in terms of their skill requirements. The failure of high technology to deliver on its job promises will undermine the incentives of students to meet the new demands of the schools and will provide increasing calls by workers for government intervention in job markets. This phenomenon will be further reinforced by the relatively high unemployment rates that are likely to be maintained in the 1980's. With the rapid economic recovery in 1983–84 fueled by large federal deficits and enormous increases in military spending, unemployment rates were expected to fall from a high of almost 11 percent at the end of 1982 to about 7.5 percent by the mid-1980's. But such a rate would be—by far—the highest U.S. unemployment rate in "prosperous" times during the entire postwar period, with over 8 million unemployed at the height of recovery. Among all youth the rates were in the 20 percent range, and among nonwhite youth they approached 50 percent. These high rates of unemployment will not be brought down by educational changes, since they largely reflect an inadequacy of jobs relative to job-seekers (Abraham 1983; Levin 1983a).

The neglect of minorities and the poor in the economy generally and the schools specifically will also serve to forge new social movements that will seek direct government intervention. The number of people in poverty in the United States rose substantially under the Reagan Administration, a result of policies accepting high levels of unemployment and promoting cutbacks in social programs. The fact that youngsters from economically disadvantaged and minority backgrounds have special educational needs that are ignored by the new educational agenda means that large numbers of such people will enter the labor market with little hope for social mobility. As long as such people can be relegated to the unemployed, employers may have little concern. But in some cities and regions minorities will represent a major share of the work force. In states such as California, it is expected that Hispanic students will become a majority in the public schools well before the turn of the century. And when school populations grow up, they become the new labor force. Thus, employers may join with these groups to push for greater equity in schooling, and there are likely to be new pressures on government by a broad coalition to promote greater equity in both labor markets and schools.

Finally, the general movement toward greater participation in the workplace associated with the overeducated worker (emphasized in Chapter 7) will also serve to undermine school reforms that ignore the democratic and egalitarian aspects of schooling. Groups that are dissatisfied with the present dynamic of schooling and the economy will likely join together with those concerned about the escalating military role of the United States, nuclear disarmament, conservation, energy, and many of the other dilemmas that have been created or exacerbated by present policies. Out of this political activity there will be new groups elected and pressures for new policies that support the broader-based concerns of a democracy, both inside the schools and in other parts of society and the economy.

Undoubtedly the most important message implied by our analysis is that democratic struggles are important for achieving the types of schools and economy that serve the broadest needs of our society and citizenry. Even under the present circumstances—when the quest for improved educational services for minorities, the poor, and the handicapped is under attack by conservative interests—it is the marshaling of social movements and democratic forces that places limits on retrenchment and makes the battle costly for the other side. But beyond this resistance, the struggle enables the tide of hegemony of the narrower interests of the wealthy to be countered in the courts, at the polls, in the media, and on the streets. Continuing struggle, together with the failures of existing policies to meet the larger concerns of a democracy, will increase the power of democratic coalitions for fairness, equity, and participation. Democratic struggles for just and meaningful schooling are effective counters to the economic forces that are attempting to gain primacy over American schools and the formation of our youth. A study of the past supports our optimism for the future.

Reference Matter

References Cited

Abraham, Katherine G. 1983. "Structural/Frictional vs. Deficient Demand Unemployment: Some New Evidence," *American Economic Review*, 83, no. 4 (Sept.), pp. 708–24.

Adizes, I. 1971. *Industrial Democracy: Yugoslav Style*. New York: Free Press.

Adler, Mortimer. 1982. *The Paideia Proposal: An Educational Manifesto*. New York: Macmillan.

Alchian, A., and H. Demsetz. 1972. "Production, Information Costs, and Economic Organization," *American Economic Review*, 62, no. 5 (Dec.), pp. 777–95.

Alexander, C. N., Jr., and E. Q. Campbell. 1964. "Peer Influences on Educational Aspirations and Attainments," *American Sociological Review*, 29, pp. 568–75.

Allen, Dwight, and Robert Bush. 1964. *A New Design for High School Education*. New York: McGraw-Hill.

Allen, Vernon L., ed. 1976. *Children as Teachers: Theory and Research on Tutoring*. New York: Academic.

Almond, Gabriel, and Sidney Verba. 1963. *The Civic Culture*. Princeton, N.J.: Princeton U.P.

Althusser, Louis. 1971. "Ideology and Ideological State Apparatuses," in *Lenin and Philosophy and Other Essays* (New York: Monthly Review Press), pp. 172–86.

Althusser, Louis, and C. Balibar. 1970. *Reading Capital*. London: New Left Books.

Anyon, Jean. 1983. "Intersections of Gender and Class: Accommodation and Resistance by Working-Class and Affluent Females to Contradictory Sex-Role Ideologies," in Stephen Walker and Len

Barton, eds., *Gender, Class and Education* (London: Falmer Press), pp. 19–37.

Apple, Michael W. 1979. *Ideology and Curriculum*. London: Routledge and Kegan Paul.

———. 1981. "Curricular Form and the Logic of Technical Control," *Economic and Industrial Democracy*, 2, no. 3 (Aug.), pp. 293–320.

———. 1982a. *Cultural and Economic Reproduction in Education*. London: Routledge and Kegan Paul.

———. 1982b. *Power and Ideology*. London: Routledge and Kegan Paul.

Argyris, Chris. 1957. *Personality and Organization*. New York: Harper.

———. 1964. *Integrating the Individual and the Organization*. New York: Wiley.

Aries, Philippe. 1962. *Centuries of Childhood*. New York: Knopf.

———. 1977. "The Family and the City," *Daedalus*, 106, no. 2, pp. 227–35.

Arnove, R. F., ed. 1976. *Educational Television*. New York: Praeger.

Aronowitz, Stanley. 1973. *False Promises*. New York: McGraw-Hill.

Arrow, Kenneth. 1951. *Social Choice and Individual Values*. New York: Wiley.

———. 1973. "Higher Education as a Filter," *Journal of Public Economics*, 2, no. 3 (July), pp. 193–216.

Averch, Harvey, *et al.* 1972. *How Effective Is Schooling? A Critical Review and Synthesis of Research Findings*. Santa Monica, Calif.: Rand.

Avineri, Schlomo. 1971. *The Social and Political Thought of Karl Marx*. New York: Cambridge U.P.

Baran, Paul, and Paul Sweezy. 1966. *Monopoly Capital*. New York: Monthly Review Press.

Barber, Randy. 1982. "Pension Funds in the United States: Issues of Investment and Control," *Economic and Industrial Democracy*, 3, no. 1 (Feb.), pp. 31–72.

Baron, Harold M. 1971. "Race and Status in School Spending: Chicago, 1961–1966," *The Journal of Human Resources*, 6, no. 1 (Winter), pp. 3–24.

Bastin, N. A. 1976. "Company Law: Some Problems of Worker Directors," *New Law Journal*, Mar. 11, pp. 271–73.

Batstone, Eric, and P. L. Davies. 1976. *Industrial Democracy: European Experience*. London: H.M.S.O.

Baudelot, Christian, and Roger Establet. 1971. *L'Ecole capitaliste en France*. Paris: Maspero.

Becker, Gary S. 1964. *Human Capital*. New York: Columbia U.P.

Beggs, David W., ed. 1964. *Team Teaching, Bold New Venture*. Bloomington, Ind.: Indiana U.P.

Behn, W., *et al.* 1974. "School Is Bad; Work Is Worse," *School Review*, 82, no. 1 (Nov.), pp. 49–68.

Berg, Ivar. 1970. *Education and Jobs: The Great Training Robbery*. New York: Praeger.

———. 1976. "Epilogue: Working Conditions and Management's Interests," in B.J. Widick, ed., *Auto Work and Its Discontents* (Baltimore, Md.: Johns Hopkins U.P.), pp. 96–107.

Bergmann, Barbara R. 1972. *Testimony Before the Joint Economic Committee, Hearings on Reducing Unemployment to 2 Percent*. Washington, D.C.: G.P.O.

Berman, P., and Milbrey McLaughlin. 1975. *Federal Programs Supporting Educational Change: The Findings in Review*, 4. Santa Monica, Calif.: Rand.

Bernstein, Basil. 1975. *Class, Codes and Control*. London: Routledge and Kegan Paul.

———. 1976. *Workplace Democratization: Its Internal Dynamics*. Kent, Ohio: Kent State U.P.

Bettelheim, Charles. 1975. *Cultural Revolution and Industrial Organization in China: Changes in Management and the Division of Labor*. New York: Monthly Review Press.

Binstock, Jeanne. 1970. "Survival in the American College Industry." Ph.D. diss., Brandeis Univ.

Bisconti, Ann S., and Lewis C. Solomon. 1976. *College Education on the Job: The Graduates' Viewpoint*. Bethlehem, Penn.: The CPC Foundation.

Blauner, Robert. 1964. *Alienation and Freedom*. Chicago: Univ. of Chicago Press.

Block, Fred. 1977. "The Ruling Class Does Not Rule," *Socialist Revolution*, 7, no. 3 (May–June), pp. 6–28.

———. 1980. "Beyond Relative Autonomy: State Managers as Historical Subjects," in R. Miliband and J. Saville, eds., *Socialist Register* (London: Merlin), pp. 227–42.

Block, James H. 1973. "Mastery Learning in the Classroom: An Overview of Recent Research." Mimeo.

Block, James H., ed. 1974. *Schools, Society, and Mastery Learning*. New York: Holt, Rinehart, and Winston.

Bloom, Benjamin S. 1976. *Human Characteristics and School Learning*. New York: McGraw-Hill.

Bluestone, Barry, and Bennett Harrison. 1982. *The Deindustrialization of America*. New York: Basic.

Blumberg, Paul. 1968. *Industrial Democracy: The Sociology of Participation*. New York: Schocken.

Bobbio, Norberto. 1979. "Gramsci and the Conception of Civil Society," in Chantal Mouffe, ed., *Gramsci and Marxist Theory* (London: Routledge and Kegan Paul), pp. 21–47.

Bordua, D. M. 1960. "Educational Aspirations and Parental Stress on College," *Social Forces*, 38, pp. 262–69.

Bottomore, Tom. 1966. *Classes in Modern Society*. New York: Pantheon.

Bourdieu, P., and J.-C. Passeron. 1977. *Reproduction*. Beverly Hills, Calif.: Sage.

Bowen, W. G., and T. A. Finegan. 1969. *The Economics of Labor Force Participation*. Chicago: Univ. of Chicago Press.

Bowles, Samuel. 1972. "Contradiction in U.S. Higher Education," in James Weaver, ed., *Political Economy: Radical vs. Orthodox Approaches*. Boston: Allyn and Bacon.

Bowles, Samuel, and Herbert Gintis. 1972–73. "IQ in the U.S. Class Structure," *Social Policy* (Nov./Dec.), (Jan./Feb.), pp. 1–32.

———. 1975. "Class Power and Alienated Labor," *Monthly Review* (Mar.), pp. 9–25.

———. 1976. *Schooling in Capitalist America*. New York: Basic.

———. 1982. "The Crisis of Liberal Democratic Capitalism: The Case of the United States," *Politics and Society*, 11, no. 1, pp. 51–93.

Boyer, Ernest L. 1983. *High School: A Report on Secondary Education in America*. New York: Harper and Row.

Braverman, Harry. 1974. *Labor and Monopoly Capital*. New York: Monthly Review Press.

Brayfield, Arthur H., and Walter H. Crockett. 1955. "Employee Attitudes and Employee Performance," *Psychological Bulletin*, 52, pp. 396–424.

Bright, James. 1958. "Does Automation Raise Skill Requirements?," *Harvard Business Review*, 36, no. 4 (July/Aug.), pp. 85–98.

———. 1966. "The Relationship of Increasing Automation and Skill Requirements," in *The Employment Impact of Technological Change* (Washington, D.C.: G.P.O.), pp. 207–21. The Report of the National Commission on Technology, Automation, and Economic Progress, Appendix Vol. 2.

Bureau of National Affairs, Inc. 1970. *Turnover and Job Satisfaction*. Personnel Policies Forum, Survey No. 91. Washington, D.C.

Burton, Nancy W., and Lyle V. Jones. 1982. "Recent Trends in Achievement Levels of Black and White Youth," *Education Researcher*, 11, no. 4 (Apr.), pp. 10–14.

Cain, Glen G. 1966. *Married Women in the Labor Force*. Chicago: Univ. of Chicago Press.

Caja Laboral Popular. 1975. *Memoria 1974*. Mondragon, Spain.

California Department of Education. 1975. *Profiles of School District*

Performance 1974–75: A Guide to Interpretation. Sacramento, Calif.

California Department of Finance. 1982. *California Statistical Abstract*. Sacramento, Calif.

Callahan, Raymond. 1962. *Education and the Cult of Efficiency*. Chicago: Univ. of Chicago Press.

Carnegie Commission on Higher Education. 1973a. *College Graduates and Jobs*. New York: McGraw-Hill.

———. 1973b. *Higher Education: Who Pays? Who Benefits? Who Should Pay?* New York: McGraw-Hill.

———. 1973c. *Toward a Learning Society: Alternative Channels to Life, Work and Service*. New York: McGraw-Hill.

Carnoy, Martin. 1974. *Education as Cultural Imperialism*. New York: McKay.

———. 1980. "Segmented Labor Markets," in M. Carnoy, H. Levin, and K. King, eds., *Education, Work and Employment—II*. Paris: I.I.E.P., pp. 9–122.

Carnoy, Martin, and Henry M. Levin. 1975. "Evaluation of Educational Media: Some Issues," *Instructional Science*, 4, pp. 385–406.

———. 1976a. *The Limits of Educational Reform*. New York: McKay.

———. 1976b. "Workers' Triumph: The Meriden Experiment," *Working Papers* (Winter), pp. 47–56.

Carnoy, Martin, and Derek Shearer. 1980. *Economic Democracy: The Challenge of the 1980's*. White Plains, N.Y.: Sharpe.

Carnoy, Martin, and Jorge Werthein. 1977. "Socialist Ideology and the Transformation of Cuban Education," in J. Karabel and A. H. Halsey, eds., *Power and Ideology in Education* (New York: Oxford U.P.), pp. 573–89.

Carnoy, Martin, Robert Girling, and Russell W. Rumberger. 1976. *Education and Public Sector Employment*. Palo Alto, Calif.: Center for Economic Studies.

Carnoy, Martin, Derek Shearer, and Russell Rumberger. 1983. *A New Social Contract: The Economy and Government After Reagan*. New York: Harper and Row.

Carter, Michael, and Martin Carnoy. 1976. "Theories of Labor Markets and Income Distribution." Palo Alto, Calif.: Center for Economic Studies, mimeo.

Cartter, Allan M. 1976. *Ph.D.'s and the Academic Labor Market*. New York: McGraw-Hill.

Charters, W. W., Jr. 1973. *Measuring the Implementation of Differentiated Staffing*. Eugene, Ore.: Center for the Advanced Study of Ed. Adm.

Childs, John L. 1939. "The Educational Philosophy of John Dewey," in P. Schilpp, ed., *The Philosophy of John Dewey* (The Library of Living Philosophers, vol. 1 [Evanston, Ill.: Northwestern U.P.]), pp. 419–43.

Chiswick, Barry, and Jacob Mincer. 1972. "Time Series in Personal Income Inequality in the United States from 1939, with Projections to 1985," *Journal of Political Economy*, 80, no. 3 (May/June), pp. 534–66.

Clark, Burton. 1960. "The 'Cooling Out' Function in Higher Education," *The American Journal of Sociology*, 65, no. 6 (May), pp. 569–77.

Cohen, Arthur. 1971. "Stretching Pre-College Education," *Social Policy*, 2, no. 1 (May–June), pp. 5–13.

Cohen, David K. 1970. "Politics and Research: Evaluation of Social Action Programs," *Reviews of Educational Research*, 40, no. 2 (Apr.), pp. 213–38.

Coleman, James S. 1968. "The Concept of Equality of Educational Opportunity," *Harvard Educational Review*, 38, no. 1, pp. 7–22.

Coleman, James S., Thomas Hoffer, and Sally Kilgore. 1982. *High School Achievement: Public, Catholic, and Private Schools Compared*. New York: Basic.

Coleman, James S., *et al.* 1966. *Equality of Educational Opportunity*. Washington, D.C.: G.P.O.

———. 1974. *Youth: Transition to Adulthood*. Chicago: Univ. of Chicago Press.

College Entrance Examination Board. 1980. *Undergraduate Admissions. The Realities of Institutional Policies, Practices, and Procedures*. New York: C.E.E.B.

Colletti, Lucio. 1972. *From Rousseau to Lenin: Studies in Ideology and Society*. New York: Monthly Review Press.

Cook, Thomas. 1975. *Sesame Street Revisited*. New York: Russell Sage Foundation.

Coons, J., W. Clune, and Stephen Sugarman. 1970. *Private Wealth and Public Education*. Cambridge, Mass.: Belknap.

Coons, John E., and Stephen D. Sugarman. 1978. *Education by Choice*. Berkeley, Calif.: Univ. of Calif. Press.

Cremin, Lawrence A. 1964. *The Transformation of the School*. New York: Vintage.

———. 1976. *Public Education*. New York: Basic.

Curti, Merle. 1963. *The Social Ideas of American Educators*. Totowa, N.J.: Littlefield.

Dahl, Robert. 1956. *A Preface to Democratic Theory*. Chicago: Univ. of Chicago Press.

Davis, Louis, and James Taylor. 1972. *Design of Jobs*. Harmondsworth, Eng.: Penguin.

Davis, Louis E., and Albert B. Cherns, eds. 1975. *The Quality of Working Life*. New York: Free Press.

Davis, Louis E., and Eric L. Trist. 1976. "Improving the Quality of Work Life: Sociotechnical Case Studies," in J. O'Toole, ed., *Work and the Quality of Life* (Cambridge, Mass.: MIT Press), Chap. 11.

Dearman, Nancy B., and Valena White Plisko, eds. 1982. *The Condition of Education: 1982 Edition*. Washington, D.C.: Nat'l Center for Ed. Statistics.

DeGrasse, Robert W., Jr. 1983. *Military Expansion, Economic Decline*. New York: Council on Economic Priorities.

Denison, Edward. 1962. *The Sources of Economic Growth in the United States and the Alternatives Before Us*. New York: Committee for Economic Development.

――――. 1979. *Accounting for Slower Economic Growth: The United States in the 1970's*. Washington, D.C.: Brookings.

Department of Trade [Great Britain]. 1977. *Report of the Committee of Inquiry on Industrial Democracy* (The Bullock Report). London: H.M.S.O.

Dewey, John. 1966. *Democracy and Education*. New York: Free Press.

Diamond, Daniel, and Hrach Bedrosian. 1970. *Hiring Standards and Job Performance*. U.S. Department of Labor, Manpower Research Monograph no. 18. Washington, D.C.: G.P.O.

Doeringer, Peter, and Michael Piore. 1971. *Internal Labor Markets and Manpower Training*. Lexington, Mass.: Heath Lexington.

Domhoff, G. William. 1967. *Who Rules America?* New York: Prentice-Hall.

Draper, Hal. 1977. *Karl Marx's Theory of Revolution, Vol. I: State and Bureaucracy*. New York: Monthly Review Press.

Dreeben, Robert. 1968. *On What Is Learned in School*. Reading, Mass.: Addison-Wesley.

Drucker, Peter. 1976. *The Unseen Revolution: How Pension Fund Socialism Came to America*. New York: Harper and Row.

Duncan, Greg. 1976. "Earnings Functions and Nonpecuniary Benefits," *Journal of Human Resources*, 11 (Fall), pp. 462–83.

Duncan, Otis Dudley, David L. Featherman, and Beverly Duncan. 1972. *Socioeconomic Background and Achievement*. New York: Seminar.

Ebel, Robert L. 1951. "Estimation of the Reliability of Ratings," *Psychometrika*, 16, pp. 407–24.

――――. 1978. "The Case for Norm-Referenced Measurements," *Educational Researcher*, 7, no. 11 (Dec.), pp. 3–5.

Economic Report of the President 1983. Washington, D.C.: G.P.O.

Edson, Charles H. 1984. "Risking the Nation: Historical Dimensions on Survival and Educational Reform," *Issues in Education* (June).

Education Commission of the States, Task Force on Education for Economic Growth. 1983. *Action for Excellence*. Denver, Colo.

Edwards, Richard C. 1976. "Individual Traits and Organization Incentives: What Makes A 'Good' Worker?," *Journal of Human Resources* 11, no. 1 (Spring), pp. 51–68.

————. 1979. *Contested Terrain: The Transformation of the Workplace in the 20th Century*. New York: Basic.

Ehly, Stewart W., and Stephen C. Larsen. 1980. *Peer Tutoring for Individualized Instruction*. Boston: Allyn and Bacon.

Eisner, Elliot W. 1973. *English Primary Schools: Some Observations and Assessments*. Stanford, Calif.: Stanford University School of Education.

Elbing, Alvar O., Herman Gadon, and John R. M. Gordon. 1975. "Flexible Working Hours: The Missing Link," *California Management Review*, 17, no. 3 (Spring), pp. 50–57.

Emery, F. E., and E. Thorsrud. 1969. *Form and Content of Industrial Democracy*. London: Tavistock.

Emery, F. E., and E. L. Trist. 1960. "Socio-technical Systems," in C. W. Churchman and M. Verhuls, eds., *Management Sciences Models and Techniques* (London: Pergamon), vol. 2, pp. 83–97.

————. 1969. "The Causal Context of Organizational Environments," in F. E. Emery, ed., *Systems Thinking* (London: Penguin), pp. 241–57.

Employment and Training Report of the President. 1976. Washington, D.C.: G.P.O.

Engles, Frederick [Friedrich Engels]. 1968 [1884]. *The Origin of the Family, Private Property, and the State*. New York: International.

Fagen, Richard R. 1969. *The Transformation of Political Culture in Cuba*. Stanford, Calif.: Stanford U.P.

Featherstone, Joseph. 1971. *Schools Where Children Learn*. New York: Liveright.

Field, Alexander J. 1974. "Educational Reform and Manufacturing Development in Mid-Nineteenth-Century Massachusetts." Ph.D. diss., Dept. of Economics, Univ. of Calif., Berkeley.

————. 1976. "Educational Expansion in Mid-Nineteenth-Century Massachusetts: Human Capital Formation or Structural Reinforcement?," *Harvard Educational Review*, 46, no. 4, pp. 521–52.

Fine, Keitha Sapsin. 1973. "Worker Participation in Israel," in G. Hunnius, ed., *Workers Control* (New York: Vintage Books), pp. 226–64.

Flanagan, Robert J., *et al.* 1974. "Worker Discontent and Workplace

Behavior." Berkeley, Calif.: Inst. of Indus. Relations, U.C. reprint 388.

Foucault, Michel. 1978. *Discipline and Punish*. New York: Random House.

Fraser, Stewart E. 1972. *Chinese Education and Society*. White Plains, N.Y.: International Arts & Sciences Press.

Freeman, Richard B. 1976. *The Over-Educated American*. New York: Academic.

Friedenberg, Edgar Z. 1963. *Coming of Age in America*. New York: Random House.

Friedman, Milton. 1962. "The Role of Government in Education," *Capitalism and Freedom* (Chicago: Univ. of Chicago Press), Chap. 6.

Fromm, Erich. 1968. *The Revolution of Hope*. New York: Harper and Row.

Fromm, Gary. 1976. "Forecasts of Long-run Economic Growth," in *U.S. Economic Growth from 1976 to 1986: Prospects, Problems and Patterns* (Washington, D.C.: G.P.O.), pp. 1–37.

Fuchs, Victor R. 1968. *The Service Economy*. New York: Nat'l Bureau of Econ. Research.

Furstenberg, Friedrich. 1977. "West German Experience with Industrial Democracy," *The Annals*, 431 (May), pp. 44–53.

"G.M. Car Project to Get Union Input." 1983. *San Francisco Examiner*, Dec. 20, p. C2.

Gallup, George H. 1977. "Ninth Annual Gallup Poll of the Public's Attitudes Toward the Public Schools," *Phi Delta Kappan* (Sept.), pp. 33–48.

Genovese, Eugene. 1965. *The Political Economy of Slavery*. New York: Random House.

Gintis, Herbert. 1971. "Education, Technology and the Characteristics of Worker Productivity," *American Economic Review*, 61, no. 2 (May), pp. 266–79.

Giroux, Henry A. 1981. *Ideology, Culture, and the Process of Schooling*. Philadelphia: Temple U.P.

Gold, D., C. Lo, and E.O. Wright. 1975. "Recent Developments in Marxist Theories of the State," *Monthly Review*, no. 5 (Oct.), pp. 29–43; no. 6 (Nov.), pp. 36–51.

Gollop, F., and W. Jorgensen. 1980. "U.S. Productivity Growth by Industry, 1947–1973," in J. Kendrick and B. Vaccara, eds., *New Developments in Productivity Measurement and Analysis* (Chicago: Univ. of Chicago Press), pp. 17–124.

Goodlad, John I., and Kenneth Rehage. 1965. "Unscrambling the Vocabulary of School Organization," in Maurie Hillson, ed., *Change and Innovation in Elementary School Organization* (New York: Holt, Rinehart, and Winston), pp. 6–11.

Goodman, Paul. 1956. *Growing Up Absurd.* New York: Random House.

———. 1964. *Compulsory Mis-Education.* New York: Horizon.

Gordon, David M. 1971. *Problems in Political Economy: An Urban Perspective.* Lexington, Mass.: Heath.

———. 1972. *Theories of Poverty and Underemployment.* Lexington, Mass.: Lexington Books.

Gordon, David, Richard Edwards, and Michael Reich. 1982. *Segmentated Work: Divided Workers.* New York: Cambridge U.P.

Gordon, David M., *et al.* 1973. "A Theory of Labor Market Segmentation," *American Economic Review*, 63, no. 2 (May), pp. 359–65.

Gordon, M. S. 1974. "The Changing Labor Market for College Graduates," in M. Gordon, ed., *Higher Education and the Labor Market* (New York: McGraw-Hill), Chap. 2.

Gorz, Andre. 1968. *Strategy for Labor.* Boston: Beacon.

———. 1973. *Socialism and Revolution.* New York: Anchor.

Graham, Patricia A. 1967. *Progressive Education: From Arcady to Academe.* New York: Teachers College Press.

Gramsci, Antonio. 1971. *Selections from Prison Notebooks.* New York: International.

Grant, W. Vance, and Leo J. Eiden. 1982. *Digest of Education Statistics.* National Center for Education Statistics. Washington, D.C.: G.P.O.

Greenbaum, Joan M. 1979. *In the Name of Efficiency.* Philadelphia, Penn.: Temple U.P.

Greenberg, Edward S. 1975. "The Consequences of Worker Participation: A Clarification of the Theoretical Literature," *Social Science Quarterly* (Sept.), pp. 191–209.

———. 1984. "Producer Cooperatives and Democratic Theory: The Case of the Plywood Firms," in Robert Jackall and Henry M. Levin, eds., *Worker Cooperatives in America.* Berkeley, Calif.: Univ. of Calif. Press.

Griesemer, J. Lynn, and Cornelius Butler. 1983. *Education Under Study.* Chelmsford, Mass.: Northeast Regional Exchange, Inc.

Griliches, Z., and W. Mason. 1972. "Education, Income, and Ability," *Journal of Political Economy* (Supplement; May/June), pp. S74–103.

Gross, Neal, *et al.* 1971. *Implementing Organizational Innovations.* New York: Basic.

Grubb, W. Norton, and Marvin Lazerson. 1975. "Rally 'Round the Workplace: Continuities and Fallacies in Career Education," *Harvard Educational Review*, 45, no. 4 (Nov.), pp. 451–74.

Gustavson, Paul, and James C. Taylor. 1982. "Socio-technical Design and New Forms of Work Organization: Integrated Circuit Fabrication." Geneva: International Labor Office, mimeo.

Gutman, Herbert. 1977. *Work, Culture and Society in Industrializing America*. New York: Vintage.

Guzzo, Richard A., and Jeffrey S. Bondy. 1983. *A Guide to Productivity Experiments in the United States, 1976–81*. New York: Pergamon.

Gwartney, James D., and James E. Long. 1978. "The Relative Earnings of Blacks and Other Minorities," *Industrial and Labor Relations Review*, 31 (Apr.), pp. 336–46.

Gyllenhammer, Pehr G. 1977. *People at Work*. Boston: Addison-Wesley.

Haber, Samuel. 1964. *Efficiency and Uplift: Scientific Management in the Progressive Era, 1890–1920*. Chicago: Univ. of Chicago Press.

Haller, A. O., and E. C. Butterworth. 1960. "Peer Influences on Levels of Occupational and Educational Aspiration," *Social Forces*, 38, pp. 289–95.

Hansen, Lee, and Burton Weisbrod. 1969. *Benefits, Costs and Finance of Higher Education*. Chicago: Markham.

Harnischfeger, A., and D. E. Wiley. 1975. "Achievement Test Score Decline: Do We Need to Worry?" Chicago: ML-Group for Policy Studies in Education, CEMREL, Inc.

Harnqvist, Kjell. 1978. *Individual Demand for Education*. Paris: O.E.C.D.

Hartmann, Heidi. 1979. "Capitalism, Patriarchy, and Job Segregation by Sex," in Zillah R. Eisenstein, ed., *Capitalist Patriarchy and the Case for Socialist Feminism* (New York: Monthly Review Press), pp. 206–47.

Hauser, R. M. 1972. "Disaggregating a Social-Psychological Model of Educational Attainment," *Social Science Research*, 1 (June), pp. 159–88.

Hawkins, John N. 1974. *Mao Tse Tung and Education*. Hamden, Conn.: Shoe String.

Hays, Samuel. 1964. "The Politics of Reform in Municipal Government in the Progressive Era," *Pacific Northwest Quarterly* (Oct.), pp. 157–69.

Hedges, Janice. 1973. "Absence from Work—A Look at Some National Data," *Monthly Labor Review* (July), pp. 24–30.

———. 1975. "Unscheduled Absence from Work—An Update," *Monthly Labor Review* (Aug.), pp. 36–39.

Henle, Peter. 1974. "Economic Effects: Reviewing the Evidence," in J. M. Rosow, ed., *The Worker and the Job* (Englewood Cliffs, N.J.: Prentice-Hall), pp. 119–44.

Herbst, P. G. 1962. *Autonomous Group Functioning*. London: Tavistock Institute.

Hernstein, Richard. 1973. *IQ in the Meritocracy*. Boston: Atlantic Monthly Press.

Herrick, Neal Q. 1975. *The Quality of Work and Its Outcomes: Estimating Potential Increases in Labor Productivity*. Columbus, Ohio: Academy for Contemporary Problems.

Herzberg, Frederick. 1968. *Work and the Nature of Man*. London: Staples.

Hirsch, Joachim. 1976. "Woram Scheitert Sladiche Reformpolitik?," *Betrifft: Erziehung* (Jan.).

————. 1978. "The State Apparatus and Social Reproduction: Elements of a Theory of the Bourgeois State," in J. Holloway and S. Picciotto, eds., *State and Capital* (London: Edward Arnold), pp. 57–107.

Hirschman, Albert O. 1970. *Exit, Voice, and Loyalty*. Cambridge, Mass.: Harvard U.P.

————. 1977. *The Passions and the Interests*. Princeton, N.J.: Princeton U.P.

Hobbes, Thomas. 1968 [1651]. *Leviathan*. Ed. C. B. MacPherson. New York: Pelican.

Holloway, J., and Sol Picciotto. 1978. *State and Capital: A Marxist Debate*. London: Edward Arnold.

Holt, John. 1964. *How Children Fail*. New York: Pitman.

Horvat, Branko. 1976. *The Yugoslav Economic System*. White Plains, N.Y.: Sharpe.

House, James S. 1974. "The Effects of Occupational Stress on Physical Health," in James O'Toole, ed., *Work and the Quality of Life* (Cambridge, Mass.: MIT Press), pp. 145–70.

Hoyle, M. H. 1973. "Transformations—An Introduction and Bibliography," in *International Statistical Review*, 41, no. 2 (Aug.), pp. 203–23.

Hoyt, Kenneth, *et al.* 1972. *Career Education: What It Is and How To Do It*. Salt Lake City, Utah: Olympus.

Hyman, Richard. 1973. "Industrial Conflict and the Political Economy: Trends of the 60's and Prospects for the 70's," *The Socialist Register, 1973* (London: Merlin Press), pp. 101–52.

————. 1974. "Workers' Control and Revolutionary Theory," in Ralph Miliband and John Saville, eds., *The Socialist Register, 1974* (London: Merlin Press), pp. 241–78.

Illich, Ivan. 1971. *De-Schooling Society*. Garden City, N.Y.: Doubleday.

Inkeles, Alex. 1966. "The Socialization of Competence," *Harvard Educational Review*, 36, no. 3 (Summer), pp. 265–83.

Inkeles, Alex, and David H. Smith. 1974. *Becoming Modern.* Cambridge, Mass.: Harvard U.P.

Jackall, Robert, and Joyce Crain. 1984. "The Shape of the Small Producer Cooperative Movement," in Robert Jackall and Henry M. Levin, eds., *Worker Cooperatives in America* (Berkeley, Calif.: Univ. of Calif. Press).

Jackall, Robert, and Henry M. Levin, eds. 1984. *Worker Cooperatives in America.* Berkeley, Calif.: Univ. of Calif. Press.

James, Thomas, and Henry M. Levin. 1983. *Public Dollars for Private Schools: The Case of Tuition Tax Credits.* Philadelphia, Penn.: Temple U.P.

Jamison, Dean T., and Lawrence J. Lau. 1982. *Farmer Education and Farm Efficiency.* Baltimore, Md.: Johns Hopkins U.P.

Jencks, Christopher, *et al.* 1972. *Inequality: A Reassessment of the Effect of Family and Schooling in America.* New York: Basic.

———. 1979. *Who Gets Ahead? The Determinants of Economic Success in America.* New York: Basic.

Jenkins, David. 1974. *Job Power.* Baltimore, Md.: Penguin.

Jensen, C. M., and W. H. Meckling. 1976. "Theory of the Firm: Managerial Behavior, Agency Costs and Ownership Structure," *Journal of Financial Economics*, 3 (Oct.), pp. 305–60.

Johnson, A. G., and W. F. Whyte. 1977. "The Mondragon System of Worker Production Cooperatives," *Industrial and Labor Relations Review*, 31, no. 1, pp. 18–30.

Johnson, T. L. 1962. *Collective Bargaining in Sweden.* London: Allen and Unwin.

Joint Economic Committee, U.S. Congress. 1976. *Broadening the Ownership of New Capital: ESOPs and Other Alternatives.* Washington, D.C.: G.P.O.

Jones, Derek C. 1977. "The Economics and Industrial Relations of Producer Cooperatives in the United States, 1791–1939," *Economic Analysis and Workers' Management*, nos. 3–4, pp. 295–317.

Jones, Derek C., and Jan Svejnar, eds. 1982. *Participatory and Self-Managed Firms.* Lexington, Mass.: Lexington Books.

Kaestle, Carl. 1973. *Joseph Lancaster and the Monitorial School Movement.* New York: Teachers College Press.

Kaestle, Carl F., and Maris A. Vinovskis. 1980. *Education and Social Change in Nineteenth-Century Massachusetts.* Cambridge, Eng.: Cambridge U.P.

Kagan, Jerome. 1977. "The Child in the Family," *Daedalus*, 106, no. 2, pp. 33–55.

Kahl, Joseph A. 1953. "Educational and Occupational Aspirations of

'Common Man' Boys," *Harvard Educational Review*, 23, pp. 186–203.

Kalleberg, Arne, and Aage Sorensen. 1973. "The Measurement of the Effects of Overtraining on Job Attitudes," *Sociological Methods and Research*, 2, no. 2 (Nov.), pp. 215–38.

Karabel, Jerome. 1972. "Community Colleges and Social Stratification," *Harvard Educational Review*, 42, no. 4 (Nov.), pp. 521–62.

Kasl, Stanislav V. 1974. "Work and Mental Health," in James O'Toole, ed., *Work and the Quality of Life* (Cambridge, Mass.: MIT Press), pp. 171–96.

Katz, Michael B. 1968. *The Irony of Early School Reform*. Boston: Beacon.

———. 1971. *Class, Bureaucracy and Schools: The Illusion of Educational Change in America*. New York: Praeger.

———. 1980. "Hardcore Educational Historiography." Review of Carl F. Kaestle and Maris A. Vinovskis, *Education and Social Change in Nineteenth-Century Massachusetts*, in *Reviews in American History* (Dec.), pp. 504–10.

Katzell, Raymond A., and Daniel Yankelovich. 1975. *Work, Productivity, and Job Satisfaction*. New York: Psychological Corp.

Katzell, Raymond A., Penny Bienstock, and Paul H. Faerstein. 1977. *A Guide to Worker Productivity Experiments in the United States, 1971–75*. Work in America Institute. New York: N.Y.U. Press.

Kay, Emanuel. 1974. "Middle Management," in James O'Toole, ed., *Work and the Quality of Life* (Cambridge, Mass.: MIT Press), pp. 106–29.

Kelly, John E. 1982. *Scientific Management, Job Redesign, and Work Performance*. New York: Academic.

Kemerer, Frank R., and Kenneth L. Deutsch. 1979. *Constitutional Rights and Student Life*. St. Paul, Minn.: West.

Ketchum, Lyle D. 1975. "A Case Study of Diffusion," in Louis E. Davis and Albert B. Cherns, eds., *The Quality of Working Life* (New York: Free Press), Chap. 11.

Kilpatrick, William. 1939. "Dewey's Influence on Education," in P. Schilpp, ed., *The Philosophy of John Dewey* (The Library of Living Philosophers, vol. 1 [Evanston, Ill.: Northwestern U.P.]), pp. 447–73.

Kirst, Michael W., and Walter I. Garms. 1980. "The Political Environment of School Finance Policy in the 1980's," in James W. Guthrie, ed., *School Finance Policies and Practices* (Cambridge, Mass.: Ballinger), pp. 47–75.

Kluger, Richard. 1975. *Simple Justice*. New York: Knopf. 2 vols.

Knowles, Asa S., *et al.* 1972. *Handbook of Cooperative Education*. San Francisco: Jossey-Bass.

Kohn, Melvin L. 1959. "Social Class and Parental Values," *American Journal of Sociology*, 64, pp. 337–51.

———. 1969. *Class and Conformity: A Study in Values*. Homewood, Ill.: Dorsey.

Kolko, Gabriel. 1963. *The Triumph of Conservatism*. New York: Free Press.

Kozol, Jonathan. 1967. *Death at an Early Age*. Boston: Houghton-Mifflin.

———. 1972. *Free Schools*. Boston: Houghton-Mifflin.

Kremen, Bennett. 1972. "No Pride in This Dust," *Dissent* (Winter), pp. 21–28.

Krug, Edward. 1969. *The Shaping of the American High School*, vol. 1. Madison, Wisc.: Univ of Wisc. Press.

Kurland, N., ed. 1977. *Entitlement Studies* (NIE Papers in Education and Work, no. 4). Washington, D.C.: National Institute of Education.

Landes, William W., and Lewis C. Solmon. 1972. "Compulsory Schooling Legislation: An Economic Analysis of Law and Social Change in the Nineteenth Century," *The Journal of Economic History*, 32, no. 1 (Mar.), pp. 54–91.

Leacock, Eleanor. 1969. *Teaching and Learning in City Schools*. New York: Basic.

Leifer, Aimee Dorr, *et al.* 1974. "Children's Television: More Than Mere Entertainment," *Harvard Educational Review*, 44, no. 2 (May), pp. 213–45.

Leiner, Marvin. 1973. "Major Developments in Cuban Education," Warner Publications, Module 264, pp. 1–21.

Levin, Henry M. 1974a. "The Economic Implications of Mastery Learning," in J. H. Block, ed., *Schools, Society and Mastery Learning* (New York: Holt, Rinehart, and Winston), pp. 75–88.

———. 1974b. "Effects of Expenditure Increases on Educational Resource Allocation and Effectiveness," in John Pincus, ed., *School Finance in Transition* (Cambridge, Mass.: Ballinger).

———. 1977. "A Decade of Policy Development in Improving Education and Training of Low Income Populations," in R. Haveman, ed., *A Decade of Federal Antipoverty Programs: Achievements, Failures and Lessons* (New York: Academic), Chap. 4.

———. 1978. "Educational Performance Standards: Image or Substance?," *Journal of Educational Measurement*, 15, no. 4 (Winter), pp. 309–19.

———. 1980. "Educational Production Theory and Teacher Inputs," in Charles Bidwell and Douglas Windham, eds., *The Analysis of Educational Productivity: Issues in Macroanalysis* (Cambridge, Mass.: Ballinger), vol. 2, Chap. 5.

―――. 1983a. "The Workplace: Employment and Business Interventions," in E. Seidman, ed., *Handbook of Social Intervention* (Beverly Hills, Calif.: Sage), pp. 499–521.

―――. 1983b. "Youth Unemployment and Its Educational Consequences," *Educational Evaluation and Policy Analysis*, 2, no. 2 (Summer), pp. 231–47.

―――. 1983c. "Raising Employment and Productivity with Producer Co-operatives," in Paul Streeten and Harry Maier, eds., *Human Resources, Employment and Development* (London: Macmillan), vol. 2, pp. 310–28.

―――. 1984. "ESOPs and the Financing of Worker Cooperatives," in R. Jackall and H. Levin, eds., *Worker Cooperatives in America* (Berkeley, Calif.: Univ. of Calif. Press).

Levin, Henry M., ed. 1970. *Community Control of Schools.* Washington, D.C.: Brookings Institution.

Levin, Henry M., and Russell W. Rumberger. 1983a. "The Educational Implications of High Technology." IFG Project Report 83-A4. Stanford, Calif.: Institute for Research on Educational Finance and Governance.

―――. 1983b. "Low-Skill Future of High Tech," *Technology Review*, 86, no. 6 (Aug./Sept.), pp. 18–21.

Levin, Henry M., and Hans G. Schutze. 1983a. "Economic and Political Dimensions of Recurrent Education," in H. M. Levin and H. G. Schutze, eds., *Financing Recurrent Education* (Beverly Hills, Calif.: Sage), Chap. 19.

Levin, Henry M., and Hans Schutze, eds. 1983b. *Financing Recurrent Education.* Beverly Hills, Calif.: Sage.

Lipset, Seymour Martin. 1963. *Political Man.* New York: Doubleday.

―――. 1972. "Social Mobility and Equal Opportunity," *Public Interest*, no. 29 (Fall), pp. 90–108.

Locke, John. 1955 [1690]. *On Civil Government.* Chicago: Regnery.

Lockwood, George B. 1971. *The New Harmony Movement.* New York: Dover.

Logue, John. 1981. "Saab/Trollhattan: Reforming Work Life on the Shop Floor," *Working Life in Sweden* (New York: Swedish Information Service), no. 23 (June).

Lucas, R. 1972. "Working Conditions, Wage Rates and Human Capital: A Hedonic Study." Ph.D. Diss., MIT.

Luft, Harold S. 1971. "New England Textile Labor in the 1840's: From Yankee Farmgirl to Irish Immigrant." Unpublished paper, Harvard Univ.

Lupton, Tom, ed. 1972. *Payment Systems.* Harmondsworth, Eng.: Penguin.

Lyons, Thomas F. 1972. "Turnover and Absenteeism: A Review of Relationship and Shared Correlates," *Personnel Psychology*, 25, no. 2, pp. 271–81.

MacEwan, Arthur. 1975. "Incentives, Equality, and Power in Revolutionary Cuba," *Socialist Revolution*, no. 23 (Apr.), pp. 117–30.

MacKenzie, Gavin. 1973. *The Aristocracy of Labor: The Position of Skilled Craftsmen in the American Class Structure*. London: Cambridge U.P.

Main, Jackson T. 1965. *The Social Structure of Revolutionary America*. Princeton, N.J.: Princeton U.P.

Marglin, Steve. 1974. "What Do Bosses Do?," *Review of Radical Political Economics* (Summer), pp. 60–112.

Marland, Sidney P. 1974. *Career Education: A Proposal for Reform*. New York: McGraw-Hill.

Marx, Karl. 1964. *Capital*, vol. 1, ed. F. Engels. New York: International.

Marx, Karl, and Friedrich Engels. 1964. *The German Ideology*. Moscow: Progress.

Mayo, John K., *et al.* 1976. *Educational Reform with Television: The El Salvador Experience*. Stanford, Calif.: Stanford U.P.

Meidner, Rudolf, and Rolf Andersson. 1973. "The Overall Impact of an Active Labor Market Policy in Sweden," in Lloyd Ulman, ed., *Manpower Programs in the Policy Mix* (Baltimore, Md.: Johns Hopkins U.P.), pp. 117–58.

———. 1978. *Employee Investment Funds*. Boston: Allen and Unwin.

Melaragno, Ralph J., and Gerald Newmark. 1971. "The Tutorial Community Concept," in James W. Guthrie and Edward Wynne, eds., *New Models for American Education* (Englewood Cliffs, N.J.: Prentice-Hall), pp. 98–113.

Messerli, Jonathan. 1972. *Horace Mann: A Biography*. New York: Knopf.

Meyer, John W. 1970. "The Charter: Conditions of Diffuse Socialization in Schools," in W. R. Scott, ed., *Social Processes and Social Structures* (New York: Holt, Rinehart, and Winston), pp. 564–78.

Meyer, Robert, and David A. Wise. 1982. "High School Preparation and Early Labor Force Experience," in Richard B. Freeman and David A. Wise, eds., *The Youth Labor Market Problem: Its Nature, Causes, and Consequences* (Chicago: Univ. of Chicago Press), Chap. 9.

Miliband, Ralph. 1969. *The State in Capitalist Society*. London: Weidenfeld and Nicholson.

———. 1970. "The Capitalist State: Reply to Nicos Poulantzas," *New Left Review*, no. 59, pp. 53–60.

———. 1973. "Poulantzas and the Capitalist State," *New Left Review*, no. 82, pp. 83–92.

————. 1977. *Marxism and Politics*. London: Oxford U.P.

Miller, Anne R. 1971. "Occupations of the Labor Force According to the Dictionary of Occupational Titles." Philadelphia, Penn.: Population Studies Center.

Mincer, Jacob, and Solomon Polachek. 1974. "Family Investments in Human Capital: Earnings of Women," *Journal of Political Economy*, 82, no. 2 (Mar./Apr.), pp. S76–108.

Ministry of Labor [Sweden]. 1975. *Proposals for an Industrial Democracy Act: A Summary of the Proposals of the Labor Legislation Committee*. Vallingby, Sweden.

Morse, Dean. 1969. *The Peripheral Worker*. New York: Columbia U.P.

Mushkin, Selma, ed. 1974. *Recurrent Education*. Washington, D.C.: G.P.O.

National Commission on Excellence in Education. 1983. *A Nation at Risk: The Imperative for Educational Reform*. Washington, D.C.: Dept. of Educ.

National Commission on Productivity and Work Quality. 1975. *A Plant-wide Productivity Plan in Action: Three Years of Experience with the Scanlon Plan*. Washington, D.C.

National Manpower Institute. 1977. *Work Education Councils: Profiles of 21 Collaborative Efforts*. Washington, D.C.

Neill, A. S. 1960. *Summerhill*. New York: Hart.

Nelson, Daniel. 1975. *Managers and Workers: Origins of the New Factory System in the United States, 1880–1920*. Madison, Wisc.: Univ. of Wisc. Press.

Newman, John E. 1974. "Predicting Absenteeism and Turnover: A Field Comparison of Fishbein's Model and Traditional Job Attitude Measures," *Journal of Applied Psychology*, 59, no. 5, pp. 610–15.

Newmark, Gerald. 1976. *This School Belongs to You and Me*. New York: Hart.

Niskanen, William. 1971. *Bureaucracy and Representative Government*. Chicago: Aldine.

Oakeshott, Robert. 1978. *The Case for Workers' Coops*. London: Routledge and Kegan Paul.

O'Connor, James. 1973. *Final Crisis of the State*. New York: St. Martin's Press.

————. 1974. *The Corporations and the State: Essays in the Theory of Capitalism and Imperialism*. New York: Harper and Row.

————. 1981. "The Fiscal Crisis of the State Revisited: A Look at Economic Crisis and Regan's Budget Policy," in *Kapitalistate*, pp. 41–61.

Offe, Claus. 1972. "Advanced Capitalism and the Welfare State," *Politics and Society* (Summer), pp. 479–88.

————. 1973. "The Theory of a Capitalist State and the Problem of Policy Formation," in Leon Lindberg *et al.*, eds., *Stress and Contradiction in Modern Capitalism* (Lexington, Mass.: Heath), pp. 125–44.

————. 1974. "Structural Problems of the Capitalist State: Class Rule and the Political System. On the Selectiveness of Political Institutions," in Klaus Von Beyme, ed., *German Political Studies* (Beverly Hills, Calif.: Sage), vol. 1, pp. 137–47.

————. 1975. "Theses on the Theory of the State," *New German Critique*, 6 (Fall).

————. 1976. "Laws of Motion of Reformist State Policies." Mimeo.

Olim, Ellis G., *et al.* 1967. "Role of Mothers' Language Styles in Mediating Their Preschool Children's Cognitive Development," *The School Review*, 75, no. 4 (Winter), pp. 414–24.

O'Neill, Dave, and Sue Ross. 1976. *Voucher Funding of Training: A Study of the GI Bill.* Arlington, Va.: Public Research Institute, publication 312–76.

Orfield, Gary. 1974. "Implications of School Desegregation for Changes in the Educational Process." Paper presented at the Conference on the Courts, Social Service, and School Desegregation, Hilton Head Island, S.C. (Aug. 18–21).

————. 1978. *Must We Bus?* Washington, D.C.: Brookings.

Ouchi, William G. 1981. *Theory Z.* Reading, Mass.: Addison-Wesley.

Owen, John D. 1972. "The Distribution of Educational Resources in Large American Cities," *Journal of Human Resources*, 7, no. 1 (Winter), pp. 26–38.

Parnes, H. S. 1962. *Forecasting Educational Needs for Economic and Social Development.* Paris: O.E.C.D.

Parsons, Talcott. 1959. "The School Class as a Social System: Some of Its Functions in American Society," *Harvard Educational Review*, 29, no. 4, pp. 297–318.

Patterson, Michelle. 1976. "Governmental Policy and Equality in Higher Education: The Junior Collegization of the French University," *Social Problems*, 24, no. 2 (Dec.), pp. 173–83.

Pearlin, Leonard I., and Melvin L. Kohn. 1966. "Social Class, Occupation, and Parental Values: A Cross-National Study," *American Sociological Review*, 31, no. 4 (Aug.), pp. 466–79.

Pellegrin, Jean-Pierre. 1974a. "Admission Policies in Post-Secondary Education," in *Towards Mass Higher Education: Issues and Dilemmas* (Paris: O.E.C.D.), pp. 63–103.

————. 1974b. "Quantitative Trends in Post Secondary Education," in *Towards Mass Higher Education: Issues and Dilemmas* (Paris: O.E.C.D.), pp. 9–62.

Pelligrin, Roland J. 1973. "Administrative Assumptions Underlying

Major Innovation: A Case Study in the Introduction of Differentiated Staffing," in W.W. Charters, Jr., *et al.*, *The Process of Planned Change in the School's Instructional Organization* (Eugene, Ore.: Center for Advanced Study of Ed. Admin.), pp. 13–34.

Petrequin, Gaynor. 1968. *Individual Learning Through Modular-Flexible Programming.* New York: McGraw-Hill.

Pigou, A. L. 1951. *A Study in Public Finance.* 3d ed. London: Macmillan.

Pincus, Fred. 1980. "The False Promises of Community Colleges: Class Conflict and Vocational Education," *Harvard Educational Review*, 50 (Aug.), pp. 332–61.

Pincus, John, ed. 1974. *School Finance in Transition.* Cambridge, Mass.: Ballinger.

Poor, Riva. 1973. *4 Days, 40 Hours and Other Forms of the Rearranged Workweek.* New York: New American Library.

Popham, W. James. 1978. "The Case for Criterion-Referenced Measurements," *Educational Researcher*, 7, no. 11 (Dec.), pp. 6–10.

Poulantzas, Nicos. 1974. *Political Power and Social Classes.* London: New Left Books.

———. 1975. *Classes in Contemporary Capitalism.* London: New Left Books.

———. 1978a. *L'état, le pouvoir, le socialisme.* Paris: P.U.F.

———. 1978b. *State, Power, Socialism.* London: New Left Books.

Prospects, 5, no. 4 (1975).

Quinn, Robert P., and Martha S. Baldi DeMandilovitch. 1975. "Education and Job Satisfaction: A Questionable Payoff." Ann Arbor, Mich.: Univ. of Mich. Survey Research Center.

Quinn, Robert P., and Linda J. Shepard. 1974. *The 1972–73 Quality of Employment Survey: Descriptive Statistics, with Comparison Data from the 1967–70 Survey of Working Conditions.* Ann Arbor, Mich.: Univ. of Mich., Institute for Social Research.

Quinn, Robert P., Graham L. Staines, and Margaret R. McCullough. 1974. *Job Satisfaction: Is There a Trend?* (U.S. Department of Labor, Manpower Research Monograph no. 30). Washington, D.C.: G.P.O.

Quinn, Robert P., *et al.* 1973. "Evaluating Working Conditions in America," *Monthly Labor Review*, 96 (Nov.), pp. 32–41.

Rawlins, V. Lane, and Lloyd Ulman. 1974. "The Utilization of College-Trained Manpower in the United States," in Margaret S. Gordon, ed., *Higher Education and the Labor Market* (New York: McGraw-Hill), pp. 195–236.

Rawls, John. 1971. *A Theory of Justice.* Cambridge, Mass.: Belknap.

Rehn, Gosta, and Erik Lundberg. 1963. "Employment and Welfare: Some Swedish Issues," *Industrial Relations*, 2 (Feb.), pp. 1–4.

Reich, Michael. 1977. "The Economics of Racism," in D. M. Gordon, ed., *Problems in Political Economy: An Urban Perspective* (2d ed.; Lexington, Mass.: Heath), pp. 183–88.

————. 1981. *Racial Inequality.* Princeton, N.J.: Princeton U.P.

Reich, Michael, *et al.* 1973. "A Theory of Labor Market Segmentation," *American Economic Review*, 63, no. 2 (May), pp. 359–65.

Riche, Richard W., *et al.* 1983. "High Technology Today and Tomorrow: A Small Slice of the Employment Pie," *Monthly Labor Review* (Nov.), pp. 50–58.

Rist, Ray C. 1970. "Student Social Class and Teacher Expectations: The Self-Fulfilling Prophecy in Ghetto Education," *Harvard Educational Review* (Aug.), pp. 411–50.

Robinson, John P., *et al.*, eds. 1967. *Measures of Occupational Attitudes and Occupational Characteristics.* Ann Arbor, Mich.: Univ. of Mich., Institute for Social Research.

Rosenthal, Edward Lee. 1977. "Lifelong Learning—For Some of the People," *Change* (Aug.), pp. 44–45.

Rosenthal, Robert, and Lenore Jacobsen. 1968. *Pygmalion in the Classroom: Teacher Expectation and Pupils' Intellectual Development.* New York: Holt, Rinehart, and Winston.

Rousseau, Jean-Jacques. 1974 [1762]. *Emile.* New York: Dutton.

Rubin, David. 1972. *The Rights of Teachers.* New York: Avon.

Rubin, Lillian B. 1979. *Women of a Certain Age.* New York: Harper and Row.

Rumberger, Russell W. 1980. "The Economic Decline of College Graduates: Fact or Fallacy?," *The Journal of Human Resources* (Winter), pp. 99–112.

————. 1981a. *Overeducation in the U.S. Labor Market.* New York: Praeger.

————. 1981b. "The Changing Skill Requirements of Jobs in the U.S. Economy," *Industrial and Labor Relations Review*, 34, no. 4 (July), pp. 578–90.

————. 1983. "Dropping Out of High School: The Influence of Race, Sex, and Family Background," *American Educational Research Journal*, 20, no. 2 (Summer), pp. 199–220.

————. 1984. "The Job Market for College Graduates, 1960–1990," *Journal of Higher Education*, 55, no. 4 (July/Aug.), pp. 433–54.

Rumberger, Russell W., and Martin Carnoy. 1980. "Segmentation in the U.S. Labour Markets: Its Effects on the Mobility and Earnings of Whites and Blacks," *Cambridge Journal of Economics*, 4, pp. 117–32.

Rumberger, Russell W., and Henry M. Levin. 1984. "Forecasting the Impact of New Technologies on the Future Job Market." Stanford, Calif.: Stanford Univ., Institute for Research on Educational Finance and Governance.

Rush, Harold M. F. 1971. *Job Design for Motivation: Experiments in*

Job Enlargement and Job Enrichment. New York: Conference Board.

———. 1973. *Organizational Development: A Reconnaissance*. New York: Conference Board.

Sarason, Seymour B. 1971. *The Culture of the School and the Problem of Change*. Boston: Allyn and Bacon.

Schauer, Helmut. 1972. "Critique of Co-determination," in Gerry Hunnius, ed., *Workers' Control* (New York: Vintage), pp. 210–24.

Schiller, Bernt. 1977. "Industrial Democracy in Scandinavia," *The Annals*, 431 (May), pp. 63–73.

Schneider, Benjamin, and Robert A. Snyder. 1975. "Some Relationships Between Job Satisfaction and Organizational Climate," *Journal of Applied Psychology*, 60, no. 3, pp. 318–28.

Schramm, Wilbur, *et al.* 1967. *The New Media: Memo to Educational Planners*. Paris: UNESCO, Int'l Institute for Educational Planning.

Schultz, Theodore W. 1975. "The Value of the Ability to Deal with Disequilibria," *Journal of Economic Literature*, 13, no. 3 (Sept.), pp. 827–46.

Schumpeter, Joseph. 1942. *Capitalism, Socialism and Democracy*. New York: Harper and Row.

Schwinger, Phinhas. 1975. *Wage Incentive Systems*. New York: Halsted.

Scitovsky, Tibor. 1976. *The Joyless Economy*. New York: Oxford U.P.

Seashore, Stanley E. 1975. "Defining and Measuring the Quality of Working Life," in Louis E. Davis and Albert B. Cherns, eds., *The Quality of Working Life* 1 (New York: Free Press), pp. 105–18.

Sennett, Richard, and Jonathan Cobb. 1972. *Hidden Injuries of Class*. New York: Knopf.

Sewell, William H., and Robert M. Hauser. 1972. "Causes and Consequences of Higher Education: Models of the Status Attainment Process," *American Journal of Agricultural Economics*, 54, no. 5 (Dec.), pp. 851–61.

———. 1975. *Education, Occupation and Earnings: Achievement in the Early Career*. New York: Academic.

———. 1976. "Causes and Consequences of Higher Education: Models of the Status Attainment Process," in W. H. Sewell, R. Hauser, and D. Featherman, eds., *Schooling and Achievement in American Society* (New York: Academic), pp. 9–28.

Sewell, William H., and Vimal P. Shah. 1967. "Socioeconomic Status, Intelligence, and the Attainment of Higher Education," *Sociology of Education*, 40 (Winter), pp. 1–23.

Sexton, Patricia. 1961. *Education and Income: Inequalities of Opportunity in Our Public Schools*. New York: Viking.

Sharan, Shlomo. 1980. "Cooperative Learning in Small Groups: Recent

Methods and Effects on Achievement, Attitudes, and Ethnic Relations," *Review of Educational Research*, 50, no. 2 (Summer), pp. 241–72.

Sharp, Rachel, and Anthony Green. 1975. *Education and Social Control*. London: Routledge and Kegan Paul.

Shirom, A. 1972. "The Industrial Relations Systems of Industrial Cooperatives in the United States, 1880–1935," *Labor History* (Fall), pp. 533–51.

Silberman, Charles. 1970. *Crisis in the Classroom*. New York: Random House.

Silvestri, George T., *et al.* 1983. "Occupational Employment Projections Through 1995," *Monthly Labor Review* (Nov.), pp. 37–49.

Skocpol, Theda. 1981. "Political Response to Capitalist Crisis: Neo-Marxist Theories of the State and the Case of the New Deal," *Politics and Society*, 10, no. 2.

Slavin, Robert E. 1983. *Cooperative Learning*. New York: Longman.

Smith, Adam. 1937 [1776]. *The Wealth of Nations*. New York: Random House.

———. 1976 [1759]. *The Theory of Moral Sentiments*. Ed. D. D. Raphael and A. L. MacFie. Oxford: Clarendon Press.

Smith, Brett A. 1976. "Worker Participation and Productivity: Another Look at the Evidence." Paper presented at the Annual Meeting of the American Economics Association, Atlantic City, N.J. (Sept.).

Sociology of Education. 1982. 55, nos. 2/3 (Apr./Jul.).

Spring, Joel. 1972. *Education and the Rise of the Corporate State*. Boston, Mass.: Beacon.

Srivastva, S., *et al.* 1975. *Job Satisfaction and Productivity*. Cleveland, Ohio: Case Western Univ., Dep't of Organizational Behavior.

Stein, Barry, *et al.* 1976. "Flextime: Work When You Want To," *Psychology Today* (June), pp. 43–80.

Steinberg, L. D., *et al.* 1981. "Early Work Experience Effects on Adolescent Occupational Socialization," *Youth and Society*, 12, no. 4 (June), pp. 403–22.

Stern, E. 1976. *Declining Test Scores—A Conference Report*. Washington, D.C.: National Institute of Education.

Stiglitz, J. 1975. "Incentives, Risk and Information: Notes Toward a Theory of Hierarchy," *Bell Journal of Economics*, 6, no. 2 (Autumn), pp. 552–79.

Susman, Gerald I. 1975. "Technological Prerequisites for Delegation of Decision Making to Work Groups," in Louis E. Davis and Albert B. Cherns, eds., *The Quality of Working Life* (New York: Free Press), pp. 242–55.

———. 1976. *Autonomy at Work: A Sociotechnical Analysis of Participative Management*. New York: Praeger.

Svejnar, Jan. 1982. "Codetermination and Productivity: Empirical Evidence from the Federal Republic of Germany," in Derek Jones and Jan Svejnar, eds., *Participatory and Self-Managed Firms* (Lexington, Mass.: Lexington), Chap. 10.

Tannenbaum, Arnold S., *et al.* 1974. *Hierarchy in Organizations.* San Francisco, Calif.: Jossey-Bass.

Terkel, Studs. 1974. *Working.* New York: Pantheon.

Thomas, Henk, and Chris Logan. 1982. *Mondragon: An Economic Analysis.* Boston, Mass.: Allen and Unwin.

Thorsrud, Einar. 1975. "Collaborative Action Research to Enhance the Quality of Working Life," in Louis E. Davis and Albert B. Cherns, eds., *The Quality of Working Life* 1 (New York: Free Press), pp. 193–204.

Thorsrud, Einar, *et al.* 1976. "Sociotechnical Approach to Industrial Democracy in Norway," in Robert Dubin, ed., *Handbook of Work, Organization, and Society* (Chicago: Rand McNally), Chap. 10.

Thurow, Lester. 1969. *Poverty and Discrimination.* Washington, D.C.: Brookings.

———. 1975. *Generating Inequality.* New York: Basic.

Tucker, Robert C. 1978. *The Marx-Engels Reader.* 2d ed.; New York: Norton.

Tyack, David B. 1972. "City Schools: Centralization and Control at the Beginning of the Century," in J. Israel, ed., *Building the Organizational Society* (New York: Free Press), pp. 57–72.

———. 1974. *The One Best System.* Cambridge, Mass.: Harvard U.P.

Tyack, David, and Elisabeth Hansot. 1981. "Conflict and Consensus in American Public Education," *Daedalus*, 110, no. 3 (Summer), pp. 1–26.

———. 1982. *Managers of Virtue: Public School Leadership in America, 1820–1980.* New York: Basic.

U.S. Congress, Congressional Budget Office. 1982. "Effects of Tax and Benefit Reductions Enacted in 1981 for Households in Different Income Categories" (Feb.). Washington, D.C.: G.P.O.

U.S. Department of Commerce. 1981. *Statistical Abstract of the United States, 1981.* Washington, D.C. 102d ed.

———. 1981. *Survey of Current Business,* 61, no. 2 (Feb.), p. 59.

———. 1982. *Statistical Abstract of the United States: 1982–83.* 103d ed. Washington, D.C.: G.P.O.

U.S. Department of Commerce, Bureau of the Census. 1978. *Historical Statistics of the United States, Colonial Period to 1970, Part I.* Washington, D.C.

U.S. Department of Education, National Center for Educational Statistics. 1979. *Digest of Education Statistics 1979.* Washington, D.C.: G.P.O.

————. 1981. *High School and Beyond, A Capsule Description of High School Students*. Review Edition. Washington, D.C.: G.P.O.

————. 1982. *Digest of Educational Statistics, 1982*. Washington, D.C.: G.P.O.

U.S. Department of Health, Education, and Welfare. 1973. *Work in America*. Cambridge, Mass.: MIT Press.

————. 1976. *The Condition of Education*. National Center for Educational Statistics, NCES 7a6-400. Washington, D.C.: G.P.O.

————. 1982. *The Condition of Education, 1982*. Washington, D.C.: G.P.O.

U.S. Department of Labor, Bureau of Labor Statistics. 1974. "Employment of Recent College Graduates, October 1972." Special Labor Force Report 169. Washington, D.C.: G.P.O.

U.S. Department of Labor, Bureau of Labor Statistics. 1976. *Occupational Projections and Training Data*. Bulletin 1918.

U.S. Department of Labor, Manpower Administration. 1968. *Historical Statistics of Employment Security Activities, 1938–1966*. Washington, D.C.: G.P.O.

————. 1974. "Youth and the Meaning of Work," no. 32. Washington, D.C.: G.P.O.

Vanek, Jaroslav. 1971. *The General Theory of Labor-Managed Market Economies*. Ithaca, N.Y.: Cornell U.P.

Verduin, John R., Jr., *et al.* 1977. *Adults Teaching Adults*. Austin, Tex.: Learning Concepts.

Wacaster, C. Thompson. 1973. "The Life and Death of Differentiated Staffing at Columbia High School," in W. W. Charters, Jr., *et al.*, *The Process of Planned Change in the School's Instructional Organization* (Eugene, Ore.: Center for the Advanced Study of Ed. Admin.), pp. 35–51.

Wachtel, Howard. 1973. *Workers' Management and Workers' Wages in Yugoslavia*. Ithaca, N.Y.: Cornell U.P.

Wachtel, Paul. 1974. "The Effect of School Quality on Achievement Attainment Levels and Lifetime Earnings." Unpublished paper, N.Y.U. Grad. School of Bus. Admin.

————. 1975. "The Returns to Investment in Higher Education: Another View," in F. Thomas Juster, ed., *Education, Income, and Human Behavior* (New York: McGraw-Hill), pp. 151–70.

Wachter, Michael L. 1974. "Primary and Secondary Labor Markets: A Critique of the Dual Approach," *Brookings Papers on Economic Activity*, no. 3, pp. 637–93.

Wade, Michael. 1973. *Flexible Working Hours in Practice*. New York: Wiley.

Walton, Richard E. 1975. "Criteria for Quality of Working Life," in

Louis E. Davis and Albert B. Cherns, eds., *The Quality of Working Life* 1 (New York: Free Press), pp. 91–104.

———. 1976. "Alienation and Innovation in the Workplace," in James O'Toole, ed., *Work and the Quality of Life* (Cambridge, Mass.: MIT Press), Chap. 10.

Weber, Max. 1946. "Bureaucracy," in H. H. Gerth and C. W. Mills, eds., *From Max Weber: Essays in Sociology* (New York: Oxford U.P.), Chap. 8.

———. 1958. *The Protestant Ethic and the Spirit of Capitalism*. New York: Scribner.

Wedderburn, Dorothy. 1977. "The Bullock by the Horns," *New Society*, 27, (Jan.), pp. 166–68.

Weiler, Daniel, *et al.* 1974. *A Public School Voucher Demonstration: The First Year at Alum Rock*. Santa Monica, Calif.: Rand.

Weiler, Hans N. 1973. *The Politics of Educational Innovation: Recent Developments in West German School Reform*. Stanford, Calif.: Stanford Univ. School of Ed.

Welch, Finis. 1970. "Education in Production," *Journal of Political Economy*, 78, no. 1 (Jan./Feb.), pp. 35–59.

Wesley, Edgar. 1957. *NEA: The First Hundred Years*. New York: Harper and Row.

White, B. L. 1960. "Job Attitudes, Absence From Work and Labour Turnover," *Personnel Practice Bulletin*, 16, no. 4 (Dec.), pp. 18–23.

Wilcox, Kathleen. 1977. "Schooling and Socialization: A Structural Inquiry into Cultural Transmission in an Urban American Community." Ph.D. diss., Dept. of Anthropology, Harvard Univ.

Williamson, Oliver E. 1975. *Markets and Hierarchies*. New York: Free Press.

Willis, Paul. 1977. *Learning to Labor*. Lexington, Mass.: Heath.

Willms, J. Douglas. 1983. "Do Private Schools Produce Higher Levels of Academic Achievement? New Evidence for the Tuition Tax Credit Debate," in Thomas James and Henry M. Levin, eds., *Public Dollars for Private Schools* (Philadelphia, Penn.: Temple U.P.), pp. 223–31.

Wilson, A. B. 1959. "Residential Segregation of Social Classes and Aspirations of High School Boys," *American Sociological Review*, 24, pp. 836–45.

Windham, Douglas. 1970. *Education, Equality and Income Redistribution: A Study of Public Higher Education*. Lexington, Mass.: Heath.

Wirt, F. M., and M. W. Kirst. 1982. *Schools in Conflict*. Berkeley, Calif.: McCutcheon.

Wirth, Arthur G. 1972. *Education in the Technological Society: The Vo-*

cation-Liberal Studies Controversy in the Early Twentieth Century. Scranton, Penn.: Intext Educational.

———. 1981. "Exploring Linkages Between Dewey's Educational Philosophy and Industrial Reorganization," *Economic and Industrial Democracy*, 2, no. 2 (May), pp. 121–40.

Wirtz, Willard, *et al.* 1977. *On Further Examination: Report of the Advisory Panel on the Scholastic Aptitude Test Score Decline*. New York: College Entrance Examination Board.

Wise, Arthur. 1968. *Rich Schools, Poor Schools*. Chicago: Univ. of Chicago Press.

Wolfe, Alan. 1977. *The Limits of Legitimacy: Political Contradictions of Late Capitalism*. New York: Free Press.

———. 1981. *America's Impasse*. New York: Pantheon.

Work in America Institute. 1982. *Productivity Through Work Innovations*. New York: Pergamon.

Wright, Eric Olin. 1978. *Class, Crisis, and the State*. London: New Left Books.

Wrigley, E. Anthony. 1977. "Reflections on the History of the Family," *Daedalus*, 106, no. 2, pp. 71–85.

Wyko, Bill. 1975. "The Work Shortage: Class Struggle and Capital Reproduction," *Review of Radical Political Economics*, 7, no. 2 (Summer), pp. 11–26.

Yankelovich, Daniel. 1974. *The New Morality: A Profile of American Youth in the 70's*. New York: McGraw-Hill.

Index

DATE DUE